The

MECHANICS

of

PASSIONS

The
MECHANICS
of
PASSIONS

Brain, Behaviour, and Society

ALAIN EHRENBERG

Translated by Craig Lund

McGill-Queen's University Press

Montreal & Kingston • London • Chicago

Translation © McGill-Queen's University Press 2020

ISBN 978-0-2280-0342-7 (cloth)
ISBN 978-0-2280-0443-1 (ePDF)
ISBN 978-0-2280-0444-8 (ePUB)

Legal deposit third quarter 2020
Bibliothèque nationale du Québec

Printed in Canada on acid-free paper that is 100% ancient forest free
(100% post-consumer recycled), processed chlorine free

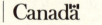

We acknowledge the support of the Canada Council for the Arts.
Nous remercions le Conseil des arts du Canada de son soutien.

Library and Archives Canada Cataloguing in Publication

Title: The mechanics of passions : brain, behaviour, and society / Alain Ehrenberg ;
translated by Craig Lund.
Other titles: Mécanique des passions. English
Names: Ehrenberg, Alain, author.
Description: Translation of: La mécanique des passions. | Includes bibliographical
  references and index.
Identifiers: Canadiana (print) 20200269569 | Canadiana (ebook) 20200269704
  | ISBN 9780228003427 (cloth) | ISBN 9780228004431 (ePDF) | ISBN
  9780228004448 (ePUB)
Subjects: LCSH: Cognitive neuroscience. | LCSH: Cognition—Social aspects.
  | LCSH: Neurosciences—Social aspects. | LCSH: Neurosciences and the humanities.
  | LCSH: Neuroanthropology.
Classification: LCC RC343.3 .E3713 2020 | DDC 362.1968—dc23

This book was typeset in 10.5/13 Sabon.

For Corinne, again

Contents

The problem of constructing a new individuality consonant with the objective conditions under which we live is the deepest problem of our times.

John Dewey, *Individualism*

There is no interval between the social and the biological.

Marcel Mauss, "Les techniques du corps"

Unravelling the mystery of these extraordinary people ... we can also learn more about ourselves, explore the "challenge to our capabilities" and uncover the hidden potential – the little Rain Man – that resides, perhaps, within us all.

Darold A. Treffert, "The Savant Syndrome"

The New Science of Human Behaviour

In advanced democratic societies, the medical and social value of the brain has steadily increased since the early 1990s. Neuroscience maintains that exploration of the brain, over time, should allow for considerable progress not only in the care of mental pathologies (like depression or schizophrenia), but also in the treatment of social problems, thus raising hope for applications that may increase efficacy in public policy, educational practices, or ways of influencing consumers or electors (neuroeconomics, neuropedagogy, neuromarketing, neurolaw, etc.). Neuroscience has become social, and the productivity in this field is so effervescent that *Nature Neuroscience* recently spoke of "an explosion of research."[1] Biologists have shown the brain to be an evolving system in constant transformation, whose function is to anticipate[2] or recognize,[3] to simulate action, to generate hypotheses, and whose fundamental property is decision-making. Do we not say now the brain perceives, decides, and acts? A new science of normal and pathological human behaviour seems well on its way to being established: cognitive neuroscience. It combines brain science with scientific, behavioural, and cognitive psychologies, which have now been brought together under the banner of "behavioural sciences."

Cognitive neuroscience is full of both expectations and fears that go well beyond the scope of discussions amongst specialists. In a global context, where psychic suffering and mental health have become a major concern, be it within a company, at work, in education, or the family, the conceptual and practical problems raised by neuroscience and its applications cannot leave public opinion indifferent. Indeed, at stake are issues as crucial as our individual and collective well-being, methods for treating psychoses, the ways in which we educate and instruct our children, how we deal with a multitude of deviances and delinquent acts, and the favouring of democratic emotions, such as empathy, or trust in one another.

In their most ambitious of aims, these disciplines are presented as a "biology of the mind," setting out to achieve the most complete understanding of the individual – a thinking, feeling and acting being – through the exploration of the brain (and the ramifications of the nervous system on the rest of the body). Such an assertion implies that neuroscience should be considered as a type of anthropology, or, in other words, a conception or certain idea of humankind. At the same time, it is reconfiguring classic distinctions between mental pathologies and neurological pathologies under the general category of brain disorders. So we have what could be called the "strong program" of cognitive neuroscience.

Not all research in this area concerns pathology, but it is the most appreciable for two distinct reasons. First, it allows for a concrete examination of a brain-mind dualism, through the twin disciplines of neurology and psychiatry. Second, it is the realm where matters of psychic suffering are settled, along with those of well-being or the improvement of individual outcomes, for which public opinion has the highest expectations.

The aim of this book is to describe this anthropology by focusing on its central issue, that of the *brain–behaviour* relationship. It begins with the premise that the brain is much more connected to the body than the outside world. Therefore behaviour, which includes thoughts, emotions, and actions, is conditioned primarily by cerebral mechanisms. The word *behaviour* is admittedly very broad; it includes, but is not limited to, all that one can fit into the "mind" – which is why I prefer to speak of the brain–behaviour problem.

FROM PSYCHOANALYSIS TO NEUROSCIENCE, FROM ONE CLIMATE OF MODERNITY TO THE OTHER

For psychopathology and Western culture in the twentieth century, as Auden wrote in regard to Freud, psychoanalysis represented "a whole climate of opinion under whom we conduct our different lives."[4] Cognitive neuroscience seems on its way to becoming the barometer for measuring behaviour in the twenty-first century.

The following work proposes to study this change in climate.

In *La Société du malaise* (2010), I described how French and American psychoanalyses brought about, each in its own way, the progressive permeation of collective representations of humankind in society through autonomy – what I call autonomy-as-condition. This occurred by placing less emphasis on Oedipal issues, in which guilt and conflict are front and centre, and more on narcissistic aspects, where shame and division take up more space. These changes in psychopathology gave rise to a recurring dispute on the virtues and vices of a new individualism upon which society was built, an individualism of the capable person. Narcissism symbolized the new malaise in the evolution of societies that have entered into the autonomy-as-condition; it illustrated that democratic apprehension, when confronted with the fear of weakening social links, could be represented. With cognitive neuroscience, it is about turning our attention to a set of disciplines manifestly more in step with these new morals. Examined through the lens of a natural science of autonomous behaviour, the objective is to highlight the designation of "natural" and to outline the project of autonomy in play.

Through the psychoanalytical versions of autonomy-as-condition, I questioned the canonical theme of the opposition between individual and society in order to show we were dealing not with a declining idea of society because of some deranged individualism, but rather a change in how we act that is embodied in the archetype of the capable individual. *The Mechanics of Passions*, which is the follow-up, tackles its neurobiological, cognitive, and behavioural versions via another major canonical theme: the opposition between biological and social, or between nature and culture. Linking the two books is the assumption that these two oppositions are tightly bonded and lead to the same vicious intellectual circles. However, it is also attached to a difference in tone adopted by the two sciences of humankind: if psychoanalysis shows us the limits of the human being, neuroscience invites us to go beyond them.

The call for cognitive neuroscience to clarify and treat a multitude of problems in everyday life raises several questions: Do they really transform our representations and understanding of human beings? Are people recognizing and identifying themselves through cerebral and cognitive language, along the lines of "it's my brain, it's not me," and what impact does this have in their lives? Are we going to use neuroscientific concepts like we did Freudian ones? Are "cognitive biases" replacing Freudian slips and is emotional management replacing the exploration of conflicting desires? Are new cognitive or behavioural psychotherapies, new medicines, or new biological techniques, which are selectively acting on one cerebral region or another, on their way to being perfected? To what extent or in what context does the brain become a reference for living, a criterion of identification for individuals who recognize themselves in their brain, be it healthy or ill?

To answer these questions, we must go beyond both the epistemological and political debates, in which cognitive neuroscience is ensnared. The epistemological debate is brought by neuroscience through the theme of "Descartes' error," to use the title of Antonio Damasio's famous book. It rejects the assumed Cartesian dualism of mind and body as a materialist monism, an indivisible unit of being, the centre of which is the brain. Also, it is supported by sociological and philosophical trends claiming to adhere to the tenets of methodological individualism. This indicates we can understand a collective behaviour only by starting with the individual, thus compensating for the supposed insufficiency of our disciplines by relying on the results of these sciences and their experimental methods.[5] The political debate is essentially sustained by critical trends within the social sciences and philosophy that claim to adhere to the thoughts of Michel Foucault or Pierre Bourdieu: they target the reductionism of neuroscience, which may lead to an expression of biopower, itself serving pervasive neoliberalism. The key question is, Are these sciences emancipatory or a new instrument of social control? These trends proclaim the birth of a "biosociality,"[6] asserting that "neurobiology is undoubtedly reconfiguring some of the ways in which individual and collective problems are made intelligible"[7] and therefore "the more relevant questions ... to work out will be how to overcome the gap between social and neural."[8]

The following study circumvents these quarrels: it seeks to shed light on overlooked connections between scientific concepts and social ideals, since neither the gap between neural and social, nor the restructuring of our governmental forms by neuroscience corresponds to what is happening in our societies concerning cognitive neuroscience.

Indeed, the manner in which things are viewed within neuroscience is certainly constrained by the concepts and methods of science, particularly the experimental, but they are also filled with moral values, ordinary social concepts, and shared ideas – what sociology calls collective representations. The heuristic value of neuroscience for a sociology of contemporary individualism resides here. Its success tells us something about ourselves as a human collective. But what? And how? The answer to these questions requires us to consider them as a space in which certain ideals of modernity are invested. But which ideals?

COGNITIVE NEUROSCIENCE AS A MORAL AUTHORITY: WHAT IDEALS OF MODERNITY? WHAT INDIVIDUALISM?

The success of cognitive neuroscience is based on a *moral authority*. That does not mean neurobiological concepts and empirical evidence do not count or are merely a rationalization. Instead, it has more to do with bringing to light the many ways specialized scientific concepts and collective representations of humans in society or ideals occur. The need is felt all the more so since these biological and psychological sciences deal directly with human matters – behaviour, psychology, mind, but also pathology, well-being, ill-being. That is why I agree with Émile Durkheim's reasoning in his conclusion of *The Elementary Forms of Religious Life*: "It is not at all true that concepts, even when constructed according to the rules of science, get their authority uniquely from their objective value. It is not enough that they be true to be believed. If they are not in harmony with the other beliefs and opinions, or, in a word, with the mass of other collective representations, they will be denied; minds will be closed to them; consequently, it will be as though they did not exist."[9] These representations have an effect not because they would constrain us from the outside, but because they are shared. Consequently, they constitute both a level of individual independent intelligibility and a system of expectations that pervades the individual, affecting one totally, even physiologically. I will use collective representations, ideals, or ideas-as-values interchangeably. The goal of this method is to understand how scientific or medical innovation, and the reasoning about these subjects and lifestyles, come together in a social and moral context in which everyone is expected to decide and act on one's own behalf, sufficiently controlling one's emotions; in short, to act as an autonomous individual.

What is the nature of this authority? To what collective sensibility does it refer? Which ideals, which collective representations of the individual in society are at work in neuroscience and cognitive behavioural science? What narrative do they propose for contemporary individualism and its tensions? In addition, which version of *naturalism* is at play?

For professional neuroscientists, the explanation of behaviours and the actions taken to possibly modify them are located preferentially in the brain and not within human interactions, yet it is these interactions that are targeted via the knowledge of how the cerebral apparatus functions and is structured. Neuroscience intentionally constructs an individual who is detached from personal relationships since it is, according to neuroscience, the best way to *scientifically* grasp the mechanisms of the individualist's behaviour. The cerebral perspective is not relational, but substantialist. Anthropologist Louis Dumont defines it as "the tendency to accentuate an agent or a unique element as a self-sufficient entity – by excluding or implicitly subordinating other agents or elements – this self-sufficient entity providing reason, the vital nucleus of the field as a whole."[10]

The sociologist can then propose an epistemological discussion describing arguments put forward, ideas formulated, and tools used to establish links between cerebral functioning and behaviour. In such a case, the sociologist views things through a true/false lens. However, since it is not sufficient for a scientific proposition to be true in order to be believed, the adopted approach here consists less in evaluating cognitive neuroscience according to these criteria, and more in outlining the collective sensibility at work and the ideals attached to it so as to demonstrate the overall consistency of its propositions. It is essential to turn to beliefs without wondering if they are true or false. It is more a matter of describing a world than it is evaluating a "knowledge-power," and therefore working like ethnologists who reconstitute the shared ideas and culture of a society by relying on the ideas and values that drive scientific articles, scholarly communications, works aimed at the general public, etc., which are direct expressions of social actors.[11]

We must not, however, completely abandon the epistemological question of true or false, since it would mean settling for a diffident sociology, but we must reconsider it by describing uses and practices that refer to cognitive neuroscience in the general context of social life. This will be the objective of chapters 5 and 6, which attempts to grasp the effect these ideas have, along with the modalities by which they fit into everyday life, and thus the whole of existence. Following the common thread of brain/behaviour connections, we will look both to describe these sciences as a moral authority based on a facet of individualist modernity, as well as to understand just how far we can take the knowledge of individuals simply by knowing their brain and body. It will then be possible to specify in what sense we must grasp Marcel Mauss's expression that "there is no interval between the social and the biological."

Members of the neuroscientific community use two main ritual sayings, two regularly uttered quasi-mantras to express the idea that the brain is the key to the discovery of fundamental truths. This regards not only mental or neurological pathology, but also all social and moral relations between human beings. First, the brain is "the most complex object in the universe," which means, on one hand, it cannot be part of a whole that would subordinate it, and, on the other, it holds the highest value. The second pertains to the temporality of the research program: "We've only just begun" – "begun" research and possible diagnostic, prognostic, and therapeutic applications, "begun" discovering human capacities of which we are possibly not yet aware.

But, some may wonder, how can you reveal ideals behind words like *mechanisms, causes, factors, variables, prediction, control, quantitative methods*, etc.? How can we see anything in this vocabulary other than a practical, technical, and consequently reductive concept of the individual in society?

My answer is we must adopt the attitude of Baudelaire, the painter of modernity, with regard to trivial life: "The painter, the true painter for whom we are looking, will be he who can snatch its epic quality from the life of today and can make us see and understand, with brush or with pencil, how great and poetic we are in our cravats and our patent-leather boots."[12] In place of cravats and black tailcoats and patent-leather boots, there are synapses, scales, tests, neuronal networks, cerebral areas, experimental devices, computer programs, etc. The idea is to extract from this mass of scientific and technical words a kind of greatness by elucidating the moral and social aspects of human life that controversy keeps us from seeing. The idea is to shed light on a rarely seen aspect of modernity: what is it?

Two characteristics of neuroscientific publications make it possible to advance a comprehensive hypothesis regarding the ideals involved in behavioural and brain sciences.

The first is that we explore rather little the meaning of existence, yet we spend ample time solving problems centred on the practical aspects of social and personal existence. The individual, whether schizophrenic, depressed, hyperactive, or of sound mind, is systematically presented as a practical subject confronted with problem-solving and decision-making by adjusting the means to serve the ends. So, the language of cognitive neuroscience is a language of action. The second aspect concerns the adjective *scientific* and the idea of nature. To study human behaviour scientifically is to consider it part of the natural world. In any case, the use of words like *behaviour, cognition*, or *brain* by experts is constantly constructing a natural science of human behaviour. Yet, the question of human nature is not limited to the problem between nature (biology) and culture (social). Following the Newtonian revolution, it concerns not only the *regularity* between the observed phenomena, but their *predictability*, as well. Empirical philosophy, put forward exemplarily by David Hume, expands this exigency to human passions that should be regulated through conversion mechanisms.

Approaching empiricism not as a philosophy but as an expression of collective sensibility makes it possible to articulate an aspect rarely seen regarding the ideals of self-reflection that characterize the modern individual. It is a way of life for which socialization through mechanisms or automatisms is a fundamental core value, and that answers problems having arisen mainly in British society. Natural sciences of human behaviour can thus be considered as a set of collective representations formulated using scientific language, which are therefore transfigured by it.

My general hypothesis, in this conversion of passions, states that a fundamental facet of democratic individualism is at stake. This facet being ordinary individuals as people of action who, as a creators of values, increases their own value through work and exchange – the Scottish contribution to modern individualism. Through ideals of regularity, we begin to see our historical representation of *character* take form, through the lens of the practical subject. These ideas developed especially in Anglo-American societies, where they were transformed in the mid-twentieth century by American behavioural social science (rational choice theory, behavioural and cognitive psychology, etc.), by the addition of choice and decision-making using a perspective of behavioural prediction and control. This inheritance was in turn modified in the 1960s and 1970s by new collective representations. These modifications made self-ownership an essential value, favouring a dynamic power of normative diversity and a multiplication of lifestyles, while placing value on individual initiative, innovation, and creativity to a degree not seen before. This widening of our ideals of liberty is indissociable from new egalitarian dynamics, the primary one of which is equality between genders (woman as individual). Borne out of the economy, the creation of value broadened when lifestyles invoked another tradition of ideals, that of modernist art and aesthetics. Modernism (from mid-nineteenth-century bohemians to twentieth-century artistic avant-gardists) built on the idea there was no border between art and life, established the artist as a hero whose lifestyle was based on personal experience and not on social conventions.[13] Having become a mainstay of everyday life, these collective representations granted everyone access to individuality. In what form were they presented?

One of the most powerful ideals of this society of generalized autonomy is the individual, whatever one's handicaps, deviances, or pathologies, who is *capable* of self-fulfillment by transforming those handicaps into assets through *creation*, thereby increasing one's personal value. We will call it the ideal of hidden potential. At the crossroads of two major individualist representations that create value (creator of wealth, creator of lifestyle), a new ideal of action was established. It associates traditional virtues of courage with newer ones of creativity, both of which socialize an uncontrollable ill, turning it into a way of life and a value of civilization. This ideal is the *specific* social form by which people diagnosed as ill, handicapped, or deviant (treated up to that point in institutions that sociologist Erving Goffman called "total institutions"[14]) became individuals capable of self-actualizing not despite their ailment, but *thanks* to it.

Cognitive neuroscience supplies this ideal (by the legitimacy from which science benefits, thanks to its fact-based propositions) with the promise of an unlimited development of human capacities against the backdrop of infinite normative diversity – shown with the autistic brain, as we will see in the first chapter. Such is the horizon of expectations that neuroscience elicits, and where they get a good deal of their authority.

To sum up the hypothesis: by following the common thread of the brain–behaviour problem, neuroscience and cognitive behavioural science are considered one of the great tales of contemporary individualism. This brings into play an anthropology of action within the autonomy society, centred on practical aspects of social and personal life, which transfigures one of the most common collective representations into scientific language, therefore possessing the highest value – that of hidden potential.

THE PROGRAM

We are going to explore the space where multiple common threads between shared ideals and scientific concepts come together. Inspired by ethnology, in the sense that information from biological and psychological literature is used to reconstitute the ideas of the protagonists studied, the purpose is to truly understand the systems of thought and reasoning that allow them to think as they do. My goal is to describe how psychologists and biologists (but also economists, who came onto the scene in the 1980s) attribute value to things, independent of any critical analysis regarding the truth of their propositions, and how these valuations are linked to powerful presuppositions shared by individuals in our societies, as well as those who create such collective expectations.

Exploration is the word that best fits this book, since it claims to open pathways by testing a hypothesis clarified and amended through empirical research.

This exploration will unfold over six chapters.

"Exemplary Brains" (chapter 1) paints a picture of two major types of paradigmatic brains of cognitive neuroscience that characterize in exemplary fashion the connections between cerebral function and behaviour: the first will represent classic individualism in its pathological form (the ailments of the practical subject), and the second will embody the new individualism of "hidden potential."

The second and third chapters take up the traits brought about by these exemplary brains in order to reconstruct the historic dimension. They will allow us to distinguish two naturalisms: a naturalism of regularity and one of foundation. The tension, ambiguity, or complementarity of these two naturalisms is the common theme in this story. "Scientific Method and Individualist Ideals" (chapter 2) describes the ideals of regularity crystalized around the adjective *cognitive*. This history, for the most part American, or Anglo-American,[15] will be viewed through the lens of character transfiguration.

"The Brain-as-Individual, a Physiology of Autonomy" (chapter 3) focuses on the substantive "neuroscience": it shifts the analysis of scientific psychology onto biological science. It demonstrates how this brain-as-individual was elaborated between the 1940s and today.

"Social Neuroscience, or How the Individual Acts with Others" (chapter 4) tackles the social according to a reading delivered by cognitive neuroscience. Neuroscience does not deny the social in any way; it reduces the social to behaviours of cooperation, also known as prosocial behaviours, which are used to discover cerebral mechanisms. It participates in the reconfiguration of the concept of character through social competence and interpersonal skills.

For what purpose? What uses does it have in social life? What types of activity? Two primary modes of action have been formulated; one that consists of obtaining, in the most mechanic way possible, cooperative behaviours, and the other consists of acquiring habits through activities designed as exercises. The first is at the centre of behavioural economics and the neuroeconomy. It will close out the chapter. In chapter 5, the second mode of action will be devoted to the neurocognitive version of exercises in autonomy, which have been developed since the early 1980s, under the designation of "rehabilitation" and "recovery." These practices were not designed to erase symptoms, but to transform them so the individual could live with them. Combining the ideal (social) of hidden potential (there are always resources within the self to improve)[16] and the facts (scientific) of cerebral plasticity, they feed the most seductive idea of autonomy-as-condition, the unlimited capacity of the individual to change, even metamorphose.

"Is It My Ideas or My Brain That Is Making Me Sick? Neuroscience and Self-Knowledge" (chapter 6) is based on three case studies (two neurocognitive narratives and a novel) to grasp to what extent and, moreover, how individuals recognize and identify themselves through cerebral and cognitive language,[17] and the way in which it fits into the whole context of life.

These last two chapters, by their object (therapeutic practices, case studies) trace a description of the way in which cognitive neuroscience has become integrated into our lives and permeates them; at the same time, this involves a reflection on the two chief ways of reconstructing one's moral self in mass individualist societies that psychoanalysis and cognitive neuroscience each embody. Where an apparently irreducible opposition is seen between these two disciplines, we will find, in reality, there is a certain sociological complementarity.

1

Exemplary Brains

From the Misfortunes of the Practical Subject
to the Heroism of Hidden Potential

The miracle is how all [the cerebral regions] cooperate, are integrated together, in the creation of a self.

Oliver Sacks, *An Anthropologist on Mars*

To develop the hypothesis of a total understanding of humankind through the understanding of the human brain, we must have pathological profiles from which the separation between neuropathology and psychopathology can be concretely elucidated. We need patients whose brains support this hypothesis (like hysteric Dora's, or "Rat Man's" did for psychoanalysis), and can embody the ambition of cognitive neuroscience; brains that play as many cognitive and affective tricks as the Freudian unconscious, which disguised the conflicts of desire and revealed the ambivalence of human intentionality.

Within the strong program of cognitive neuroscience, brains are considered exemplary when they allow us to display the separation between neurology and psychiatry and, in turn, make inroads on the key issue of opening doors onto the missing links between brain and behaviour. Following our approach, these brains tell a tale in which collective representations and scientific concepts are indissociable.

Traditionally, neurological patients are not well suited for such a process. Paralyses, aphasias, trembling – such symptoms are more evocative of disabled individuals, unwell people with deficits: something within that is missing. Therefore, they cannot embody the intricacy of brain science and the understanding of humankind. In the disabled patient, illness demonstrates cerebral mechanics that have become dysfunctional following a lesion. Situated on an infra-personal level, the lesion attacks the motor or cognitive capacities, which is why neurologists speak of focal symptoms. The illness is situated on a personal level, so the psychiatric patient suffers as an individual, but the symptoms are universal. This problem needs to be solved in order to fill the gap between neuropathology and psychopathology.

Answers will be found in pathologies that affect what neurologists call higher brain functions, bringing will or perception into play, thus appearing as disorders teetering between neurology and psychiatry.

This chapter has been split into two parts. The first looks at the brain that embodies "Descartes' error," which is to say the cognitive neuroscientific patient, who has concretely caused problems with causal relationships between cerebral function and mental disorder, and upon which hypotheses were built, making it possible to eventually obtain the most complete knowledge of humankind through the brain. It describes neurological patients who resemble psychiatric patients because they demonstrate a personality and behavioural disorder, and not a deficit in motor skills or mental functions. The illness has caused them to lose their moral conscience, itself inseparable from the demands of social life, and by which one can recognize them as responsible for their own actions, beings who can be trusted, who are reliable. True, they do not have the benefit of satisfying their own interests in everyday interactions, which is why their behaviour is considered pathological: this brain embodies the misfortunes of a practical subject. Here, Antonio Damasio will serve as our inside source.

The second part sheds light on another strategy in our search for the missing connection: the individualization of the neurological patient. Using this expression, I am identifying types of cerebral pathologies from which clinicians have shown that the patient's personality and history affect how neurological symptoms are expressed. Physiology, or rather pathophysiology, is personalized. From this personalization comes an element that clinicians, attentive to the needs of their patients, started to notice as early as the 1920s: pathologies are not merely deficiencies (an injury that lessens function), since patients possess qualities on which clinicians can depend. A researcher looking for connections between brain and mind can then attempt to understand how individual singularity shapes pathophysiology.

Next, we will go from patient individualization to a new individualism emerging in the 1960s and 1970s: the ideals of personal self-actualization broaden to new populations – ill, handicapped, deviant, disabled – living a negative experience whose fate was often institutionalization. Self-actualization is taking negativity and transforming it into a valued and socially accepted lifestyle: self-fulfillment, not impeded by the illness, but *thanks* to it, by discovering one's own hidden potential, has become one of the most powerful ideals of the autonomous condition. The psychiatric and neurological patients start to free themselves as individuals, which means their status shifts toward moral and social *partners* who are *capable* of demonstrating their autonomy through a *skill*. This transformation of the individual's role is what we wish to describe – a transformation inextricably linked to the new moral and social context. The brain's hidden potential will be exemplified by autism. In the 1980s, it began occupying a strategic position at the intersection of neuroscientific ideals (or the brain–behaviour problem), and ideals of new individualism. The brain supports a form of singular life (a singular brain, a direct expression of a singular individual) in a world that increasingly values diversity, innovative behaviour, and creativity. Oliver Sacks (1933–2015), the great storyteller of hidden potential, will be our second source.

From the pathology of the practical subject to the discovery of hidden potential, we will explore the "paradox of little Rain Man."

THE MISFORTUNES OF THE PRACTICAL SUBJECT

The earliest example of a model patient of cognitive neuroscience, one who shows a close connection between brain and behaviour, did not take place in Vienna in the 1890s, but rather in Vermont in 1848. A century and a half later, Antonio Damasio intricately described the example in the opening chapter of the book that would make him famous, *Descartes' Error*.

Phineas Gage was a railroad construction foreman. He was a remarkable worker whose physical qualities and sense of responsibility and organization were lauded by his superiors. Following a rock explosion, an iron rod drove through his brain. Miraculously, he survived and recovered within a few weeks. Even if his cognitive capabilities (in modern parlance) remained intact, his change in personality caught everyone off guard: "His disposition, his likes and dislikes, his dreams and aspirations are all to change. Gage's body may be alive and well, but there is a new spirit animating it."[1] He became vulgar, unstable, uninhibited, the opposite of everything he was prior to the accident. The doctor who treated him remarked that "the equilibrium or balance, so to speak, between his intellectual faculty and animal propensities"[2] had been broken. He lost what the neuroscientific community would today call his sense of social cognition: he was no longer reliable.

Gage is cited in numerous neuroscientific works and articles, both scholarly and non-academic, and is almost systematically presented by those discussing the social brain.[3] Why Gage? Because his is the first case to encapsulate the brain–behaviour connection of neuroscience: personality and the self appear manifestly dependent on their material basis – the brain. He is not similar to habitual neurological patients whose disorders are motor related (like with hemiplegia) or who have a perturbed brain function (like with aphasia). Actually, he does not appear to have a brain disorder, but rather some kind of strange psychology, an inconsistent nature, an unstable personality. He is *like* a psychopathological patient, since his behaviour involuntarily involves moral and social norms. It is a borderline case, teetering between neurology and psychiatry.

This brings Damasio to "tell a sad story":

> While other cases of neurological damage that occurred at about the same time revealed that the brain was the foundation for language, perception, and motor function ... Gage's story hinted at an amazing fact: ... there were systems in the human brain dedicated ... in particular to the personal and social dimensions of reasoning. The observance of previously acquired social convention and ethical rules could be lost as a result of brain damage, even when neither basic intellect nor language seemed compromised. Unwittingly, Gage's example indicated that something in the brain was concerned specifically with unique human properties, among them the ability to anticipate the future and plan accordingly within a complex social environment: the sense of responsibility toward the self and others; and the ability to orchestrate one's survival deliberately, at the command of one's free will.[4]

All of these traits were part of the previous Gage, a man ascending the social ladder thanks to his own personal qualities. His behaviour became irrational, and he was incapable of making any decisions[5] advantageous to himself. Hence, making good choices is a sign that one's personal and social abilities are intact. The criterion of his pathology, as it deals with moral and social behaviour, is that he acts systematically to his own disadvantage. It is the only criterion put forward by Damasio, and it is clear he makes the distinction between *pathological* behaviour and *amoral* behaviour, in which subjects act in their own best interests. Gage lost his sense of what today is called social cognition, and he could no longer function in society. He was no longer a rational being. It is essential to integrate social normativity into a clinician's reasoning. Moreover, it is affirmed explicitly.

But to say the brain is at stake is not enough, since the anatomical question is, Where in the brain? "But to understand Gage's behavioural change," Damasio continues, "would have meant believing that normal social conduct required a particular corresponding brain region, and this concept was far more unthinkable than its equivalent for movement, the senses, or even language."[6] Much more unthinkable because social behaviour did not concern, at that time at least, neurology. The part of the brain affected was the prefrontal cortex. Hannah Damasio re-examined Gage's skull (kept at Harvard Medical School) using state-of-the-art neuroanatomic imaging equipment. The examination confirmed it was not the regions dedicated to motor function and language that were hit, but a part of the prefrontal region, the ventromedial area of the cortex, where the frontal lobes are located.[7] They occupy close to half of the human brain, and are therefore much larger than that of other primates, and do not exist in other mammals. Gage appears to be a paradigmatic case for social neuroscience: "Our recent investigations have highlighted as critical for normal decision-making, the ventromedial prefrontal region."[8] The frontal lobe, the part of the brain that separates humans from other mammals, plays a crucial role in "executive functions," meaning the multiple requirements of individualized action, especially anticipating the effects of those actions. It plays a decisive role in socialization. The normal traits destroyed by the pathology do not produce symptoms of a guilty conscience, unconsciously conflicted between right and wrong. Instead, we find practical subjects whose brains, because they are ill, irrationally associate a means to an end. They systematically fail themselves by acting against their own interests. This brings the concept of self-regulation into play.

So here, nestled between neurology and psychiatry, is a prime example. The symptom demonstrates sufficient subtlety, since there are no obvious signs the aphasic individual has difficulty with speech, yet there is a particularly destructive disorganization as it negates the interpersonal life of the affected subject.

Two points need stressing. The first has to do with the language used by Damasio: associating means and ends, the rationality and irrationality of decisions, acting in one's best interest, and consideration for the consequences of one's actions. Here we can detect vocabulary and ideals developed in the Anglo-Scottish eighteenth century and later influenced by American behavioural social sciences starting in the 1940s. Gage's brain refracts these ideals. Therein lies a decisive point of order in understanding the type of moral authority upon which neuroscience is based. It will be situated in its historical context in the next chapter.

The second relates to frontal lobe sequencing and decision-making, as well as decision-making and social behaviour: we will follow this path to arrive at a better understanding of humankind through the brain. It is the path of emotions, but to find and recognize it, we need a living patient. We will get there.

Personality Disorders Reviewed through the Lens of the Practical Subject

Gage's case is paradigmatic because it raises both neurological questions (a rod through the brain) and psychological questions (his altered personality or behaviour), which boil down to a loss of normal social behaviour. It is the social being that preoccupies Damasio: "Gage lost something uniquely human, the ability to plan his future as a social being."[9] Of course, Gage was a neurological patient, but the lesson to be learned, Damasio thinks, goes beyond the brain: "There are many Gages around us, people whose fall from social grace is disturbingly similar." But not all of them have experienced lesions or trauma, they are not affected by neurological disorders, "and they still behave like Gage, for reasons having to do with their brains or with the society into which they were born."[10] These Gages are not insane: they are not schizophrenic or paranoid; they do not have somatoform disorders or types of hysteria; they are not obsessed, nor are they neurotic. They have behavioural disorders and are among the morass of personality disorders. The harmful consequence of "irrationality"[11] for those afflicted with it is due to desocialization, which they cannot keep from adopting.

If there are several Gages in our society, it is because his brain speaks to us, in the language of cognitive neuroscience, about the vast field of personality disorders (antisocial behaviour, behavioural disorders, psychopathies, narcissistic pathologies, borderline personalities), which play a central role in contemporary psychopathology and in the individualist psyche of our societies. There are multiple symptoms regarding personality disorders caused by frontal lesions: "indifference, puerilism, mood swings, behaving contrary to social norms."[12] This list, made by a neurologist, can be applied to psychopathic behaviours as well as pathological narcissism and borderline personalities. These make for interesting cases in that they bring to mind familiar figures of psychopathology, figures at the core of psychoanlysis from the 1950s and 1960s who were under intense media scrutiny. They brought a psychopathologic approach to neurological patients.

Personality disorders increasingly caught people's attention in the United States in the 1950s via psychoanalytic debates on borderline personalities and pathological narcissism.[13] These are traits commonly found in everyday life, easily recognized, rightly or wrongly, in the person sitting next to you. They even had their own dedicated axis in the DSM-III (1980) – the famous *Diagnostic and Statistical Manual* published by the American Psychiatric Association – and their numbers increased considerably with the following versions (the fifth was published in 2013). In the 1980s, these patients, who embody the psychoanalytic shift in interest away from Oedipal neuroses and toward personality neuroses (pathological narcissism and borderline personalities), made up the bulk of psychoanalysts' clientele in the United States. Since then, these patients, although at the core of the psychoanalyst's profession, are themselves part of a study reconfigured from a cerebral perspective.

These individuals, these many Gages, who are without any apparent neurological disorders, but with emotional and psychological issues, personify a neuropsychiatric conception of mental disorders, in terms of border disorders: "The distinction between diseases of 'brain' and 'mind,' between 'neurological' problems and 'psychological' or 'psychiatric' ones, is an unfortunate cultural inheritance ... It reflects a basic ignorance of the relation between brain and mind. Diseases of the brain are seen as tragedies visited on people who cannot be blamed for their condition, while diseases of the mind, especially those that affect conduct and emotion, are seen as social inconveniences for which sufferers have much to answer."[14] The argument is brilliantly simplistic: if the symptom is psychological in origin, it appears to be imperceptible, and its pathological dimension doubtful, whereas if the disorder is cerebral, it has an actual pathological foundation.

Emotion, Cognition, Behaviour:
The Golden Triangle of Cognitive Neuroscience

Taking an interest in the pathological consequences of patients who have sustained frontal lobe lesions, Damasio had the opportunity to observe subjects like Gage, which is to say apparently demonstrating the distinction between neuropathology and psychopathology.

Elliot was in his thirties. He had also "undergone a radical personality change" despite being in possession of his intellectual faculties. Suffering from meningioma (a benign growth in the meninges), the operation to remove it was considered a success, and yet his personality had changed: "Elliot was no longer Elliot."[15] His "social cognition" was also affected and he became incapable of making rational decisions. Cerebral imaging showed only the prefrontal cortex was affected, mainly in the ventromedial area. Neuropsychological tests indicated normal intellectual function, but an inability to make decisions regarding personal and social matters.

Nevertheless, another element intervened, which struck Damasio: Elliot recounted his tragedy with extreme detachment. "He was always controlled, always describing scenes as a dispassionate, uninvolved spectator."[16] "He seemed to approach life on the same neutral note,"[17] and Damasio felt more for him listening to his tragic tale than did Elliot. He allowed Damasio to explore an issue he could not with Gage: emotions. Their absence did not allow Elliot to *weigh* decisions, to attribute differential values to them and, consequently, to behave in a rational manner, not against his own self-interest. He had lesions, which are neurological, but they generated emotional problems, which are psychological.

From Gage to Elliot, we find our way to a set of three terms: *emotions, decision-making, frontal lobes,* even if other regions are involved in the making of emotions. So cognition (the faculty to reason in order to make decisions) and emotion form an indissociable pair that conditions behaviour. Cognition-emotion-behaviour is the golden triangle of cognitive neuroscience, and within it we find it possible to open decisive perspectives by building the unified science of the individual who thinks, feels, and acts.

Let's continue investigating the role these regions have in moral and social behaviour. Elliot suffered cerebral damage as an adult. The psychological lab tests showed he was capable of authentic social knowledge, such as evaluating the consequences of a decision, and therefore his lesion did not alter the memory of this knowledge. However, it is learned knowledge, purely formal since, in real life, he was incapable of using it. So what happens when the cerebral injury occurs during childhood? An article written by Damasio's team, published in 1999 in *Nature,* considers that "information about the early onset condition is vital to the elucidation of how social and moral competencies develop from a neurobiological standpoint."[18] Childhood allows us to introduce the developmental dimension. Two patients were examined. The first (twenty years old) received a blow at the age of fifteen months. From the age of three, she showed indifference to reprimand and punishment. Then, in her pre-adolescence, her behaviour became increasingly disruptive. Her teachers considered her to be intelligent and scholastically capable, but constant lying, stealing, running away, etc., hindered her life. She was totally dependent financially on her parents and social services; she had no prospects for the future. The second patient (twenty-three years old) underwent surgery at the age of three months to remove a tumour in the right frontal lobe. At the age of nine, he started having outbursts of anger and behavioural issues; he became obese, began lying, and started committing petty crimes. He showed no sign of guilt or remorse for his actions and had no plans for the future. Their social and familial status is in no way at fault: both patients were brought up in stable, middle-class households with attentive and dedicated parents, and their siblings enjoyed a normal development. By eliminating any potential social factors, it was concluded the brain was the cause.

"The neurological evaluation was normal in both patients, except for their behavioural deficits."[19] Their cognitive capacities were not at fault and therefore could not explain their issues. However, they were handicapped when put in social situations; they failed tests having to do with conduct; their level of moral reasoning was that of a ten-year-old child and, when we examine their decision-making, they always made choices that went against their own best interests. The MRI showed both patients had lesions in the prefrontal region of the brain, known for being associated with emotional difficulties and decision-making.

Compared with patients whose pathologies start in adulthood (like Gage and Elliot), their cerebral injury was more severe: they developed antisocial behaviours and were incapable of accessing and grasping rules on a simple declarative level (Elliot understood rules on a declarative level, but failed on an emotional one, and was unaffected by this failure).

If Elliot and Gage were two inconsequent beings who were a nuisance to themselves, the other two patients faced problems that were more dramatic. In effect, they "bore considerable similarity to those of patients with psychopathy or sociopathy ('Conduct Disorder' or 'Antisocial Personality Disorder,' according to the DSM-IV nosology), another early onset disorder characterized by a pervasive disregard for social and moral standards, consistent irresponsibility and a lack of remorse."[20]

Then there is the *extensive hypothesis* of behavioural neurology: the deregulated cerebral mechanism takes into account psychopathology. The authors are quick to add, "Psychopathy may be associated with dysfunction in prefrontal regions, especially in persons without predisposing psychosocial risk factors."[21] This essentially means not in a social environment that is unfavourable and unstructured.

The two cases of frontal lesions during childhood suggest "early dysfunction in certain sectors of the prefrontal cortex seems to cause abnormal development of social and moral behavior, independently of social and psychological factors, which do not seem to have played a role in the condition of our subjects. This suggests that antisocial behavior may depend, at least in part, on the abnormal operation of a multi-component neural system ... The causes of that abnormal operation would range from primarily biological (for instance, genetic, action at the molecular and cellular levels) to environmental."[22]

Since these subjects did not respect common rules, their behaviour was relative to social life, and this absence of respect was a symptom (it was systematically to their personal disadvantage), and so we have fallen into the realm of psychopathology. Expanding to include the social appears to be necessary for the identification of cerebral knowledge and knowledge of self.

In all these cases, establishing correlations between behavioural disorders and lesions in certain cerebral areas leads to the inevitable conclusion: "There appears to be a collection of systems in the human brain consistently dedicated to the goal-oriented thinking process we call reasoning, and to the response selection we call deci- sion- making, with a special emphasis on the personal and social domain."[23] Is knowing this personal and social domain through the brain merely a manner of speaking, a metaphorical language, or does it point to an authentic reality?

Like Freud's patients, this new neuropsychiatric patient can serve as a support upon which concepts and theories are elaborated. It is like a weaving loom, thanks to which a series of scientific threads will be woven, and will help give substance to our golden triangle of emotion-cognition-behaviour. The theory will develop from related concepts found in all variants of cognitive neuroscience, forming several branches that stem from the same trunk.

The condition for the project's success is finding actual markers indicating the links between body, mind, and world. The "somatic marker" hypothesis is Damasio's main theory, which features a personal system that aids individuals in decision-making. Before performing a cost/benefit analysis, there is a brief unfortunate reac- tion that takes the form of an unpleasant feeling in the gut. This marker is an alarm preceding any actual reasoning, allowing for the reduction of possible solutions to the problem: "Somatic markers do not deliberate for us. They *assist* the deliberation."[24] These markers are the body's knowledge, an unconscious knowledge modifying the body's state through chemical and neural channels.[25] The principal marker used in experimental settings is skin conductance (a mea- sure of the variation of moisture secreted by sweat glands), which informs the autonomic nervous system. In a device displaying both disturbing and neutral images, patients suffering from frontal lobe lesions are compared to patients suffering from lesions elsewhere in the region, as well as healthy subjects. The results can hardly be contested: those with frontal lobe lesions show no variation in skin conductance, whereas the two other categories do. However, these are merely traditional psychological measures used for decades in experimental cognitive psychology, and not markers of a mechanism that triggers response X.

In researching biomarkers, "biological signatures" of mental pathologies have been part of biological psychiatry research since at least the 1970s. They are the subject of several experimental works, especially since they received heavy financial backing from the National Institute of Mental Health (NIMH): in psychiatry, the ambition was to be able to go from clinical diagnostics, derived from indicators displayed by the subject, to biological diagnostics, as is done in other fields of medicine. More broadly, the challenge of bio-markers is to make sense of the cerebral part of human behaviour, which is to say the way in which the outside world is *represented* within the subject.

For Damasio, the marker is a bodily indicator of a deliberation that in turn leads to a decision. This deliberation consists of theorizing the problems and weighing the solutions. In order to perceive anything, individuals must theorize their own psychology and that of others, since, "on the basis of those theories we can predict what theories others are forming about our own mind."[26] This theory allows the individual to make accurate *predictions* and, consequently, behave in a *rational* manner. We come to view the idea (which we will come back to) that social competence consists of being able to put oneself in someone else's place, this capacity demonstrated in the concept of empathy, which itself involves a theory of mind.

This theory is a cognitive conception of perception: to perceive X is to know it, and to know it is to be able to visualize it. At the root of this system are "neural representations." The thesis is as fol-lows: for a central nervous system to be in possession of a mental function between stimulus and response, the "essential condition" is "the aptitude to create internal images," to elaborate "neural representations which can become images." "Herein lies the center of neurobiology as I see it: ... the process that allows for invisible microstructural changes in neuronal circuitry (in cell bodies, den-drites and axons, and synapses) becomes a neural representation, which in turn becomes an image we each experience as belonging to us."[27] The approach is very materialistic and is based on the areas of sensory input that process information in order to pro-duce motor output and mental images. This information is "stored, dormantly and abeyantly, in the form of 'dispositional representa-tions' ('dispositions,' for short) in the in-between brain sectors."[28] However, one step is missing so these representations can be our own. Subjectivity is "a key feature of consciousness," as Damasio notes. Therefore, "those neural representations must be correlated with those which, moment by moment, constitute the neural basis for the self." But this self "is not the infamous homunculus ... It is, rather, a perpetually re-created neurobiological state."[29] It is an activation system that comprises "dispositional representations" controlled by "topographically organized representations,"[30] which are controlled on a superior level, the entire process ending in representations in the form of words, phrases, and arbitrary symbols of thought, all elements that are conceived as images. "Surely nobody will deny that thought includes words and arbitrary symbols. But what that statement misses is the fact that both words and arbitrary symbols are based on topographically organized representations and can become images."[31]

The extensive hypothesis of behavioural neurology is based on existent, putative somatic markers that research will one day discover.[32] According to the mantra repeated within the neuroscientific tribe, "We've only just begun."

BRAINS OF HIDDEN POTENTIAL, OR DEMOCRATIZING THE EXCEPTIONAL

For a biology of the mind to have any chance of coming into existence, the brain used to support it must be full not only of mystery, but of force, power, and ability. Neurologist Oliver Sacks, attentive and empathetic clinician, admirable storyteller, and prolific author who started in the early 1970s, became the herald of colourful neurological patients. He is *the* mediator between research, clinic, and public. His life's work was built around finding an alternative to "neurology's favorite word," which is "deficit."[33] It is because of Sacks that the neurological patient appears in the public eye[34] as an individual who is singular, in both senses of the adjective: as a unique individuality and as an eccentric being (when considering shared norms). Two books, which present stories of particular cases, caught the public's attention: *The Man Who Mistook His Wife for a Hat* in 1985 and *An Anthropologist on Mars*, which came out in 1995. They played a part in showing peculiar brains and patients with extravagant personalities. Sacks is most certainly the leading neurologist thanks to whom "the neurological patient became a thing through which humans fashioned their sense of identity."[35] What identity? That of hidden potential, which can reveal itself only through a system of collective expectations resolutely centred on valuing individual differences. These expectations themselves demonstrate a shift in the concept of human capacity, according to a typical/atypical polarity embodied by the autistic individual.

From Type to Individual

The neurological disorder from which Gage and Elliot suffered is a personality disorder of sorts. However, they lacked personality. They displayed the characteristics of an organism with mechanical behaviour, through which Damasio explores the neurophysiology rather than the psychology underlying the symptomatology. They are types, not individuals. For the extensive hypothesis of behavioural neurology to account for the entirety of the pathological spectrum, neuro and psych, and therefore uncover the missing links between brain and mind, we need something neurophysiology cannot bring to the table: a collaboration with patients in their own words. This implies there is a clinician in front of them willing to listen. Listen to what they offer as much as to what they are.

Among the first to promote neuropsychology were 1920s clinicians, like Soviets Lev Vygotsky and Alexander Luria or the German Kurt Goldstein, who remarked that the personality of neurological patients should be taken into account when considering their treatment. Early in his career, Luria worked with blind and deaf children. He focused more on their strengths than on their handicaps, looking for the unique in each case, since each child acquires this strength through personal means that go against established norms. Sacks describes Luria as an activist for "a new view of the brain, a sense of it not as programmed and static, but rather as dynamic and active, a supremely efficient adaptive system geared for evolution and change, ceaselessly adapting to the needs of the organism – its need, above all, to construct a coherent self and world ... The miracle is how they all (the cerebral areas) cooperate, are integrated together, in the creation of a self"[36] – *the* problem of neuroscience. Sacks situates himself explicitly in the tradition of Soviet neurology: in his books, he hammers home the idea that "the patient's essential being is very relevant in the higher reaches of neurology, and in psychology; for here the patient's personhood is essentially involved, and the study of disease and of identity cannot be disjoined. Such disorders, and their depiction and study, indeed entail a new discipline, which we may call the 'neurology of identity,' for it deals with the neural foundations of the *self*, the age-old problem of mind and brain."[37] In this text, we are definitely reading the plea of a clinician particularly mindful of the fact that patients are best cared for when there is a good understanding of their specific needs. However, there is something more to be said regarding brainpower, which can be used by neuroscientists to raise serious questions on the human condition by treating it empirically (in contrast with the philosophers to whom they are the heirs). With these excessive pathologies, neuroscientists have at their disposal individual supports helping them understand human nature.[38] This implies the method of meticulously describing cases Alexander Luria reintroduced and to which he attributed the word *neuropsychology.*

Will *without Ability, the Cornerstone of* Individualizing the Neurological Patient

Paradoxically, it was a pathology with a presentation of profound impairment that uncovered the issue of patient individualization. Sacks wrote an entire book, *Awakenings*, on the subject of encephalitis lethargica (EL), also known as sleeping sickness, a pandemic that lasted for about ten years starting in 1917.

Interestingly, there may be no other pathology more motor deficient than encephalitis lethargica. In the acute phase, patients show symptoms of akinesia, characterized by an absence of voluntary motor functions, catatonia, lethargy, or even a state of comatose – some of those affected fell into comas lasting decades, until prescribed L-Dopa to bring them out of it, though often only temporarily. In the post-EL phase, symptoms persist at a less intense rate, with Parkinsonian symptoms. By radically affecting motor functions, the pathology also radically creates deficits.

This was the first neurological syndrome to serve as a prime example linking motor and psychic disorders[39] because, although it has an organic origin (virally transmitted), both motor and psychiatric symptoms occur together. Neurological pathology is of interest to us because several patients showed symptoms present in psychiatry. Now, the specificity of the psychiatric symptom shown by neurological patients is such that they, unaffected by disordered thinking, appear to be reliable witnesses. Their reasoning, their thinking, or their personality has not been brought into question. By listening to patients we are able to access the *mechanics* of their psychiatric symptoms. Therefore, it is possible to find a material basis for the common symptoms of the two classes of pathology. Between the two world wars, French and German psychiatrists contemplating the possibility of cerebrally locating psychiatric diseases published several articles.

The disease does not affect the prefrontal cortex, where higher functions supposedly reside, but the parts of the brain where the vegetative functions, which regulate multiple vital physiological functions, are located. They are the foundation of the brain's base – without vegetative functions there is no living body.

The symptom of akinesia (impairment of voluntary movement whose severity can go as far as quasi-immobility) exists in schizophrenia and Parkinson's disease. Neurologists and psychiatrists took an interest in educated patients who were able to give an account of their state. Albert Hauptmann, a psychiatrist best known for his work on patients post-EL, elaborated a theory in the 1920s on subcortical activity, in which the self does not direct the mental process of will, but results from a chain of reflex actions and automatic processes regulating human physiological functions: "It appears that 'I' move myself, but I am in fact moved." Akinesia presents as an "impulse disorder" that prevents motion from happening. Cases published from patient reports showed there was no link between their personality before the disease and the motor and psychiatric symptoms following it. In other words, there was no psychiatric predisposition.

EL opened pathways linking motor function, shared by all living beings, and will, the greatest characteristic of human existence. A post-EL patient affected by Parkinson's in one arm had to show phenomenal willpower to move the affected arm. The patient declared resolutely that his will was unchanged; it was just that one of his limbs was sick. For Hauptmann, the explanations consisted of affirming "only the unconscious process that links the *will to move* and the *movement itself* was affected by EL."[40] For these patients, the will was not disturbed; only its execution was compromised. He observed that their emotional and intellectual lives remained rich – one of them, a scientist, was able to write many articles *thanks* to the solitude created by the reduction of sensation. Other patients showed a more advanced akinesia as well as a decrease in thinking and affect. They were affected by an "impulse insufficiency": although they were aware of their disability, they were devoid of emotions and presented no depressive symptoms. They may have appeared to be suffering from dementia, but in fact, it was a lack of interest, not intelligence, that was the cause.

A French psychiatrist, who was hit with the disease over a three-week period in 1920 and suffered from the after-effects for three decades, contested the slowing of the mind as well as impulse insufficiency. On the contrary, he showed mental hyperactivity (publishing numerous articles and books), and emotional outbursts. Other patients were recognized as showing inconsistencies in their behaviour, abruptly going from a state of emotional excitement to one of clear judgment regarding themselves. Through a catatonic-like state, there was an awakened consciousness, but one that felt beside itself, like a spectator to what was happening, as if cut into sections foreign to itself, yet observed without folly, and with great accuracy. But it is thanks to these patients, whose intelligence remained intact, that psychiatrists hoped to gain some insight into the complexity of motor symptoms in schizophrenia.

Here, neurology brings two elements that specify what it means to access the "mechanics" of a symptom that could not be accessed in a schizophrenic patient – provided the symptom has the same function in both cases, which is far from consensus. An impaired will that presents without intellectual disturbance – without the disorganization characteristic to so many schizophrenic patients – makes it possible to isolate the *doing* aspect of will: patients want, but are unable, to execute their will. It becomes possible to break down mental entities into simpler elements. The contrast between apparent immobility and richness of personal life has thus placed EL into a "prototype of a neurological disorder in which the actual patient does not reflect specifically the internal person and his psychological dynamic."[41] The second contribution is that shared mechanisms can be involved, either because the motor symptoms would be analogous in psychiatry and neurology, or because they are susceptible to being the basis of psychic symptoms in psychiatry and neurology alike. Some sixty years later, starting in the 1990s, psychiatric symptoms of Parkinson's disease, after having been thought not to affect the senses and personality, have been more closely scrutinized: it is one of the disorders on the fence between psychiatry and neurology.[42] It is not the only one.

In EL, the motor has broken down and there is no longer any will being relayed from brain to body. We could make do, as with aphasia, with a mechanistic and deficient form of neurology: the patient is akinesic, abulic, etc. When these patients were prescribed L-Dopa in the 1960s, their awakening was accompanied by hyperkinesia, hyperbulia, etc. The deficit-causing disease became a disease of excess. What does this spectacular reversal tell us about brainpower? "We are forced," writes Sacks, "to move from a neurology of [diminished] function to a neurology of action, of life," the life of the mind in everyday situations of affected people. This form of neurology "is forced upon us by diseases of excess" since they reveal "instinct in all cerebral functions, at least higher functions such as those of imagination, memory and perception," which are "highly personal."[43] Indeed, diseases of excess possess a paradoxical feature: they often create "a wonderful feeling of health and well-being," and therefore the individual is confronted with "dilemmas ... of an extraordinary kind: for patients are here faced with disease as seduction."[44] The disease does not only appear as an illness having affected the subjects from the outside, but as an element of their selves, of their personality. The same goes for neuroses in which the disease possesses secondary benefits. Do certain neurological illnesses strike a Freudian note? Does the psychoanalytical "dynamic" work discretely – unconsciously – on neurology's "mechanism"?

From Deficit to Asset: Tourette Syndrome as New Individualism

Gage and Elliot are types, because Damasio describes them, very classically, as patients with deficits. For Sacks, patients who have suffered losses (in function) or, on the contrary, those who were affected by excesses, transports, possessions, are shown as individuals whose personality comes out *through* their brain: "It is, then, less deficits, in the traditional sense, which have engaged my interest than neurological disorders affecting the self."[45] Here, at the focal point of cognitive neuroscientific preoccupations, Sacks's stories paint the picture of people at "the far borders of human experience,"[46] by following a common thread: the disease's creative potential. "Defects, disorders, diseases, in this sense, can play a paradoxical role, by bringing out latent powers, developments, evolutions, forms of life, that might never be seen, or even be imaginable, in their absence. It is the paradox of disease, in this sense, its 'creative' potential, that forms the central theme of this book."[47] By nature, a disease is something described according to normal/pathological criteria, but, and herein lies the cultural innovation, it shows paradoxes that change its trajectory: the paradoxical condition is thought of in interdependent terms of disability and asset. And so the approach to problems switches from a mechanical perspective to a dynamic one, in which the affected subject demonstrates creative abilities brought out by confronting the disease.

Creative abilities: this topic proves to be decisive for transforming neurological, but also psychiatric, patients into autonomous
individuals, capable of finding their own way in life despite being
afflicted. "Creativity" has provided a moral context that creates
a space for the development of rehabilitation and recovery practices that treat the mental or cerebral patient as a moral or social
partner (see chapter 5).

Psychiatric aspects of neurological disorders did not generally garner much attention, since their characteristics are focal (function is
affected) and not global (personality is affected). Neurology is first
and foremost motor focused, and neuropathology deficit focused.

Within neurological disorders, excesses have a special place, since
they seem to affect personality and "challenge the basic mechanistic
concepts of neurology." Sacks believes these "disorders of excess"
force us to explore the life of the mind, whereas deficits seem more
mechanical, more linked to a disturbance in cerebral programming.[48]

"Such cases are exciting and precious, for they serve as a bridge
between the physical and personal, and they will point, if we let
them, to the neurology of the future, a neurology of living experience."[49] They show the existence of a personal dimension analogous
to what is found in psychopathology. As privileged material establishing links between mind and body, the self or the personality, they
belong to a neurology of the self.[50]

Among such cases is Tourette syndrome. The disorder is characterized by motor and vocal tics, strange noises, swearing, and insults.
Since the symptomatology is on the fence between neuropathology
and psychopathology, it "constitutes a sort of 'missing link' between
body and mind."[51] Indeed, "Tics can have an ambiguous status, part-
way between meaningless jerks or noises and meaningful acts ... One
such patient ... kept making an explosive, guttural, trisyllabic noise,
which revealed itself, on analysis, as a very accelerated, crushed ren-
dering of 'Verboten!' in a convulsive parody of his father's constantly
forbidding German voice."[52] The symptom is set off by a cerebral
malfunction, but its form is Freudian since it is directed: it does not
appear to be merely motor; it is marked by an intentional element
making it a neurological syndrome whose expression is Freudian. In
the United States, it went from being considered a psychosomatic
pathology, taken on by psychoanalysis during the 1940s, to a neurologic pathology around 1970 when patients given haloperidol (an
antipsychotic) had significant results.

"Witty Ticcy Ray" was twenty-four years old when he met Sacks. He suffered from "multiple tics of extreme violence," which started when he was a young boy. He was fired from several jobs because of them. Yet he created an asset from his symptoms, which allowed him to make a living: a "jazz drummer of real virtuosity, famous for his sudden and wild extemporizations, which would arise from a tic or a compulsive hitting of a drum and would instantly be made the nucleus of a wild and wonderful improvisation, so that the 'sudden intruder' would be turned to brilliant advantage." In music, his tics were transformed into a skill, better yet, a gift. But it is relative, since Ray was a man in despair: "He scarcely knew whether it was a gift or a curse."[53] Sacks prescribed him an antipsychotic, but the medicine made him feel numb and without the secondary benefits from the syndrome. Like the Freudian subject, the Tourette's subject is ambivalent toward the symptoms since the negative and the positive are inextricably linked.

Sacks proposed a therapy to "examine the role and economic importance" of the syndrome and "how he might get on without [its] affects]."[54] During treatment, the exploration that ensued dissolved his "resistance." Ray was put back on the antipsychotic, which relieved him of his tics, but this time it was without the side-effects from his first treatment. The medicine was effective because he had arrived at a level of maturity that allowed him to forego the symptoms. Nine years later, he was a married father, who enjoyed spaciousness, freedom, and work, and played an important part in his community. Still, he had lost some of his drive, impetuousness, vivacity, some of the benefits of the syndrome, out of which came a compromise: he would take his medicine during the week and allow himself two days of impetuousness on the weekends. As in psychoanalytic treatment, according to Freud, he had a newly found "freedom to decide one way or another."[55]

"When the galvanized Touretter sings, plays or acts, he ... is completely liberated from his Tourette's. Here the [self] vanquishes and reigns over the 'It.'" The brain appears to be an instinctual motor: "The 'It' in Tourette's, like the 'It' in Parkinsonism and chorea, reflects what Pavlov called 'the blind force of the subcortex,' a disturbance of those primitive parts of the brain which govern 'go' and 'drive'"[56] – the subcortex, where the limbic system is located and where, according to Damasio, basic emotions are programmed.[57]

However, with Tourette syndrome, something else is happening along with the patient's individualization through listening: the emergence of a new individualism coming from the margins of society. The paradoxical polarity of disability and asset is progressively placed at the centre of the individualist notion of autonomy in that it challenges – paradoxically – the limits of human capacity, and thus reveals the hidden potential of each individual.

Furthermore, it was the first neurological syndrome that brought about patient activism and mediatization in the 1970s. A group of parents, whose children were treated with antipsychotics prescribed by several psychiatrists (the Shapiros, very hostile toward psychoanalysis), created the Tourette Syndrome Association (TSA) in 1972. They promoted the disorder as organic. The TSA gathered professionals, patients, and their families. They put out information regarding the disorder as well as advertisements to recruit those suffering from multiple tics. Tics were rare, but publicity demonstrated they were much more common than previously thought. To organize is to emancipate, but it also serves a larger purpose, getting a wider range of research, even on themes as diverse as the linguistic structure and genetic basis of tics. "Never before have patients led the way to understanding, become the active and enterprising agents of their own comprehension and cure."[58] The fact they put it together collectively as a social movement, as an advocacy group, as a mutual aid system, was new.

For the Touretter, the turning point was not only individualization as *heard* patients, by adapting therapy to their needs, but also as individuals *like any other*, capable of self-actualization. Since the symptom is not merely negative, it also can be treated as an asset, as it was for Ray, making it possible to socialize the disorder – he is a better drummer because of the syndrome. A new economy of affection comes into being – this is the pathology's paradoxical side, highlighted by Sacks.

There is a two-fold shift occurring from Tourette syndrome, which concerns the ideals of treatment and of the individual. Turning the disabling symptom into an asset is a theme that became central to rehabilitation and recovery practices: it is at the core of what can be called exercises in autonomy (see chapter 5, in which the cognitive version will be discussed).

In order to grasp the shift in individualist ideals, we should go back to how Ray was described. The patient is elevated through a double reference: to his intelligence, which is creative, and to his courage, which is heroic. Creativity is linked to the way in which Ray found a compromise with his symptoms, which allowed him to lead a fulfilling life despite his affliction, a life anyone can recognize as having value. The heroic character comes through in the last paragraph of the chapter: "The super-Touretter, then, is compelled to fight, as no one else is, simply to survive – to become an individual, and survive as one, in face of constant impulse ... The miracle is that, in most cases, he succeeds."[59] He succeeds because he demonstrates courage and creativity greater than his affliction, qualities that elevate him to a level of dignity surpassing the disorder: he is cured by *socializing* his ailment, by finding a *form of life*. He met the illocutionary conditions that turned his actions into successful actions: he can be admired, despite his quirkiness, as a talented individual, instead of arousing the compassion one should have toward someone who is not well.

Touretters were henceforth linked to creative and heroic figures, a social movement, bringing them into the public eye. By association, they rose out of their invisibility, and in doing so, shed light on the moral qualities of courage and inventiveness, both of which are ordinary and essential. They no longer were subjected; they chose and decided for themselves. Touretters socialized the negative aspects of social life, the disorders defined as deviances, the pathologies or disabilities that could not be controlled, and thus spread the individualist ideal by enriching what we included in humanity, what we considered as partaking in the ideals of ordinary humanity. That was new.

This style of socializing the evil is in accordance with a new moral, social, and political context; it is a shift in the collective sensibilities beginning in the early 1960s: the new individualism imbued with ideas-as-values brought together under the concept of autonomy. This can be characterized by two fundamental traits. The first is a new egalitarian dynamic marked by the huge upheaval of equality of the sexes; in other words, that women be recognized as individuals equal to men. This dynamic brings to the social table a series of social groups who found themselves marginalized: in the United States, it is minority groups; in France, it is the immigrant worker. The institution of valuing choice and self-ownership engendered a dynamic of normative diversity and a multiplication of lifestyles that were still unknown fifty years ago in North America and Europe. Beginning in the 1960s, in Europe and the United States, people started leading lives that belonged more to the artist (the bohemian), thereby marking a softening of bourgeoisie and middle-class social codes. These innovative groups promote ideals of creativity, originality, experimentation; they explore new forms of experience and action, *new forms of personal life*. These ideals were aptly summed up in a famous article written by Tom Wolfe, published in 1976 by *New York Magazine*, "The Me Decade," which was a brilliant (but hardly original) accusation against therapeutic culture. He characterizes it as an inheritance of mystic gnosticism from the beginnings of Christianity, whose message proclaims each person possesses a dormant divine spark at the summit of the soul. In this new context, each person can awaken this spark hidden within, not by refusing the physical world and body, but quite the opposite, by scratching the surface of civilization to fulfill one's life by taking total possession of one's body *in* the world.[60] The creative figure became central to contemporary ideals (giving rise to ways of life as well as markets).

These new collective representations of humans in society place an emphasis on the individual's ability to act as well as on creative and innovative behaviours. Individual choice, creativity, initiative: here we are entering into what could be considered an individualism of capacity. Adopting a personal course of action has become important. Hidden potential is a particularly salient aspect of it.

The "super-Touretters" are the heroes of this new individualism since they are capable of awakening the dormant spark that makes them *them*. They are not only the survivors of trials undergone, they are also individuals who self-actualize, not despite the disorder, but in all probability thanks to it. This double locution (despite/thanks) extends access to individuality to new populations – deviant, ill, disabled – since these are ideals for action: it opens a pathway beyond the normal/pathological polarity, inherent in the very concept of illness, by subjecting it to the paradoxical perspective in which a disability is prone to transform into an asset: individuals were patients who needed to be treated; now they had become individuals whose potential was to be developed in order to create a form of life, a potential that will act, if need be, on the ailment. There has been a hierarchical reversal in our collective representations of individuals in society. A major consequence is the emergence of a new form of social access to a successful and socialized individuality; they are *recognized* as players with skin in the social game. In chapter 5, we will examine behaviours through practices conceived to help individuals help themselves, so they make the right choices when faced with adversity and are able to be their own agents of change.

However, the coming together of individualist ideals of hidden potential and cognitive neuroscientific concepts, having the biggest impact on the patient, will derive from the high-functioning autistic individual and, more specifically, her brain.

The Autistic Brain as a Cultural Commodity

Autism has undergone a spectacular transformation: from the depths of mental handicap and institutionalization to being elevated to a way a life, the names of which clearly refer to cognitive science and neuroscience: "different cognitive styles" and "neurodiversity." These qualifiers define autistic intelligence as a special intelligence created by brains with a singular organization. This is why autism is a textbook case for issues concerning the brain–behaviour relationship. It becomes *the* reference for a reorganization of the relationship between normal and pathological, resulting in the disorder being transfigured into a different form of life. In short, it is the key element that took a purely defective pathological condition and transformed it into a paradoxical condition. From the 1980s, it had the particularity of being thought of as a pathology, characterized simultaneously as a major disability and a powerful asset.

Temple Grandin was the first well-known, high-functioning autistic, diagnosed with (what is now called) Asperger's. A professor of animal science at Colorado State University, and recognized the world over as a specialist on livestock handling, she co-wrote the first story "from the inside," *Emergence*, published in 1986.[61] This work demonstrates the emergence of her autistic subjectivity, and she continues to publish books today. For Oliver Sacks, this book was both "unprecedented because there had never before been an 'inside narrative' of autism; unthinkable because it had been medical dogma for forty years and more that there *was* no 'inside,' no inner life, in the autistic."[62] Yet something else comes from these stories: the feeling of being foreign to humankind, like being *An Anthropologist on Mars*,[63] an expression coined by Grandin that gave the book its title. It is worth noting, and this is no trivial detail, that feeling foreign among humans is a *very* human feeling, an ordinary feeling, which can be felt by anyone in any number of circumstances.

Grandin's brain allows us to illustrate the way in which, using cognitive neuroscientific vocabulary, the ideal of the individual is refracted. The individual is self-reliant and can self-actualize, despite disability or illness, provided she is able to transform the deficit into an asset; to do this implies a *competency* that makes it possible to play such a social role.[64]

To describe a human group that defines itself with factor X is to describe how the group attributes supreme value to the entity it finds most important. The criterion for this supremacy is that the entity in question cannot be integrated as part of a superior whole that encompasses it. Yet Temple Grandin sees the world through the prism of the brain. Her case allows us to grasp both the conditions under which one can live with language derived from cognitive neuroscience, and the effect it has on the individual to see the world, and herself, through her brain. The issue is to know how an entity, like the brain, develops cultural value.

A quick comparative detour allows us to specify what I want to put forward. The book written by Edward Evans-Pritchard on the Nuer of South Sudan,[65] a masterpiece of British anthropology, is useful to this point because the Nuer see the world through an entity, their cattle.

The Nuer are a "pre-eminently pastoral" people, writes Evans-Pritchard, "for at heart they are herdsmen, and the only labour in which they delight is care for cattle. They not only depend on cattle for many of life's necessities but they have the herdsmen's outlook on the world. Cattle are their dearest possessions ... Most of their social activities concern cattle" (16). And he gives a bit of advice for those who want to better know the Nuer: "*Cherchez la vache.*" It is through cattle that a person can get in touch with his ancestors, a fundamental activity in a lineage-structured society. The Nuer are obsessed with their cattle as, for example, an American may be with liberty, or Christians with their love of God. "Their social idiom is a bovine idiom" (19), and this plays an essential role in Nuer culture. Here the key word is *culture.* Therefore, "A cow is never to them just a cow, but is always a good cow or a bad cow." In other words, it possesses a symbolic value. "Irrespective of use, they are in themselves a cultural end" (40). Yes, the cattle allow the Nuer to live materially, but also spiritually – and the two aspects are inseparable and mutually reinforcing.

Let us crack open Grandin's latest book, *The Autistic Brain*, published in 2013. "In this book," she writes, "I will be your guide on a tour of the autistic brain. I am in the unique position to speak about both my experiences with autism and the insights I have gained from undergoing numerous brain scans over the decades, always with the latest technology … Seeing the detailed anatomy of my brain was awesome. My many brain scans have provided possible explanations for my childhood speech delay, panic attacks, and facial-recognition difficulties."[66] A bit further, she adds a sentence representative of autistic pride: "Do not allow a child or an adult to become defined by a DSM label."

In 1987, she was one of the first people to undergo an MRI. Upon getting out of the machine, "I hopped off the gurney and headed straight for the technician's room, and there I received my reward: I got to see my brain. 'Journey to the center of my brain' is what I call this experience. Seven or eight times now I have emerged from a brain-imaging device and looked at the inner workings that make me *me*: the folds and lobes and pathways that determine my thinking, my whole way of seeing the world."[67] This technique allowed her to describe her brain with the same attention to detail that the Nuer describe their cattle, with features like cowhide spots, horn convolution, ear shape, etc. What follows is a several-page description of cerebral areas and associations that are presented under the aegis of a principle: "But it's the overall complex relationship between the various parts of the brain that make us each who we are" – known in neuroscience as "distributed knowledge" (see chapter 3). These successive journeys to the land of cerebral imagery are journeys of her brain, a famous brain that in turn made her famous. The identification between Grandin and her brain is a theme woven throughout the text: "Because my brain has become fairly well known for its various peculiarities, autism researchers have contacted me over the years to ask permission to put me in this scanner or that. I'm usually happy to oblige. As a result of these studies, I've learned a lot about the inner workings of my own brain." They learned that her cerebellum is 20 per cent smaller than normal, that her visual cortex responds better to objects than faces, that her association fibres are hyperconnected between two areas of her cortex (which is why she thinks through images, by representing things that words designate). They discovered that her left ventricle is larger than her right by half, whereas in "control subjects" it is only 15 per cent larger – a finding that was "particularly gratifying," and that her intracranial volume, brain, and amygdala are larger than normal. She does not have a brain like most do; her brain *is* her: it is not only a part of her, but it is an entity through which she self-identifies, a like being. Her idiom in search for an explanation is exactly that of cognitive neuroscience.

Discussing the size of her amygdala and therefore the question of the relationship between neuroanatomy and behaviour, which is, may I remind you, the central issue in cognitive neuroscience, she hopes to eventually have cerebral diagnostics:

> Personally, I like to know that my high level of anxiety might be related to having an enlarged amygdala. That knowledge is important to me. It helps me keep the anxiety in perspective. I can remind myself that the problem isn't out there – the students in my parking lot under the bedroom window. The problem is in here – the way I'm wired. I can medicate for the anxiety somewhat, but I can't make it go away. So as long as I have to live with it, I can at least do so secure in the knowledge that the threat isn't real. The feeling of the threat is real – and that's a huge difference.[68]

The cognitive neuroscientific language makes it so she can invoke the entities responsible for her condition and relativize their negative effects. It's a way to cope. That is why Temple Grandin's brain is, like cattle for the Nuer, a supreme value: it organizes their world.

"No sight so fills a Nuer with contentment and pride as his oxen. The more he can display, the happier he is."[69] The attention to detail with which a Nuer can speak about a cow or an ox is absolutely phenomenal: where we see a simple animal, they see what they hold dearest to their hearts, something without which their life would not be worth living. There is nothing taking up more space in Temple's life than her brain, besides animals, of course: her neuroanatomic differences regarding the norm are the subject of interpretations concerning what she herself is. Here, neuroanatomy is psychology, or maybe ontology even. If Temple Grandin's brain is precious to her, like cattle to the Nuer, this is because it is *more* than just her brain. It is a form of life, a way to live in the world and manage within it. "Neuroanatomy isn't destiny ... So what I want to do here is focus on how the autistic brain can build up areas of real strength – how we can actually change the brain to help it do what it does best."[70] This rich description is the rhetorical process by which the brain appreciates in value, in a register that no longer belongs to biology, but to ideals, or rather, that of the idealization of biology. The brain is a value in that it delivers an essential message: even in the worst conditions, there are still resources within individuals to find a way out and take their lives into their own hands.

Defining oneself via the brain is not arguing in favour of some thesis, but living in a way that makes the language of cognitive neuroscience one's own, and living thanks to it: functional neuroanatomy is the basis on which she describes herself. The pieces of neuro-imagery are references to her psychology. She thinks of herself in the language of neuroscience, whose concepts are ideals for action, thus making it possible to lead a fulfilling life by insisting on a radical difference concerning traditional social (and medical) convention. This brain personifies a new horizon of expectations and possibilities for personal fulfillment, dominated by normative pluralization, which consists of reconfiguring numerous pathological conditions and turning them into socializable differences.[71] And what does this brain tell us about ourselves, if not that there are challenges in every life that need to be confronted, and that each individual can achieve fulfillment with what each has been given?

From the Autism of Yesterday to the Autism of Today

For Grandin to be able to speak like this without coming across as someone who is disturbed, our ideals had to change in the way we already indicated. A thorough reconceptualization of autism was also necessary.

The contemporary concept of autism was formulated in British child psychiatry.[72] Between the 1920s and the 1960s, it was considered an early infantile psychosis, since it triggers very early in childhood, whereas schizophrenia becomes apparent during adolescence. Psychosis means the disorder is characterized by hallucinations, difficulties connecting with others, and an unconsciousness of one's own subjectivity. In the 1960s, authorities started closing asylums en masse, and populations once institutionalized had to be cared for by the general public with other means. Psychiatric epidemiology developed within this context and completely redrew the lines of autism. "Instead of measuring child development and its anomalies via theoretical models of an individual child's successive attempts to engage with reality through his or her relationships with people and objects, these studies measured child development and its anomalies as behavioural variables within a total population that represented the norm."[73] Autism is thus radically distinguished from psychosis, with its emotional causality and hallucinatory aspects. It is defined as a pediatric developmental pathology whose primary symptoms are language deficiencies (delayed access followed by anomalies), communication deficits, and stereotyped behaviours. In 1979, Lorna Wing, a British psychiatrist, redefined autism through the criteria of "social deficits." Her argument was that social disability is a better indication for stereotyped behaviours as well as communication difficulties. She put forward the hypothesis that the authors hypothesized "certain areas or functions of the brain are responsible for the development of social interaction and symbolic imaginative activities."[74] Two years later, she coined the term *Asperger's syndrome* for the diagnosis of subjects with normal intelligence.

Throughout the 1980s, two theories emerged accounting for autism, one explaining social deficit, and the other special intelligence. The theory of mind is the capacity to put oneself in someone else's place and to infer someone else's thoughts. Autistic individuals suffer from a theory of mind deficit, and because of that, they do not possess certain social keys and are unable to unlock codes from everyday life, or implicit situations that are self-evident to most. Whereas Gage or Elliot transgress social norms, autistic individuals, through naïveté, display normocentrism. They thus satisfy our ideals of openness to the pluralization of norms and values, making us sensitive to the diversity of human forms of life possessing value. The theory of mind allows us to understand social disability, but not the existence of assets – we will come back to this theory in chapter 4.

From the traditional figure of the "idiot savant" first noticed in the nineteenth century, an alternative theory emerged. Around 10 per cent of autistic individuals, essentially affected by Asperger's, have major disabilities along with major talents, or competencies, which can sometimes reach levels far superior to the norm. In order to account for this polarity, we must consider that they are interdependent. British psychologist Uta Frith proposed to define autism as a "weak central coherence." The expression describes the capacity to collect information according to context and to understand what is most important in a given situation, often at the expense of attention to detail and memorization. People who have autism, however, pay close attention to detail at the expense of global configuration and contextual meaning. They cannot see the big picture without first paying exclusive attention to the parts that make it up. The inability to integrate information is a major causal factor in their social ineptitude.

Thinking in parts is pathological, since the information received by the subject is not incorporated into a coherent whole. Yet certain autistic individuals possess the ability to see the whole from its parts: their weak central coherence has its disadvantages, but it also has its advantages. The theory states it is possible to predict "that people with autism and their relatives will be characterized by expertise only with those mechanical systems where focus on detail is an advantage."[75] It is their cognitive style.[76] Talent functions in separate ways, like modules that exist independently. From here, there is ongoing debate around whether it is a central mechanism or a system functioning separately, or differences scattered within the cerebral organization. Sacks writes, their talents

> do not seem to develop as normal talents do. They are fully fledged from the start ... Savant talents, further, have a more autonomous, even automatic quality than normal ones. They do not seem to occupy the mind or attention fully ... Savant talents do not seem to connect, as normal talents do, to the rest of the person. All this is strongly suggestive of a neural mechanism different from that which underlies normal talents ... It may be that savants have a highly specialized, immensely developed system in the brain, a "neuromodule," and that this is "switched on" at particular times – when the right stimulus (musical, visual, whatever) meets the system at the right time – and immediately starts to operate full blast.[77]

An alternative explanation to weak central coherence suggests, rather, that those with autism are perfectly capable of thinking in totalities, but with a particularity linked to their cerebral organization. In order to see autistic intelligence, cerebral organization must be divided into its different functions: if autistics are better than the norm at certain tasks and worse in others, it is because their brain favours more areas and visual networks than it does those linked to language – Grandin thinks in pictures, for example. This provides an advantage for any activity associated with perception. Laurent Mottron, professor of psychiatry, who heads a cognitive neuroscience lab in Montreal, brought eight autistics into his research team: "I believe that they contribute to science because of their autism, not in spite of it." They are not autistics who demonstrate extraordinary abilities. "They are 'ordinary' autistics, who as a group, on average, often outperform non-autistics in a range of tasks, including measures of intelligence." If 90 per cent of autistics do not speak and 80 per cent of them depend on their parents into adulthood, "in my experience," he writes, "autism can also be an advantage."[78] This is true for scientific research. His main collaborator, Michelle Dawson, who has been part of the team since the early 2000s (they have co-written thirteen articles), is herself autistic.

How are these people able to contribute to research thanks to their autism? What can autistic creativity achieve by committing itself to scientific activities? "From a young age, they may be interested in information and structures, such as numbers, letters, mechanisms and geometrical patterns – the basis of scientific thinking. Their intense focus can lead them to become self-taught experts in scientific topics,"[79] as is the case with Dawson. Their capacity to pay close attention to detail can allow them to connect X to Y in a manner that would have gone unnoticed by normal, or "neurotypical," people. From this viewpoint, it may be said they possess a mind whose style is that of British empiricist philosophy: they are keen observers of patterns that escape those who do not possess their special cerebral mechanisms.

If IQ can vary much more than among normal people, it is because the style of intelligence is different: "There are autistics with IQ's of 47 and autistics with IQ's of 150. When these scores are divided into their component parts, a unique and characteristic profile of autistic intelligence (Asperger syndrome has its own profile) emerges across all levels of intelligence. Declaring that autistics differ from non-autistics in level of intelligence is false, except in that the range in autism is extraordinary. It is accurate to say that in autism, the *kind* of intelligence is different."[80] The gap between the two extremes is key: mentally slow or genius, mechanical repetition or inventiveness, etc. As a paradoxical condition, it shatters the usual polarities, giving it a unique place. This is strengthened by the affirmation that autistic individuals are undeniably different from one another, just as if autistics replicated, in their own unique way, the infinite diversity of *ordinary* people. Such a representation can satisfy only the expectations of an individualist society. It is a new biological interpretation:

"Without question, autistic brains operate differently."[81] The brain is wired, structured, and organized differently; the singularity of autistic intelligence is inscribed in its functional cerebral anatomy. Here, harboured in a natural foundation, ideals are strengthened on a biological level – we will see in chapter 3 how neuroscientists came to think all brains are anatomically different from each other and that these differences are significant.

If these brains arouse scientific interest, it also can be affirmed that they are of notable interest on a human level. As we explore them, "we can also learn more about ourselves, explore the 'challenge to our capabilities' and uncover the hidden potential – the little Rain Man – that resides, perhaps, within us all."[82] Here we are at the heart of the paradoxical condition in that the little Rain Man in us is the linchpin from which we can just as easily descend into intellectual deficiency as we can elevate to social and personal fulfillment.

Through the brain, we discover not only a form of life, but also a civilization, a system of ideas-as-values that push the individual to discover powers hidden behind the symptom, the illness, or the disorder. The new opinion is not to eliminate it entirely in order to be cured, but to create from it a life measured by the capacity to be autonomous. It is from this paradigm that neuroscience secures its moral authority: sustaining those collective beliefs upon which the highest value is bestowed, with the unequalled demonstrative resources of science.

Hidden Potential: A Specific Social Form of Entrance into Modernity

The autistic brain and those of Gage and Elliot are central to cognitive neuroscience since each allows us to uncover missing links between brain and behaviour. However, unlike Gage and Elliot, the autistic brain is representative of a positive, heroic figure, one with whom anyone can identify, whether odd, eccentric, original, *or* normal. The scientific and social lessons are one and the same. They represent a way of overcoming adversity, to "reconstruct one's moral being." "But I have confidence that whatever the thinking about autism is, it will incorporate a need to consider it brain by brain, DNA strand by DNA strand, trait by trait, strength by strength, and, maybe most important of all, individual by individual."[83] This is the last sentence in Grandin's book. It flawlessly outlines a personal course of action for an autonomy-as-condition society as it possesses an aptitude so engrained in her disease that to remove it would mean eliminating the aptitude. Her reputation around the globe regarding her thorough knowledge of animal behaviour and her peculiarity toward humans are inextricably linked. She fulfills perfectly the characteristics of the paradoxical condition.

Painting the Baudelairian picture of modernity, Walter Benjamin wrote, "The hero is the true subject of *la modernité*. In other words, it takes a heroic constitution to live modernity."[84] Baudelaire, for example, elevates the unsung blue-collar worker to a hero of modernity, who every day does the work of a gladiator, but with none of the glory. The pantheon of heroism is democratized by the introduction of the lay person[85] – the labourer, "ruffian," or prostitute – onto the stage of greatness. Here, another democratization is demonstrated: these people accomplish the feat of creatively solving problems traditionally considered acts of passion. Today, we can apply Baudelaire's thoughts on suicide in the middle of the nineteenth century to these individuals: "The conquest of modernity in the realm of passion."[86] In this, passion is thought of in the sense of pathos, agony, suffering, but with an active dimension that progressively infiltrated the moderns, starting in the late seventeenth century. Without delving too deeply into a historic and philosophical discussion – passion, emotion, affect, affectivity – these words share a mix of passivity and activity.[87]

Through courage and inventiveness, these new heroic representations affirm individual singularity in the world by transforming their ailment into a socially valuable form of life. They appear as artists of a diminished life. High-functioning autistics symbolize this because they are a unique mix of disability and asset. If the vast majority of those afflicted do not fall within these parameters, these exceptional examples increased the ability of those affected and their families to pursue specific treatments beginning in the 1990s. Their representativity is not demonstrated in statistics, but in the democratic ideal: it broadens the horizon of action. Transforming representations of the self in society and changing how we think about treatment are two sides of the same coin. The main lesson brought by Grandin, writes Oliver Sacks, is that "she and other autistic people, though they unquestionably have great problems in some areas, may have extraordinary, and socially valuable, powers in others – provided that they are allowed to be themselves, autistic."[88] To become yourself by transforming the constraints of disability into a lifestyle chosen by you and recognized by others, being yourself not only despite the disability, but thanks to it. A perfect example of modernity triumphing in the realm of passion.

Hidden potential is the social form by which those afflicted with deviant behaviours, illnesses, or disabilities have become modern individuals (or subjects, if you prefer the philosophical trope) by emancipating themselves from the purview of total institutions. More specifically, it is the social condition by which they have established themselves as individuals.

These new individualist representations serve as backdrops that give direction and meaning to the many ways in which the normal/pathological polarity can be reconfigured into an asset/disability polarity. The lesson is clear and simple: You must be yourself, and to be yourself, you must find your hidden potential, and awaken the divine spark residing within. These grand models with which everybody can identify demonstrate the diversity of ways in which anybody can turn bad into good by simply having self-confidence. They are models of *being*: they create viable, credible pathways to a utopic society organized around the individual.[89]

With this perspective, Grandin represents an Emersonian version of the brain, a brain of *self-reliance* (one of *the* texts of American existentialism, published in 1841),[90] of the individual who dares, who is not timid, as Emerson states, who can rely on herself in any circumstance. The autistic brain is the expression of the reconfigured normal–pathological relationship in a moral and social context characterized by freedom of choice and the diversification of lifestyles. An inheritor of the Me decade, Grandin's is the emancipated brain that found the (cerebral?) spark that makes her *her*; she checks off the conditions that allow her to make her autism an asset by finding her personal course of action – her style of life. A culture of normative diversity without which individual capacity could not be recognized: the model is not in the disorder, but is the oppressed, unrecognized minority. It is an individualism that relies on science because neurobiology is the language that makes it possible for some to live a fulfilling life by increasing their capacity to maintain hope in humankind and play a part in society. These concepts and tools serve as a blueprint for how to lead a life in which individuals are more or less capable of finding their niche in a more open world, with more or less social backing, since there is always a question of degree in autonomy. However, the change in collective representations is undeniable.

The symptomatology of these patients is characterized by the extraordinary in that it challenges the canons of ordinary life. Something is shown in the pathology, something that, if not more complex, is at least more intangible, and therefore more indicative of humanity than what the afflicted patient could reveal. Entwined in these cases is the strangest, and yet the most human, the farthest from and the closest to ordinary. They no longer represent "the far borders of human experience," because these borders have come closer together. Much like Grandin wrote, we went from the wings to centre stage.

Coincidentally, it becomes possible to transform the brain into a highly colourful character, an individual, a partner, an idea we talk about and that floats around in conversation, an autobiographical or fictional narrative. Since increasing the brain's value helps account for humans in their entirety, we can personify it: the brain thinks, acts, decides. With this new brain we can ask *the* big questions of the body–mind relationship, those of which psychiatric disorders – insanity – or neuroses were the focus up to this point. With high-functioning autistics, the brain has become a character of the contemporary individualist imagination, which shows us to what point radical diversity – each autistic is unique – is a way to put our capacities to the test.

Neurology of the self is a story of the individual as a creator of values, the created value being a way of life, a style, a form with inherent worth. This story emerges from a period of history in which innovation is becoming an important cultural element. To the prototypes of the practical subject, devised according to the characteristics of the relation between means and ends (Gage and Elliot), we add a new heroic figure, one who integrates and surpasses an ailment through personal creativity and courage – creativity and effort feed into one another. The manner of being ill and the manner of living a normal life change as a result. Those patients *capable* of adopting a personal course of action, and awakening their hidden potential when confronted with adversity, are individuals with whom anyone can positively identify. However, if we can identify with that person, it means *we* have already entered into a shared mindset, a system of collective representations of humans in society that encourages us all to explore the little Rain Man within – at your own risk, of course, but whoever said it would be easy?

These patients are on the same level as neurotic Freudian patients, every single one of them demonstrating the same strangeness, the same singularity, and therefore the same humanity. The blind force of the brain can emulate in value the instinctual force of the Freudian unconscious.

We previously mentioned that two traits were recurrent in Damasio's vocabulary: the moral dimension corresponded well with British empiricist and utilitarian thought of the eighteenth century, but not to Kantian duty and categorical imperative. This dimension found its place in behavioural social sciences developed between the 1940s and 1960s in the United States, which then is compartmentalized into rational choice theory, decision theory, and everything represented in the "cognitive revolution," to use the experts' expression.

The next chapter will develop these concepts. It will situate these collective representations crystallized by our exemplary brains in the history of their social origins, a story in which the methods adopted by science and social ideals intertwine. We could thus uncover the different stylings encapsulated in the adjective *cognitive*. In chapter 3, we will examine the cerebral basis of the individual by centring it on the noun *neuroscience*. This will allow us to link collective representations and the history of science.[91]

2

Scientific Method and Individualist Ideals

Converting Passions, from the Scottish Enlightenment
to New Individualism

Nothing has a greater effect both to increase and diminish our
passions, to convert pleasure into pain, and pain into pleasure, than
custom and repetition.

David Hume, *A Treatise of Human Nature*

Psychology cannot tell people how they ought to live their lives. It
can, however, provide them with the means for effecting personal
and social change.

Albert Bandura, "Behavior Theory and the Models of Man"

The brains of Gage, Elliot, and Grandin are specimens of the anthropology underlying neuroscience, since their cerebral functioning conditions their behaviour. They form two cases of this biology-based
naturalism, the scientific aim of which is to explain humankind by
understanding the brain. Both Damasio's scientific argument on
somatic markers and Grandin's stories depicting her unique brain
carry us precisely in this direction. But which anthropological concept are we talking about?

In this chapter, we will retrace the social origins of these ideas
in order to identify the style of individualism at hand, and the element of modernity that falls within the concepts of neuroscience and
scientific psychology. We will develop the idea that the brain, as cognitive neuroscience conceives it, was passed down through forms of
behavioural self-regulation that appeared during the eighteenth-century Scottish Enlightenment with a rather generic term: *passions*.

That will cover the first part. Next, we will describe how these forms shifted with the introduction of the concept of behaviour in the United States beginning in the early twentieth century and continuing through the 1970s, creating a new individualism of capacity imbued with the ideas and values of autonomy.

The importance of this outline is to provide historical perspective to cognitive neuroscience by rooting it in culture, thereby identifying the affinities between scientific and social ideas.

The purpose here is to shed light on the fact that a naturalism, one very distinct from how it is defined today by cognitive neuroscience, was at work: not a biology-based naturalism, but one based on *regularity*, the main tool of which was *exercise*, and the sought-after effect was the formation of *habits*. For Aristotle, a habit was second nature. At its core is this aptitude, which David Hume ably stated was a "very powerful principle of the human mind." This alternate naturalism shows how certain aspects of the history of scientific psychology correspond with the transformation of collective expectations. These aspects remain somewhat obscured when approached exclusively from an epistemological history of science. At the same time, they enrich this history, since the forms of regulating behaviour and the forms of collective representations of the individual in society are interwoven. It is impossible to understand the authority neuroscience has acquired if we do not consider it as a behavioural science intertwined with scientific psychology, from which it gets not only the essentials for its ideas of the individual but, moreover, the style of practice it advocates. Regularity, exercise, habit – the way in which neuroscience combines these words undoubtedly resides in the social basis of its moral authority, considering these words are the common key to unlocking both self-control and successful action.

Through the ideals of regularity, we will uncover the history of our representations of *character*, examined through the lens of the practical subject, from the Scottish Enlightenment of the eighteenth century to the new individualism of the 1960s and 1970s. From the beginning of the twentieth century, these ideals became entangled with the extraordinary fate of the word *behaviour*, the uses and meanings of which continued to expand and diversify.

THE MECHANICS OF CONVERTING PASSIONS: THE ORDINARY INDIVIDUAL AS A PERSON OF ACTION AND CREATOR OF VALUES

From behaviourism in the beginning of the twentieth century to behavioural sciences today, American scientific psychology has been part of the tradition of experimental observation unlocked by empirical philosophy (of which David Hume was a forefather). This is a well-known fact among historians of psychology,[1] but here our goal is to look at philosophical and scientific concepts promoted by this family of ideal individualists, of which the empirical philosophers are the conceptual expression. Through them, we can articulate the key ideas-as-values of the anthropology of action, which is cognitive neuroscience.

Philosophers do not ponder in the land of pure ideas, but troubleshoot from concrete problems and dilemmas, thereby delineating preoccupations and debates in their society. "The eighteenth-century philosopher is not an isolated hero giving shape to what would otherwise be unintelligible, but a cultural spokesman who explores the ways in which everybody *already does* make sense of the world."[2] This is precisely the path taken in this book. Their thought process evolved in societies where freedom of thought and behaviour developed and, consequently, where people were no longer directed by the commandments of religion or royalty. The metaphysical question of freedom arises in close connection with emergent ways of acting in society. Crucially, these new values and ideals had a social and political foothold that differed somewhat, depending on the society. France and the United Kingdom came up with two major ways of thinking about the association of free people, developing two solutions to the philosophical and social problem at the centre of individualism. It was formulated as follows.

Freedom of conscience and behaviour created a new blueprint of reality:[3] the world did not exist solely according to a hierarchical interdependence of an ordered society (nobility, clergy, and the third estate), but also according to an equal independence of free individuals. Therein lies the inner workings of the sociological and philosophical question of individualism, characterized by a two-fold nature: it is a value (of freedom and equality), yet this value also risks social dissolution; it does not stipulate how to construct social order. Individualism is both the principle and the problem of modernity. No society can function on principles of freedom and equality (principles of independence) alone; there also needs to be social order (principles of interdependence). There must be both liberty and order, independence and interdependence. That is why, as Tocqueville wrote, the art of association is the mother science. So, how do we achieve individual freedom and social order at the same time?

Overcoming the Dichotomy of Natural and Artificial

Individualism is a way of understanding and articulating independence and interdependence. The French and Scottish came up with two ways to interconnect free people, two distinct arts of human association, representing two variations of modern individualism. Both assert it is possible to reject the idea of subordination to a power that compels obedience. From the moment that freedom of consciousness and behaviour entered into the collective sensibility, people could no longer be governed by divine or royal commandments any more than by reason. The question of will thus became central.

The French school of thought, from Rousseau to Durkheim, employs the concept of obligation, which is linked to free will, and assumes a representation of the individual as will.[4] The novelty of Rousseau's *The Social Contract* was conceiving convention as a general will (to form an association), rather than a consent (to authority). His logic begins with the social totality, the act by which a people is a people, to use the phrase from his work. This totality encompasses and supports, rather than acts as a power that dominates and compels. The sociology of Durkheim completes the Rousseauian idea of obligation by making moral authority the acting force of society, the main attribute of which is not obedience, but respect.

The Anglo-Scottish school of thought, which we owe to David Hume, Adam Smith, and other philosophers and publicists, begins with the individual, refers to a logic of parts, and understands moral concepts as mechanisms. The British philosophical approach consisted of applying the scientific method of observation to moral deeds. These "Newtons of the mind" empirically observed human nature and the attraction between people, represented as life in society, by using the law of universal gravitation from the physical world. Their empiricism is first and foremost an experimental philosophy, a method for observing regularities. To establish morality as an observational science – a Newtonianism – we must dissect the complex into simple elements, and the simplest observable element is the individual.

Nothing that originates from reason is non-causal, nor does reason direct the will. The Scottish argue, "This power belongs to affections or passions, since only they can function as motives."[5] Everything begins with individual experience, and this experience is passionate because the individual, from birth, is immersed in an ocean of sensory impressions, causing either pain or pleasure. For this reason, individuals are pulled out of their original passivity and put in motion, causing them to act on these effects in accordance with the logic of mechanical forces. In empiricism, the individual is an affected being. Human nature is passionate.[6] It is important to note that the notion of passion underwent changes during the seventeenth and eighteenth centuries: it was no longer simply pathos, suffering, and subjugation. It was also detached from the types of activity that linked it to fury, mania, or anger. Lastly, from a positive viewpoint, it spread beyond its monopolization by the heroic grandeur of nobility. The distinction between interest and passion, then good and bad passions propelled the notion to develop into an idea of passion as a source of creative energy inciting action.[7]

To grasp the naturalism that is not upheld by neuroscience, it would be useful to turn to Hume, who characterizes the natural by what it is not: "Natural may be opposed, either to what is *unusual, miraculous*, or *artificial*."[8] The opposition of artificial and natural requires that what is natural does not depend on works and is observed independently from human will. Religion and politics, having their origins in projects, are artificial. Habit, as opposed to the unusual, is the second criterion of nature: "Nature may certainly produce whatever can arise from habit: Nay, habit is nothing but one of the principles of nature, and derives all its force from that origin."[9] For Hume, nature is fundamentally regularity.[10]

However, nature is also physiological for Hume: "Nature, by an absolute and uncontrolable necessity has determin'd us to judge as well as to breathe and feel."[11] Breathing and feeling are two physiological activities of the same automatic nature: we cannot keep ourselves from breathing any more than we can from thinking. Thinking is a physiological activity like any other, an automatism.[12] We cannot not think just as we cannot not be affected. Here, perception is key. Inversely, intentionality is marginal.

A paragraph on custom in one section of the book on passions, dedicated to the will, sums up the alchemy of repetition: "But nothing has a greater effect both to increase and diminish our passions, to convert pleasure into pain, and pain into pleasure, than custom and repetition. Custom has two *original* effects upon the mind, in bestowing a *facility* in the performance of any action of the conception of any object; and afterwards a *tendency* or *inclination* towards it ... By degrees the repetition produces a facility, which is another very powerful principle of the human mind."[13] Negative passions (suffering, anger, envy) are converted by custom, which is acquired through repetition. Repetition creates a natural tendency toward action, making that action easier. Through custom and repetition, our thoughts and actions eventually become one with us. Humean ideals assume it is human nature to develop abilities through *habit* and *exercise*, and *habit* then becomes an *automatism* of thought and behaviour, much like breathing. Likewise, the laws of human nature are characterized by their consistency and not by their intelligibility. This consistency is tightly linked to a conception of knowledge as inference: "And even after all, the inference is nothing but the effects of custom on the imagination."[14] These ideals put much more emphasis on regularity and the coupling of exercise and facility than they do on intelligibility.

The same goes for human association, because it is necessary to account for social order, since "men cannot live without society, and cannot be associated without government."[15] While Rousseau refers to a totality – the act by which a people is a people, the social contract by which a people constructs shared laws and foster a common spirit – Hume thinks of association according to a logic of parts. Humean convention uses a paradigmatic example of two rowers who adjust their own movements to the movements of the other, and this has a cooperative *effect*. Both rowers gain an advantage they could not have gotten on their own. For Rousseau, totality is consciousness within the parts, whereas for Hume totality is the unconscious effect of the parts' action. "Individual interactions produce cohesion and paradox, from any point of view, which respond to no *specific* intention ... In other words, looking for reasons in how effects are structured must begin from a logic of parts."[16] Conventions are formed tacitly in everyday interactions through reciprocal expectations, establishing sequences of cause and effect. Social interactions, independent from our thought and reasoning, are natural. They regulate passions through mutual influences, transforming them into experiences that in turn make humans more mature. The Scottish shed light on a class of phenomena that resisted the dichotomy between *natural* and *artificial*. Philosopher Adam Ferguson defined it, through his famous expression, as "the result of human action, but not the execution of any human design."[17]

The major difference between the French and Scottish was clearly laid out by Adam Smith when he compared, in his *Theory of Moral Sentiments* (1759), the French Enlightenment to a game of chess, in which "every single piece has a principle of motion of its own," and the Scottish Enlightenment to a watch, in which "they are put into action by a spring, which intends the effect it produces as little as they do."[18] Rousseau's (the French) question is how to connect people by compelling their will, by calling on the individual's free will. The Anglo-Scottish question is how to connect people by converting their passions through operators or mechanisms – Mandeville, Hume, Smith, Hutcheson, Ferguson, Bentham, James Mill, etc. are philosophers of action – action in a society for which they seek principles. Government does not result from the moral nature of humankind (who delegate their rights to representatives), but from their social nature, from the diversity of activities in which they are engaged – both social and natural considerations make government necessary. Political institutions are a problem of government, not of sovereignty – "natural society" has a commercial nature, in both senses of the word when it was put in use: social commerce, which civilizes, and "commercial" commerce.

Yet it is imperative for us to have a mechanism at our disposal that can account for the universal law of attraction between people and their moral compass. This mechanism is a process of the imagination that both Hume and Smith called sympathy. It is fundamental to understand that it "is not a moral sentiment, but a mechanism, an operator" that, writes Smith, may be used to denote "our fellow-feeling with any passion whatever." It "seem[s] to be transfused from one man to another."[19] For Hume, it is the first of two principles that are "very conspicuous in human nature,"[20] and this allows us to understand how passions are passed from one person to the next and how relationships among individuals are established spontaneously or automatically. From the given of the individual who self-constructs through experience, passions can be adjusted, thanks to an "affective intensity regulator," also known as sympathy, which connects people through a chain of mechanisms. The concatenation of passions[21] makes it possible for us to ponder the interdependence of relationships using an entity approach.

Virtue or Character: A Central Conflict for
Transitioning into Modernity

In what type of society were such questions raised?

The given from which the subject is constituted is undoubtedly a lesson straight from Newton's method, but the way in which this given is presented marks the birth of an individualist collective representation of people in society, of a shared mindset. The scientific method of philosophers and the individualist ideal of Anglo-Scottish society are profoundly linked. After two revolutions that, during the seventeenth century, brought all authority into question and instilled a freedom of thought (and more specifically, religious pluralism) in the individual, making people their own judge. The Anglo-Saxons began a financial revolution in the 1690s, a discovery in economics that would come to be called capitalism at the end of the eighteenth century.

The crucial point is that this discovery was, as shown in great detail by British historian John Greville A. Pocock, "traumatising" and was the subject of a "gigantic quarrel" regarding the relationship between virtue and commerce, and therefore between two valuations of the individual that lasted from the end of the seventeenth century to the 1770s. On one hand, there is the civic patriot, who possesses a title of nobility, owns land he received as an inheritance and therefore cannot sell (landed propriety), has power over other men, and takes up arms to defend his nation. This is the ideal of a unified personality, one in which personality and property are inseparable. On the other hand, the private investor, whose properties are mobile and exchangeable, separates the person from the property, thereby making the individual's personality the sole foundation of rights. The first was conceived from a viewpoint of civic virtue, the second of *character*. Freedom was no longer about being self-sufficient, but had to do with an increase in exchange and sociability. This debate took place in several European societies, but the United Kingdom (which came into being in 1707) was the first society that, after the Netherlands, experienced a sharp upturn in commerce and credit, thereby discovering the modern idea of contingency, which mobilized the intelligentsia to a degree never before seen. The Anglo-Scottish found themselves facing something hitherto unknown: an open, undefined future in which people could become something they were not by increasing their own value through the creation of riches.[22]

The financial revolution of the 1690s introduced a system of public credit built on financial obligations allowing people to lend to the government, on which the state would pay interest; these obligations could in turn be exchanged on a market, and therefore be subject to *speculation*. However, speculation did not yet refer to any rational calculation, but to a sense of fantasy, imagination, or passion. Public credit placed British society on a new temporal axis: an open future, which reason was powerless to shape and Christian faith could not master. The discovery of capital was not, at first, calculated interest, but a new way of living in which "not only was every man in debt to every other man, but every man was judged and governed, at every moment, by other men's opinion."[23] From there the question of confidence was raised, of how much credit one can extend to another, which then became a question of regularity and predictability. In this new society, "obliging men to credit one another with capacity to expand and grow and become what they were not,"[24] and the ability to self-expand along with the credit, faith, and confidence that can be bestowed upon others, and that others can bestow, go completely hand in hand.

The idea of credit opened people to an entirely new experience of the future that led to intense preoccupation with contingency plans. The relationship between motive, action, and consequence, as well as an action's intended purpose and the result, increasingly became a focus.[25] For empiricism, as Gilles Deleuze reminds us, "the essence of action is found in the nexus between means and end. To act is to assemble means in order to realize an end."[26] Means/ends and end/result are very concrete issues in this new society that opened up the possibility to personal choice and multiplied the opportunity to act on one's own behalf: individuals who act must weigh their options according to the purpose they give themselves. That is the sociological meaning behind the association of ideas: selecting means between alternatives with a specific purpose in mind. The question of action is raised in terms completely different from those of action stipulated by a moral sense of duty or loyalty to a society of orders. In this new collective experience, in which trust was granted to all people, credit and reliability were the centre of everyone's concern. "If speculative man was not to be the slave of his passions, he had to moderate these by converting them into opinion, experience, and interest, and ... the reification followed by exchange of the objects on which his passions focussed was an excellent means of socialising them."[27]

To socialize them, i.e., to allow for a regulated self-expansion, was precisely the *social* idea from the British. The morals of converting passions are the morals of inclinations, happiness, and choice. Virtue went to the ideal of a unified personality – "civic patriots," owners of land, having power over others, and taking up arms to defend their country; it would go to the people of average station, who were neither noble nor poor, but who could create wealth; not lavishness, but a *common wealth*, based on individual action. "Commerce, and the complexity of exchange which it generates, teaches both rulers and subjects the conventions according to which government must be conducted. Being rooted in experience, these lessons take the form of opinion,"[28] an opinion well thought out. In Scottish philosophy, like in Scottish society, human commerce, through its own working, leads individuals to display sociable behaviour; it civilizes them, teaches them the social *sentiments* essential for prospering both morally and materially.

This type of sociability must distinguish between impersonal and personal relations in such a way that trust reigns. In Britain, it puts a fresh face on the stranger: a "stranger is not a friend from whom we can expect any special favor and sympathy. But at the same time he is not an enemy from whom we cannot expect any sympathy at all. Everyone in society is as independent of every other as a stranger, and is equal with every other [because] they can [imagine the] exchange [of their] situations,"[29] thanks to sympathy, which is the "principle of communication." For British philosophers, the confusion between interested and uninterested actions, which characterizes the relationship of personal dependency between nobility and other social bodies, comes undone in the commercial society with the emergence of "weak ties,"[30] in which relations are structured in such a way that strangers can be indifferent to one another in a "technical sense."[31] The mechanisms for sympathy and interest are new details for regulating behaviour, which accompany these new collective representations founded on trust and exchange.

With sympathy, there is a principle of communication that makes it possible to account for the individual's social (sociable) nature. However, there needs to be a moral principle that regulates human behaviour.

Virtue frames the individual's character in the ideal of the civic patriot. However, based on the 1714 publication of Bernard de Mandeville's famous essay, *The Fable of the Bees or Private Vices*,

Publick Benefits, moral virtue, which does not need to be approved by others, and social character, which, on the contrary, demands it, are separate. Mandeville argues that private vices lead to public benefits. He supported the idea put forward by the French Jansenists that there could be a disparity between apparent virtue, which was publicly approved of, and actual motive. The discovery of society around 1700 is two-fold: individuals are driven both by a passion for financial gain and wanting approval from others. The well-known philosophical expression that "human minds are mirrors of each other" gets its entire sociological meaning from this context: it is the expression of a theatrical concept of the passionate individual.

In opposition to Mandeville, for whom the spectator is partial, in the sense that one does not refer to social morality when judging one's own conduct. Adam Smith states, in *The Theory of Moral Sentiments*, that "we examine our own conduct, and endeavour to view it in the light in which the impartial spectator would view it" (44.7.2.4). Society is a game of smoke and mirrors in which reputation is fundamental for individualization and where the individual needs certain criteria in order to self-evaluate and evaluate others. Adam Smith's position regarding the impartial spectator was in response to this problem: "We begin ... to examine our own passions and conduct, and to consider how these must appear to them ... We suppose ourselves the spectators of our own behaviour, and endeavour to imagine what effect it would, in this light, produce upon us. This is the only looking-glass by which we can, in some measure, with the eyes of other people, scrutinize the propriety of our own conduct."[32] Impartial spectators are definitely a modest concept, and they possess a strong regulating power, but we must make do with the means available.

Sociologically, this concept assumes a certain type of social life without which it could not be conceived.[33] Indeed, the character that intense sociability requires was established according to a criterion of trust, without which there could be no guarantee of ensuring stability and regularity in relationships. It is presented also as individuals who know their role. Spectators are not only the reference of moral principle that completes the principle of communication, otherwise known as sympathy, forming a second mechanism, but they are also the ones who are practising to become actors. Is learning a role not the association of ideas according to observation and experience, which is necessarily a social experience? To achieve this, it is necessary to practise. Theatre's role was fundamental to bringing in these new morals, as a British historian so aptly pointed out: "Encounters in the theatre offered a model for the rehearsal of public expression, where members of the audience could conceptually remove themselves from their companions, and then, in imaginative isolation, experience those states of feeling whose appropriately performed outward signs were evidence of a distinguished sensibility."[34] The spectator is, from the empirical philosopher's standpoint, observing regularities, but the stage of observation is composed of multiple moral and social dilemmas that the actors debate and resolve.

Individual as Creator of Values or the Socialization of Self-Expansion

How to create wealth was one of the major debates of the eighteenth century. Smith's answer was it is not nature nor the earth that provides subsistence (as it was for the physiocrats), but humankind. In "Smith's solution," Louis Dumont notes, "the individual as creator of values [is] similar to the theists' insistence on God as creator."[35] Individuals as *creators of values*, viewed through the lens of the God-as-creator model, increase, through the same operation, their own value and simultaneously contribute to the common wealth. This was the major discovery given to us by the Scottish and is among the strongest of individualist ideals. Its singularity was having devised a general form of regulating behaviour through operators and mechanisms, to avoid resorting to a superior authority whenever possible, instead calling on individual will, since such an authority would apparently be a constraining power – from there Rousseau was able to enter into the Anglo-Saxon world as a "totalitarian" philosopher.

Reference to a moral mechanism is a way of recognizing social interdependence, since the mechanism is independent from individual will, and subordinating the individual, who simultaneously supports natural rights and the natural given. As supporters of rights, the individuals' freedom is not to be limited by law, and we must bend their nature by converting their passions. This is a question of "socializing by means of automatic mechanisms."[36] Recognizing the social as a level existing independently from individuals is shown in the form of an operator and a mechanism. Dumont suggests this regarding Mandeville, who opened the Anglo-Scottish discussion at the beginning of the eighteenth century: "Mandeville admits the existence of something beyond every individual man, something that, for this reason, could be called social ... The mechanism by which specific interests align [is not] something designed and thought of by men, but something that exists independently from them."[37] We have fully shifted from the perspective of a social contract that, by definition, is "something designed and thought of."

The methodological individualism of the British (human beings within the impressions constituting them) is the expression of a moral individualism: it is a manifestation, using a scientific and philosophical approach, of ideals in which ordinary people are encouraged to follow their inclinations to generate wealth and increase their own value. Here we are dealing with a morality that differs from that of Kantian duty. Anglo-Scottish ideals value ordinary individuals as people of action, and civil society as a level of exchange between people in order to satisfy needs and desires through interest and sympathy. It is through these ideas from Scottish philosophers that the collective representation of the ordinary person, as a creator of values by way of work and exchange, developed in the West. It is, as Albert O. Hirschman wrote, "a demolition of the hero"[38] and underlies the rise of character at virtue's expense. The condition for creating value is, on one level, the mechanism by which passions are converted, and on another, a new morality that rejects abnegation by the promotion of personal inclination, a morality of *good*. Furthermore, abnegation, sacrificing one's own interest on behalf of some superior ideal, is there only to serve the interests of the higher classes. "The fundamental moral notion was no longer that of obligation," wrote Élie Halévy at the beginning of the twentieth century, "but change; the motive for moral action was no longer fear, but trust."[39] With trust as a criterion, when compared with obligation, we are still within contingency, and in the realm of extending credit to people.

For Hume, the social was structured by generalizing individual tendencies that were in agreement with the opinions of others (like in the case of the rowers). There is one constant here. We could define the British view of the relationship between independence and interdependence by using Jeremy Bentham's expression from 1814: "To give, in a word, to the social, all the influence of the personal motive."[40]

It is obvious that therein lies a perspective other than that of freedom à la française understood as willpower that *wants* to be linked with and *consciously* decide in all shared domains. To compel free will or convert passions, now there are two ways of recognizing the necessity for a supra-individual reality in an individualistic society, two styles of collective representation of the individual in society, and two conceptions of the relationship between independence and interdependence. In the United Kingdom, individualism takes shape through the economy (*common* wealth) and the mechanics of converting passions; in France, through politics (a person is first a citizen, then French) and the artificiality of the contract. All this language pertains to the individual of action established in Britain by the philosophy of human nature.

The Rise of the Altruism/Egoism Polarity and the Moral Moment of Character

The modern question of character came about when it was perceived of as a theatre of passions. Character (social) opposes virtue (moral). It marks the concern individuals of action have for their reputation, which is crucial to confidence. Personal motive is utilitarian: individuals are the best judge of their own self-interests, which make up the principal motive for action, or active passion.

The language of action underwent multiple transformations throughout nineteenth-century Britain, during which character was reconfigured into a purely moral concept.[41] This change is linked particularly to the rise of a new concept, altruism, a term coined by John Stuart Mill in Great Britain in the 1850s. Progressively, altruism's popularity would lead to identifying personal interest with egoism, and the altruism/egoism polarity defined the entire moral spectrum, and as a result marginalized *amour-propre*. Egoism became the sign of a lack of character and emerged as an insufficient motive for making people act. Emphasis was placed entirely on will: a weak will became the primary concern and marked the forming of "implicit Kantism."[42]

The rise of character took place after Romanticism, for which the emphasis on introspection surfaced as a risk for self-absorption. "The Victorian intellectual, believer or sceptic, did not have a constant impulse to serve, he ... had a constant anxiety about apathy and infirmity of the will." Character, as a moral concept, also corresponds to an emerging middle-class that was hostile toward the unwarranted privileges of the well-born and who developed competition as a struggle against oneself and one's own weakness. Character represented "an ideal particularly suited to a future of unknown circumstances."[43] It was a "second-order" virtue, a general aptitude, which could support first-order virtues in "a society which paradigmatically envisaged the individual – often an isolated individual ... – confronting the task of maintaining his will in the face of adversity."[44] A colonial, industrial, and commercial endeavour favoured a representation of individuals confronting themselves, namely their will.

The development of psychologies starting at the end of the nineteenth century relativized a focus on will and shifted the question of character toward one of personality. With psychology, a two-fold idea surfaced: the bulk of the individual's mental powers does not reside in the conscious, but in the unconscious; and psychological techniques make it possible to access it. Psychoanalysis and scientific psychology, as well as several other forms of psychology, rooted in the popular culture of the United States and Great Britain, arise as practices for the new urban-industrial civilization.[45]

FROM SOCIAL ENGINEERING TO SELF-FULFILLMENT (1900–1970): THE THREE AGES OF BEHAVIOUR

We will follow this language of action to the United States, from the beginning of the twentieth century to 1970, using the emblematic word *behaviour*, which left a mark on scientific psychology that became a sociological hallmark. First associated with behaviourism, which became, from the turn of the twentieth century to the 1930s in the United States, the main academic branch of psychology and the only one able to claim the adjective *scientific*, the word *behaviour* was profoundly varied and went well beyond the behavioural school of psychology. Behaviourism is mainly an American phenomenon that marginally touched European psychologies, including the British.[46]

Its history accompanies a debate that went on for decades and could be called, to use John Dewey's book, published in 1930, *The Lost Individual*. It addresses the individualism specific to America as it became an industrial and urban society focused on mass production and consumption. The nation entered the "era of organization" and turned to the "visible hand" of experts. New collective representations of individuals in society accompanied this change. "The problem of constructing a new individuality consonant with the objective conditions under which we live is the deepest problem of our times."[47] The objective conditions are, broadly speaking, those of a "corporate civilization" in which "associations tightly and loosely organized more and more define the opportunities, the choices and the actions of individuals."[48] The expression "lost individual" is to be understood in two ways: "Individuals vibrate between a past that is intellectually too empty to give stability and a present that is too diversely crowded and chaotic to afford balance or direction to ideas and emotion."[49]

During this transition from old to new, the debate on the individual was formulated via a recurring question until the 1950s: Is the individual inner-directed or other-directed? Scientific psychology and behavioural science offered a possible answer to this question.

The word *behaviour* went through three different stages from the time of its introduction up until the 1970s. The first represented behaviourism symbolized by the stimulus-response polarity. Its primary emphasis was understanding how human beings are shaped by their environment. The second stage came with the emergence of behavioural social sciences in the 1940s, which, unlike behaviourism, was about understanding the ways individuals shape their environment through their choices, decisions, intelligence, and rationality, all while being shaped by it. This would eventually come to be called their cognitive system. The representation of the individual is that of a citizen of the free world, who chooses and makes decisions. The model for this individual is that of the scientist, who embodies the values of reason. The third stage was marked by the integration of this new individualism into scientific psychology, which emerged during the 1960s: behaviour regulation shifts toward self-regulation. It is no longer a question of governing individuals' conduct, but allowing individuals to acquire skills in such a way that they are able to effectively achieve self-fulfillment in their choices by adopting a personal course of action. Self-regulation was a regulation of behaviour based on the idea that individuals were agents of their own change.

If there is a mission for which scientific psychology takes credit, from behaviourism at the beginning of the twentieth century to cognitive neuroscience and behavioural science of the twenty-first century, it is resolving social problems scientifically by focusing on practical aspects of existence. How does scientific psychology suggest we complete this mission?

Behaviourism: Reforming Individualism in Mass Society by Directing the Individual from the Outside

The word *behaviour* became prominent at the beginning of the twentieth century as a category used by scientific psychology in the United States to define its subject. It was established in opposition to the two-sided idea in Anglo-Saxon psychology that prevailed at the end of the nineteenth century: knowledge of one's own mind is based on introspection; knowledge of another's mind is based on inference.

The meaning of the word is firstly physiological. It designates the behaviour of an organism in terms of its adaptation, aim, and organization. It was introduced through concepts shifting away from physiology and toward psychology, by moving the lines of these disciplines to a comparative perspective between people and animals – the book that advanced behaviourism, *Animal Behavior*, by Edward Thorndike, was published in 1898. Organism and stimulation are the main ideas that emerged. They made it possible to encompass animals and people in a single category with the concept of dependence upon the environment: an organism creates a system with its environment, its milieu. Stimulation was used in questions, central to scientific psychology, of learning and memory. Motive and emotion, and more generally, human behaviour would be interpreted as a response to a stimulus. The historian of psychology Kurt Danziger considers that "this term, perhaps more than any other, expressed fundamental convictions about the status occupied by subjectivity in the natural order."[50]

Here, however, *nature* has two meanings: one basing behaviour in a materialist and mechanic perspective (everything reduced to physical movements), and the other of applied behavioural science, one of control and prediction. The latter definition would appeal to behaviourism as a natural science.[51] Danziger insists, "'Behavior' had come to mean any aspect of human activity that could be predicted and controlled by psychologists."[52]

John B. Watson, the popular founder of behaviourism, was very successful intellectually and philosophically – his theories were discussed among the greatest minds of the time. He was *the* behaviourist. In "Psychology as the Behaviorist Views It," published in 1913 and still famous even today, he defines his discipline: "Psychology as the behaviorist views it is a purely objective experimental branch of natural science. Its theoretical goal is the prediction and control of behavior."[53] He was the one who carved in stone an "objectification" of psychology, which was largely initiated in the United States starting at the end of the nineteenth century. Objectification is, in other words, the study of human behaviour without reference to consciousness or introspection.

Behavioural psychology was a social engineering project organized around prediction and control, and centred on learning and memory. The fundamental idea was that organisms (animal or human) learn to solve problems through trial and error, and not through understanding their environment. Learning is adjusting behaviour through repetitive acts so that eventually the organism is able to give the correct responses to stimuli, which then imprint in the memory. A subject learns by a repetition of trial and error, by direct experience, in which responses to stimuli are attained using association of ideas. To condition is to create habits that facilitate action. Habits and "conditioned responses" are equivalent. Therefore, we should consider historian Kerry W. Buckley when he wrote of Watson that, for him, "only the unexamined life was worth living."[54] When life is not going well, rather than trying to determine what is not working, perhaps a change of surroundings would be better for receiving new stimuli and choosing a different path in the maze of life.

The stimulus-response pairing is a metalanguage into which all psychological concepts must be translated, and the aim of experimental mechanisms is to study what an individual can instinctively do with a stimulus. Next, it is about exercise so the individual develops methods in order to adjust to the demands of society. For behaviourists, everything (dreams, imagination, etc.) must be reformulated according to the "S-R" paradigm, and such a reformulation makes it possible, in the lab, to formulate hypotheses on humans based on animals – going from simple to complex.

The word *behaviour* was not used only in a scientific setting. It appeared when new morals were being developed as well. Behaviourism rose and developed in an America that, from the 1860s to the First World War, went from a rural society to one that was industrial and urban, but also from a rather homogeneous population, Yankee and Protestant, to one that was much more diversified. The ideals of this rural society, in which personal character, self-reliance, merit, and entrepreneurial spirit made up its foundation, became blurred in this new mass society – the individual became lost. During this period, the United States experienced its first great industrial wave (the Fords, Rockefellers, etc.), the birth of Taylorism and assembly lines, which profoundly changed the way work was organized, and the beginning of mass consumption with the emergence of marketing and advertising, as well as accelerated urbanization and immigration.[55]

The complexities of life in big cities and large companies could not be mastered by following the individualist plan that pervaded agrarian society in small, self-governing cities. Here, we see a three-fold shift in collective representations: the big city favours anonymity when meeting strangers,[56] the big factory creates major models for mechanizing action, and mass consumption opens a new, vast horizon of desire. From rural to urban-industrial America, it is the anonymity of strangers meeting (urban society), the mechanization as a sign of entering into the era of organization (industrial society), and a new world of imagination. These changes in how people act echo the Humean idea of a being immersed in a frenzy of impressions. Machines, speed, rhythm, anonymous masses, mass production and consumption: new modernity is a frenzy of stimuli. Modernity *is* chaos. These are ingredients recycled by behaviourism – ingredients that comprise a new society of elementary particles.

Watson was a rural man (born in South Carolina), a stranger to this new urban culture. For him, behaviourism was "an attempt to produce a psychology appropriate for urban life":[57] "The most fruitful starting point for psychology," he wrote in *Behaviorism* in 1924, the book that would bring him into the public eye, is "not the study of our own self, but of our neighbor's behavior,"[58] behaviour whose code must be cracked. Social individuals remain spectators who must first perceive; they are empiricists observing regularities and irregularities in order to reduce possible contingencies before taking action.

Over a forty-year span, from a rural society to an urban-industrial society, there was a profound feeling that time was moving faster and mores were rapidly changing. In this context, the question of the type of individual likely to adjust to these new conditions was the subject of intense reflection. The self was defined as a "character," one of austere puritan asceticism and a pioneer's morality (at the end of westward expansion); it was henceforth considered a "personality." Character is defined by the moral dimension of good and evil. Personality possesses a psychological dimension. Watson himself had made a distinction between character, which fell under what should be morally evaluated, and personality, which was more a scientific matter. This shift created a hierarchical reversal: moral rectitude was progressively subjected to psychology, or more precisely two psychologies: behaviourism *and* psychoanalysis,[59] both having emerged at the same time in the United States and propagated as two primary and complementary responses to these changes. Historians of American psychology have known this for quite some time, as one of them wrote in 1966: "The simultaneous popularity of two psychologies, behaviorism on the one hand, and psychoanalysis on the other, are related to these two features of mind associated with the growing urbanization of our society, behaviorism articulating with the need for mastery, and psychoanalysis with the need for rescuing the personality from the impersonality of the society ... The alienation which was a common experience of the new people who entered upon the cities in the late 19th and early 20th centuries generated both an intense internal preoccupation and an intense effort to control the behavior of others."[60] Behaviourism and psychoanalysis are thus the manifestation of a change of the individual's course of action in society. Both are responses to the "problems of living in the city [which] forced a turn either inward or outward."[61] Even though these psychological conceptions are opposed to each other, they are nevertheless sociologically complementary.

It should be noted that the end of the nineteenth century saw the emergence of both neurasthenia, the first pathology resulting from this new *environment* of modern life, and psychotherapies that were essentially a "moral treatment," the practice of which was directing consciousness.

A recurring theme was the major transformation of social relationships: personal relationships were replaced by impersonal ones. Although the latter freed individuals from any obligation that accompanied the "character" of Protestant, pioneer society, it also disoriented them. Compared to the supposed tight-knit relationships found in rural towns, the impersonality of relationships introduced uncertainty and new contingencies. The reciprocal adjustment between strangers became a practical issue for controlling behaviour – in the big city, like in the big Taylorized factory, everyone must keep up, obey without taking the slightest initiative, and refrain from developing personal intelligence.

The two disciplines brought answers to new societal problems by providing tools, concepts, and ideas. One did so by focusing on its

capacity to transform the evil within the individual through sublimation, and the other did so by focusing on the mechanics of behaviour,
which, when conditioned, could produce habits. Each could thus be
involved in moral and social reform, or social engineering projects.

Watson, Buckley wrote, "said with authority what many in
America had already come to believe. It made adjustment to the
world simpler and human nature more helpful."[62] Understanding
the human being via animals was not all for naught. In a book published in 1928, Watson compares himself to a scientist from Mars
looking down on the confused, frantic movements of humans and
likening them to ants in a maze. It was *the* symbol marking the similarity between animal and human societies.

The maze was the perfect metaphor for the Great Society that
detached individuals from their relationships: the common people, the
simple people seek to find themselves in the maze of the world. This
mechanism depicts the passionate situation of people immersed in a
frenzy of impressions, in their initial passivity from which they are torn
and forced to choose between two paths.[63] The world according to the
behaviourist was a maze in which individuals had to detect signals in
order to adjust, but it was an environment that could be modified at
leisure to change people from the outside.[64] This two-sided characteristic appealed to the psychology of the industrial realm, with the
prospect of predicting and controlling worker or consumer behaviour
by conditioning them, along with the political realm, where progressives focused on projects of social reform, since the word *control*
sits at an intersection of multiple meanings. Progressives, considered
advocates for social reform, shared something sociologically essential
with psychology reformers: an environmental approach, so long as it
is controlled, organized, and supported by the attentive observation of
facts, can change individuals and society.

In 1917, John Dewey, addressing the American Psychological
Association on its twenty-five-year anniversary, concluded his speech
by repeating a phrase he had stated to the association in 1899: "The
psychologist in his most remote and technical occupation with
mechanism may be contributing his bit to that ordered knowledge
which alone enables mankind to secure a larger and to direct a more
equal flow of the values of life." The "ordered knowledge" of social
life was articulated aptly in this technical work dedicated to studying the mechanisms of behaviour. Social life required a "scientific
treatment of collective human nature," and this treatment needed

"psychology in building up the new social science."[65] He gave credit to the "behavioristic movement" for having turned attention to "the specific processes of interaction which take place among human beings." He recognized its primary quality of having clarified and simplified the approach to human nature and having made its reorganization operational through acquisitions obtained in activities with others. Behaviourism made possible the establishment of a direct alliance between education and social reform through the lingua franca of psychology: "To form a mind out of certain native instincts by selecting an environment which evokes them and directs their course; to re-form social institutions by breaking up habits and giving peculiar intensity and scope to some impulse is the problem of social control in its two phases."[66] A pragmatic program of controlling forces that make up society, this was what behaviourism could bring to the progress of humankind and society.

Watson saw psychology "both as a vehicle of social mobility for a professional rising class and as a means of providing direct services of social control for and emerging corporate society that sought stability and predictability."[67] Scientific psychology offered resources to the new class of professionals (marketing people, accountants, engineers, etc.) who found unprecedented career opportunities in organizations (corporate society). They made up the "visible hand"[68] in the era of organization. They were experts of instrumental wisdom, bearers of knowledge that could make individuals efficient. These learning methods could be used to condition the behaviour of factory workers, market consumers, or kids in school. In this environment, Watson published a manual on childhood education that would go on to have wide commercial success.

With behaviourism came the rising instrumental trend of knowledge and expert advice. Watson, "preaching a gospel of achievement through self-control,... became the first 'pop' psychologist to the newly urbanized middle classes."[69] Psychologists themselves became professionals by developing scholastic and IQ tests, and creating selective criteria for personnel within a company or the army. Moreover, it was after the First World War that psychologists started using objective methods for evaluating aptitudes and predicting outcomes, and behaviourism really gained a foothold in the public eye.

The attraction provoked by behaviourism was "above all, a faith in radical environmentalism that invested man with the ability to make and shape his own world, free from the authority of tradition and the dead hand of the past."[70] New society had modified the meaning of contingency. The tool represented by the S-R system had the huge advantage of providing simple means not only to help people adapt to an unstable environment by directing them from the outside, which attracted industry, but also to reform harmful or unfavourable environments, which attracted those in favour of social reform, like Dewey. "The new point of view treats social facts as the material of an experimental science, where the problem is that of modifying belief and desire – this is to say mind – by enacting specific changes in the social environment."[71]

Paradoxically, personality is central to this approach, because it is targeted indirectly, covertly, by controlling the environment. It is targeted through Watson's message, according to which people possess the capacity to change their world and shape it to themselves.

Furthermore, we can understand what happens sociologically with scientific psychology only if we incorporate psychoanalytical appeal into the analysis: an enrichment, provided its concepts can be tested and supply methodological purity.[72] Behaviourists reintroduced "personality" during the interwar period, but in their own way. In 1916, Watson himself proclaimed a "central truth" from Freud: "Youthful, outgrown, and partially discarded habits and instinctive systems of reaction can and possibly always do influence the functioning of our adult systems of reactions, and influence to a certain extent the possibility of our forming the new habit systems which we must reasonably be expected to form."[73]

Many behaviourists recognized that psychoanalysis possessed tools to aid insight, but criticized it for lacking scientific methods of observation. It offered perspectives for broadening the conclusions of their own psychology and provided hypotheses for their experimental work. The preoccupation with translating psychoanalytic concepts into the behaviourist language of habit formation through conditioning (methods vary according to the type of behaviourism) appeared very early. Throughout the 1930s, behaviourists elaborated so-called intermediary variables between S and R. They thought to expand the scope of what scientific psychology called high-level processes, which are by definition complex and therefore must be broken down into simple elements, variables, or factors, in order to be tested in an experimental setting.

Behaviourists defined "personality" as a *"tout de coalition,"* within which tendencies or components came together and gave rise to quantification. The introduction of intermediary variables made it possible to study correlations and factorize dispositions (innate as acquired by education), thereby influencing the determinants of behaviour. Everything that happens between S and R or between independent and dependent variables could therefore be interpreted in terms of intermediary variables, which made it possible to use a richer, more flexible scientific diction.[74]

Neo-behaviourists complexified the S-R system and dependency regarding the environment by adding the concept of an organism's internal strength, using triggers as a model for the mechanisms of a machine. They used terms such as *instinct, impulse, need,* or *motivation* as types of energy to be managed. Thus, in the 1930s, a group of behaviourists at Yale University brought together by Clark Hull, with whom several students started psychoanalysis, endeavoured to test psychoanalytic concepts by conveying them as compatible with experimental methods. They went concept by concept, and one of the most successful attempts was tackling the concept of drive, understood as a Freudian instinct. It was known as the frustration-aggression hypothesis. Someone who is frustrated responds with aggression, frustration being the stimulus, and aggression being the response. This hypothesis was quite popular in most psychological circles. Indeed, it was used to motivate American troops in the 1940s.[75]

Personality thus became the subject that historian Kurt Danziger aptly called "unification by naming."[76] It became a neutral term that could refer to any branch of psychology. From character, which holds up on its own, to personality, which needs some support, the new conditions for freedom made the expert's visible hand necessary to reform individualism in this world of new complexities.

If the transition to the Great Society witnessed the rise of the word *behaviour*, postwar scientific psychology was present for the rise of *personality. Behaviour* was drastically disrupted as a result. It integrated the self, thanks to new tools and concepts. It would subsequently set off to garner support by opening itself to a market beyond the academy: supporting individuals in their life choices.

The Self of Behavioural Social Sciences

The question of whether humankind is inner-directed or other-directed got its strongest backing from public opinion with sociologist David Riesman's 1950 publication, *The Lonely Crowd*, a book organized entirely around that question. It had widespread commercial success throughout the social science community. The work was published at a time when American society was well into its phase of mass production and consumption; the transition to the Great Society was complete. In the former society, social conformity was obtained by reinforcing the inner life, which made the individual relatively indifferent to the approval of others, an indifference indicating the capacity of self-reliance: the individual was inner-directed. In this new society, conformity went essentially through the approbation of others (other-directed), according to Riesman: "It is perhaps the insatiable force of this psychological need for approval that differentiates people of the metropolitan, American upper middle class."[77] He saw signs of this everywhere – at school where teachers took increased interest in how their students interacted, and therefore in their personalities; in companies that invited white-collar workers and their superiors to mould themselves and adjust to each other, etc.: "But the product now in demand is neither a staple nor a machine; it is a personality."[78]

Riesman's book was published the same year as the American translation of *The Authoritarian Personality*. Written by Adorno and his team from the Frankfurt School, it used a Freudian perspective to shed light on what could have caused Germans to plunge into Nazism. The team conducted myriad inquiries, interviews, and projective tests enabling them to spot character traits like intolerance or rigidity. Apart from acknowledging an evolution in morals, a second element of change cropped up that made the uncontrolled use of "control" progressively delicate: Nazi and fascist totalitarianisms were overcome, but a new adversary sprang up in the form of communism, which set off the Cold War in 1946.

Under these new circumstances, science was not merely an epistemological and empirical issue, it was also a cultural and political battle between democracy and totalitarianism.[79] The scientific ideal and the democratic idea feed off each other's will to forge open personalities. The appeal of these new theories stemmed from the fact that their science laid out both facts – what is – and principles of action – what should be. One of the founders of mathematical psychology, a discipline producing the behavioural economics of Amos Tversky and Daniel Kahneman, wrote in 1970, "Decision theory is the study of how decisions are or ought to be made. Thus it has two faces: descriptive and normative."[80] The emergence of behavioural social sciences became the cornerstone of a two-sided battle for scientific rigour and democracy. The project was to forge a science of human nature richer than that proposed by behaviourism.

The question of what type of personality should be favoured became a major political and scientific issue: simply adjusting to society was no longer acceptable if adjusting to either totalitarianism or democracy was the same thing. There needed to be a concrete theory of human nature to combat the theory of the individual's infinite malleability advocated by totalitarianism. During the war, the system of expectations concerning individuality was not completely the same. In the upheaval of the 1940s and 1950s, behavioural sciences shifted the conception of the other-directed individual toward the concept of inner-direction, but with an inflection that transcended the old individualism of character. This modernized idea of individuals structuring their environment thanks to "internal models" became associated with a brand new concept: the computer "program," which transforms the computer as an instrument of calculation into one that solves problems. The topic of control was reconfigured through the problem of choice and decision, on the one hand, and intelligence and "bounded rationality" on the other. Between stimuli and responses, the new science of human nature introduced a double mediation: intelligence, via the adjective *cognitive*, and freedom, via the nouns *decision* and *choice*. Two types elucidate these ideals: the scientist and the economic individual, both models of the intelligent nature of humankind. They are *practical* subjects seeking to solve problems, introspectively speaking, who have goals and the means to achieve them (exteriority of choice and action). But they are also *democratic* subjects, who are rational, this time in terms of freedom. Scientific psychology and economy were therefore on a path to experience two broad lines of complementary change. They find themselves brought together by the new conception of information technology, conceived as a program that solves problems – like humans acting as machines that problem solve. The individual-as-machine system tends toward replacing the rat in the maze – even though it can still be used to help understand shared behaviours in people and animals.

A DECIDING PERSON CHOOSES FREELY:
INTRODUCING SUBJECTIVITY AND ACTIVITY

Choosing freely and choosing rationally are one and the same. That is one of the main ideas coming from this period. Rational choice theory (RCT) is a case in point.

Starting in the 1940s, army research agencies and major American foundations played an important role in directing American social sciences to evolve toward behaviour. This evolution went from disciplinary reasoning (sociology, psychology, etc.) to problem-solving reasoning, with new statistical methods and multidisciplinary teams referring to models stemming from the natural sciences or mathematics. Several institutions of science and behaviour were created between 1945 and the 1960s, with social relations often part of their programs. They brought together theoretical research and practical applications, the solving of practical problems through pluri-disciplinary research. "Social" and "behaviour" were inextricably linked. Under the umbrella of interdisciplinarity, an alliance between math, psychology, and economy was progressively put in place – which would eventually link up with brain science.

Neoclassical economics posed problems of optimization and eliminated behaviour from its theory. During the 1940s, neoclassical economists participated in attempts to understand the mechanisms utilized by individuals to shape their world through solving problems. Notably, this occurred through decision-making when faced with choices whose consequences were uncertain, leaving in place the contingency of action as the common thread of this anthropology. Rational choice theory was developed to solidify the philosophical basis of the free world. It promoted a liberal political vision and behavioural psychology. The liberal conception was one of radical negative liberty: it opposed any idea of constraint. The strategically rational actor, characterized by personal interests, whether egoistic or altruistic, became the main representation for reconfiguring Enlightenment concepts and issues of societal governance: the issue was to find a scientific foundation of human nature by discovering its laws.[81] This headlong rush toward scientism recovered a political ideal to more strongly root democratic ideals: laws of (free) behaviour were thought better able to resist onslaughts of totalitarianism than the old political concepts of the Enlightenment, like sympathy or civil society – the society of cultural passions. Rational choice theory was at the heart of this changing sensibility in which individuals were shaped less by their environment than they were by themselves, making do with what they had. This theory applied to both individual and collective action.

Collective action refers to the problem of cooperation. This subject is particularly sensitive politically because free people cannot be forced to cooperate. The decision or choice must necessarily be rational, since they make individual freedom effective, and social order can only be a spontaneous effect of individual decisions. Looking through the prism of the economic individual, what is at play here is the *sacralization of choice* that is not merely free, but rational, and therefore intelligent: deciding is what free people do in life. Anything that can evoke "general will" or authority in society is suspected to be limiting: only individual freedom is rational, whereas communism, in this language, is quite simply irrational. The fundamental work on this concept was von Neumann and Morgenstern's 1944 book *Theory of Games and Economic Behavior*. Game theory allows us to go beyond solving problems of optimization in the economy and expands it to treat all decision-making as situations of incertitude. It developed mostly in the 1940s and 1950s and extended to political science (both political theory and public policy), sociology, and psychology. Insomuch as it is a collective action, the authors speak of social sciences. The only acceptable scientific method, which is to say compatible with democracy, is methodological individualism. This is how "social" and "behavioural" intersect.

These ideas were based on an identification of the citizen and the consumer, the former providing the gauge by which the latter is composed. In 1951, Kenneth Arrow mathematically defined the sovereignty of citizens as equivalent to the sovereignty of consumers who are free to choose their own products at the market. His famous impossibility theorem stated that it is impossible to glean collective preference from an aggregate of individual choices, which implies that the necessity of a welfare state cannot be rationally deduced. His theory was built on "the conviction that the individual is the absolute and final arbiter of his own preferences."[82] Citizens' sovereignty, consumer sovereignty: the only approach that freedom can tolerate is methodological individualism – without limitations à la Rousseau (political obligation is a constraint) or Kant (moral obligation of duty is a constraint). It remains a question of favouring intelligence, a sign of liberty, rationality, and open personality.[83]

Individual action is taken using inferential statistics and new methods for calculating probability[84] and, accordingly, by broadening the concept of utility to expected utility, thereby introducing a psychological dimension. Psychological mathematicians shifted the economy toward a theory of human behaviour, toward psychology, which is decision theory with the initiative to solve problems. They called it the "theory of expected utility" – expected and therefore subjective. This theory could be tested using experimental methods found in scientific psychology thanks to new mathematical tools: probability and statistics, which were up to that point used in objective incertitude, and were thus broadened to include subjective probability. What is important here is that experimental psychology turned its attention away from perception and toward decision-making.

Inferential statistics are a metaphor for cognitive processes: the mind decides that X is a stimulus rather than a noise. Like a scientist deciding between two hypotheses, these theories attributed a cause (inferred) from an effect. They gave rise to a widespread idea of "the mind as intuitive statistician" – an expression from Amos Tversky, who founded behavioural economics with Daniel Kahneman (see chapter 4). Stochastic probability deals with situations in which the individual shows a slight preference for A over B, yet has difficulties perceiving this difference. If the choice is repeated several times over and the subject prefers A over B, this preference is stochastic. "Stochastic preference eliminated the concept of indifference,"[85] technically demonstrating the social value of individual choice. The scientist (economist, mathematician, or statistician) is the moral authority from which human differences are evaluated. The question of knowing what happens when people do not do what decision theory normatively predicts was not asked until the 1970s, in the context of a moral and social reorientation of individualism. It would be the big question of cognitive biases in behavioural economics, but also in cognitive neuroscience: not everyone generally behaves rationally since all are subjected to cognitive biases that keep them from satisfying their own personal interests (see chapter 4).

THE "COGNITIVE REVOLUTION" OR THE SCIENTIST AS A MODEL OF ORDINARY INTELLIGENCE

In 1971, the behaviourist Burrhus F. Skinner formulated this key idea in *Beyond Freedom and Dignity*: "A person does not act upon the world, the world acts upon him."[86] This idea has lost much of its social *and* scientific credibility over the last decade.

To elevate scientific psychology to the level of science (which is reason) and democracy (which is freedom), it was necessary to abandon the behaviourist pair of stimulus-response. It was the condition for taking into account human intelligence and creativity, using methods that made standardization possible.

In 2003, George A. Miller took a retrospective view of the 1950s: "If scientific psychology were to succeed, mentalistic concepts would have to integrate and explain the behavioral data. We were still reluctant to use such terms as 'mentalism' to describe what was needed, so we talked about cognition instead." Mentalism or cognition, no matter the word as long as we have the thing. But what is this thing? Miller summarized the "cognitive revolution" as "the original dream of a unified science that would discover the representational and computational capacities of the human mind." "This original dream," he continued, "still has an appeal that I cannot resist."[87] The concept of the computer put forth by Herbert Simon is key to realizing this dream.

Herbert Simon embodied the shift in social sciences toward behavioural social sciences. He was the man of the behavioural revolution in social sciences, a revolution whose goal was to construct a unified science of human behaviour. He took on a wide variety of subjects, like political science, math and computer science, psychology, and economics (for which he was awarded the Nobel Prize in 1978). In 1961, he declared, "Psychologists think that I am an economist, but economists think I am a psychologist. In fact, I feel allegiance to none of these academic tribes, but regard myself as a citizen of the world – a behavioral scientist."[88] Not a behaviourist, but an actual behavioural scientist. Mathematics, which Simon identified as human reason, is the key discipline in this interdisciplinarity geared toward real world problem solving. Simon particularly stands out when it comes to behavioural social sciences as he linked what was happening in economics and psychology through a freshly blazed trail of cybernetics, the science of machines. With it, historian Hunter Crowther-Heyck writes in his biography, "the new model of the human would be ... *Homo adaptivus*, the active problem solver of finite, but real, powers."[89]

At the same time, adaptation mechanisms for which the economy was unable to account were sought in psychology via learning processes: to learn is to adapt according to one's choices. "Learning theory thus blended with the ideas Simon had drawn from the science of machines. Their confluence taught him many things, but probably the most important was that learning to solve problems was not an optimizing process. Like other adaptive processes, it was about finding a viable ... solution. There was no test beyond survival."[90] The project was no longer to elaborate mathematical models of decisions in order to attain an optimum, but to use computer science as a simulation instrument for solving problems. The concept of *program* filled the gap between formal models of economics and empiric experiments of agents. From that moment, this work fed a new interdisciplinary research program that eventually allowed scientific psychology to introduce human intelligence between stimuli and responses with the adjective *cognitive*.

The computer and the computer program were tools and metaphors for reintroducing the mind (via decisions) to scientific psychology. A few decades later, it was easy to see a more reductionist vision of the individual in it. However, this gaze was anachronistic: the computer program and computer associated with the scientific model represented a clear shift toward a richer, more realistic conception of scientific psychology, at least according to criteria of the practical subject of empiricism.

They made it possible to add communication to adaptation and therefore make hypotheses on the ways in which individuals understand the world – how they transform information coming from the world in order to solve problems.

Individuals react to stimuli, and will act upon the world by transforming stimuli into information thanks to internal models. For behaviourists, actions are repetitive behaviours that characterize the animal side of humankind. Behaviours involving the superior activities of the mind, and more precisely language, the most complex behaviour, are out of reach. The keyword of these models is *representation*. Philosopher Daniel Andler, one of the players involved in bringing cognitive science to France, stated it clearly: "It is undeniable that the centre of gravity in cognitive science is situated on the axis, traditional in Western philosophy, of representation, seen as a relationship between independent reality and a subject in search of an accurate image of this reality, and is more or less well-equipped to obtain it."[91]

For George Miller, the process by which this accurate image is made possible is called recoding: this concept describes the way in which information is treated by the receiver – and not only emitted by the source. It introduces activity – of thought – to the agent. Recoding follows the empiricist method, which goes from simple to complex. Linguist Noam Chomsky's grammar and Herbert Simon's program would provide the tools for recoding.

Chomsky's argument is that individuals learn things by remembering kernel sentences – prototypes – and so grammar, and not the learning of words, is the basis for creating meaning. This argument was elaborated upon starting from this kernel and according to rules for generating phrases. Grammar was derived from a universal "transformational grammar" that is innate in all of us. Therefore, a natural generation of systems makes it possible to imagine the world from within the self. Chomsky promoted the idea that learning is active, that it is not just about acquiring words, but about "operating like a scientist by actively developing a theory of how to speak properly."[92] His theory of grammar is equivalent to an extremely complex mechanism. Miller's idea of recoding was tightly entwined in this idea of grammar, which itself was identical to that of a computer program.

Chomsky's natural grammar had both a scientific and political advantage: scientifically, it allowed for psychology to operationalize complex behavioural analysis, since language is the most complex of behaviours; politically, its innatism was perhaps philosophically naïve, but sociologically it had highlighted the fact that humans are sufficiently autonomous to not have to depend on the environment and could not be changed as easily as behaviourists may have thought.

Simon promoted a new computer concept: not a super-calculator, but a program facilitating the transformation of the computer into a machine that generally treats symbols able to simulate situations and therefore solve problems by implementing choices among several possibilities. Problem-solving requires intelligence, adaptability, and creativity. Where behaviourism once used science as a means of measurement, it was then substituted with an idea of science as creative, as logical discovery, and replaced the individual as a receptacle of stimuli with an individual of "limited rationality" whose mind constructed world models. "A problem exists," he wrote in a report for the Rand Corporation in 1958, "whenever a problem solver desires some outcome or state of affairs that he does not immediately know how to attain. Imperfect knowledge about how to proceed is at the core of the genuinely problematic." In Simon's program, problematic knowledge equates to introducing creativity, meaning to solve problems that do not demand automatic solutions. Such knowledge does not rely on determinist or logical methods, but on methods Simon called "heuristics": they "seldom provide infallible guidance; they give practical knowledge, possessing only empirical validity." They can "aid discovery."[93] They are the means, for a people of limited rationality, to find what they are seeking. "The story is an allegory ... intended to illustrate Simon's theory that the human actor is a simple creature motivated by a few basic drives that attempts to achieve its goals largely by trial and error, guided only by rough heuristic lessons drawn from experience."[94] Quite possibly a good part of the scientific psychology community shares this conviction of ordinary individuals seeking to find themselves in the maze of the world.

In a famous article written in collaboration, Miller developed the argument that "thinking and understanding were much like constructing an internal model of the world,"[95] an essential idea to cognitive neuroscience – cognitive being this internal model. He called "image" the symbolic representation of the world and "plan" the mechanism that transforms the image into behaviour. "The notion of a Plan that guides behaviour is ... quite similar to the notion of a program that guides an electronic computer."[96] This perspective implied that "learning was not so much a process of acquiring facts about the world as of developing a skill ... with a conceptual tool that could then be deployed creatively."

"The scientist is Everyman, looking just like you and me. We look for the things we want, and when we find them we find part of ourselves."[97] Embodying both the individual's reason and freedom, it is the ideal of human nature on which the analysis of complex behaviours of every one of us is constructed.

The economic and psychological transformations of the 1940s and 1950s had an underlying scientific and socio-political representation of the individual, free to think and act, who deliberates and, when faced with choices, makes decisions while relying on the scientific model that seeks truth, and using the model of the economic person capable of making decisions in incertitude. This perspective is situated in the legacy of the practical subject as an intelligent being who depends on the principle of utility, which is to say who organizes the means with an end in view. These two models of rationality also come in contact with a new science, computer science, and a new object, the computer, to which something new is attributed, "thought." They come together through the adjective *cognitive*, which designates rationality in rational choice theory and a subject's reflexivity, the individual's mind, in cognitive science. Rational or mental, depending on the case.

Proponents of the cognitive revolution thought that the study of human minds, rather than those of rats, made it possible to focus on values scientifically and consequently to emphasize what is specifically human – behaviourists studying what is shared between human and animal. The values of truth, rationality, enquiry, honesty... these are things that could mobilize a research program of the human mind – an open mind program. On the one hand, objectivity, attention to exact observation (empiricism), theoretical rigour, and on the other, freedom, decision, choice – scientific and democratic values woven into one another to such an extent it becomes difficult to separate and distinguish them.

The New Individualism of Scientific Psychology: Everyone Becomes His Own Psychologist

Expert systems envisage the individual as an expert (scientist, researcher, engineer) who solves problems using practical intelligence and the means available, thus expressing the idea of limited rationality of the ordinary person. If they made for, as proponents claimed, a social engineering more efficient than the one proposed by behaviourism, they left these psychologists ill-equipped to face practices that were being established in American society after the war – psychotherapies. Their widespread development, in psychiatric institutions as in private practices, was the third major change during this time, with the end of the transition toward the Great Society and the beginning of the Cold War. Psychotherapies opened new prospects for ideals that the most efficient conditioning was far from achieving: well-being through self-understanding – intelligence applied to the self. Yet the issue with scientific psychology was that it did not have therapeutic applications, it could not be used to cure people of their ills – despite attempts to use one form of conditioning or another as therapy. A true rooting in society, beyond the academic milieu, demanded that scientific psychology had something to say and do regarding everyday life.

These new ideals make up the third phase of behaviour: if winning over academic opinion was already underway, public opinion would have to go through a double interdependent phase of scientifically appropriating the self *and* developing a clinic for the laity to fulfill their lives effectively.

Two presidential addresses given before the annual congress of the American Psychological Association (APA), one in 1960 by Canadian neuropsychologist Donald O. Hebb, and the other in 1969 by George A. Miller, express this double phase in clear terms. The first opens the decade by declaring it is absolutely imperative to bring the self into the fold of scientific psychology, and the second closes it with the claim that this is not only to serve individual well-being, but also that these tools should be available to everyone.

Donald O. Hebb was a chief player in the history of cognitive neuroscience, beginning with the arrival of *Organization of Behavior* in 1949. He linked many concepts of psychology and physiology, notably synaptic plasticity, which successfully detailed how the brain "learns" and promoted the idea that the brain can change itself (as we will see in the next chapter). A neuropsychologist, in the strict sense of the term, he was as much a psychologist as he was a neurologist. He declared in "The American Revolution" that "the failure of experimental psychology to deal with the 'I' or the 'ego' is a cause of its continued inadequacy with regard to clinical matters." Therefore we must "throw new light on the problems of mind and consciousness – or if you prefer, of the complex function of mediating processes."[98] It is vital to adopt the right method and to make it possible to replace philosophical terms, like *conscience*, with those from science, like *mediation process* or *higher cortical functions*. No entity is more hypothetical than the self, but none has more theoretical value for the clinician. It is among the most esoteric problems we face, which is why Hebb affirms, "Freud is the great man of the psychological world," but "psychoanalysis is still not part of the mainstream of psychological thought." His pre-eminence in this field helped fill the gap left by the absence of "motivation" in academic psychology at the beginning of the twentieth century, and gave us the theory that all behaviour has a motive. However, psychoanalysis is absent here, as there is a disinterest in "the mechanics of behavior" that did not utilize the scientific method. However, Hebb notes, scientific psychology should not brag too much, since it has progressed little on the mechanics of thought: "If we do not like the looks of psychoanalytic theory, what better tools have we to offer the psychiatrist?" To ask this question is, as he himself says, "to take the bull by the horns."

Behaviourism, during the first phase of the psychological revolution, "banished thought, imagery, volition, attention, and other such seditious notions. The sedition of one period, however, may be the good sense of another": "My thesis, in this address is that an outstanding contribution to psychology was made in the establishment of a thoroughgoing behavioristic mode of thinking. But this has been achieved, too frequently, only by excluding the chief problem of human behaviour":[99] the process of thought. The task of the second revolution was to refine a systematic, behaviourist approach for the mechanics of thought, allowing psychologists, who claim to have an authentic behavioural science, to sway public opinion won over by psychodynamic psychologies.

Retrospectively, the contribution from the first revolution was to shed light on behaviours dominated by the senses, those common to animal and human, *non-cognitive* behaviours. The S-R formula presented two advantages, thought Hebb: first, it provided "a reasonable explanation of much reflexive human behavior," which then provided "a fundamental analytical tool, by which to distinguish between lower (noncognitive) and higher (cognitive) forms of behavior."[100] The second psychological revolution needed to tackle higher processes that were specifically human, *cognitive* behaviours. "Cognitive" thus came to designate what was specifically human, and this specificity itself possessed a unique characteristic: creativity.

During the 1950s,[101] the world of psychotherapy was composed of diverse practices, like psychoanalysis, used mainly by physicians. New methods were proposed by post-Freudians (for which dissident institutes trained psychoanalysts who were not physicians), like Erich Fromm, at the height of his career in the 1950s (a proponent of the social origins of neuroses); the humanist psychology of Carl Rogers (and his "person-centred therapy"); or Abraham Maslow, who left his work on primates for the development of human potential (in 1954, he published *Motivation and Personality*, in which self-actualization was placed atop his hierarchy of needs). These psychologies, although offshoots of psychoanalysis, fell under Freudian sensibility – psychodynamics – and for the public, the psychoanalyst was the embodiment of the clinical psychologist. Between psychotherapy and psychoanalysis, the lines became blurred. Centred on the individual, the aim of psychotherapy was well-being for all by proposing a practice of self-understanding. Its goal reinforced the self. Whatever the method, it fell under the same label of "psychodynamics." Psychotherapy stimulated the human psyche, increased the capacity for self-reflection, and consequently had a reach that went beyond psychopathology. Such therapy was generally practised in private, but also offered counselling, guidance, and support services for universities and companies, and for people who were not affected by any psychopathology. It was not aimed solely at neurotic illness, but could be used to increase everyone's possibilities, in work, studies, love life, or family. Psychotherapy developed to such a degree that in 1965 sociologist Philip Rieff denounced the "triumph of the therapeutic,"[102] which would become a way of being in a world centred on the only thing that counted: the individual self – so sought after, yet so elusive for the scientific psychologist.

The distance between the strong academic legitimacy of the behavioural paradigm and its weak social legitimacy represents all that underlies Hebb's address. That is why it is so important to continue to explore the thought process with any means at our disposal.

Almost absent from the expanding world of psychotherapy, scientific psychology was also confronted with a turnaround in collective sensibilities regarding control: its traditional testing segment came under intense scrutiny. During the 1960s, the testing market, which was highly developed, notably in school and work settings, became the subject of increased suspicion. Personality tests especially, with the intimate questions they ask, would come to be thought of as illegitimate social control. This led to recurring debates throughout the 1960s over constitutional rights and privacy – both houses of Congress set up hearings, and *American Psychologist*, the journal of the profession, dedicated an entire instalment to the subject in 1965.[103] If the word *conditioning* had already been receiving negative press for some time, *control* was next in the firing line.[104]

In 1969, for the first time, the APA's annual convention did not have research results or conceptual issues, but a subject that today would be called societal: "Psychology and the Problems with Society" – in other words, the social role psychology needs to work for the individual.[105]

The presidential address given by George A. Miller, entitled "Psychology as a Means of Promoting Human Welfare," exemplifies the pervasiveness of new ideals in scientific psychology. Not only did Miller emphasize the fetishization of technology as a solution to social ills, he also went one step further and denounced the obsession with prediction and control. To his peers, he proposed a reflection on what the relationship should be between psychology and society. Like Hebb ten years earlier, he referred to Freud, the great temptation of scientific psychologists, but with a fresh perspective that no longer criticized its absence of scientific method. Its support went much further, since scientific psychology had something decisive to lend to it, an idea of the individual: "The impact of Freud's thought had been due far less to the instrumentalities he provided than to the changed conception of ourselves that he inspired." His impact on society in general made people more aware of "the irrational components of human nature and much better able to accept the reality of our unconscious impulses. The importance of Freudian psychology derives far less from its scientific validity than from the effects it has had on the shared image of man himself." This was how scientific psychology needed to take hold, but in such a way that it had an "effect on the way we behave in our daily affairs and in our institutional contexts." A new concept had "immediate implications for the most intimate details of our social and personal lives."[106] It was imperative to sway public opinion, which was won over by Freudian thought and humanist psychology, in order to convert the idea that only psychodynamic psychology treated and ameliorated the human mind, and that scientific psychology did what it could to control it. "Freud has already established in the public mind a general belief that all behavior is motivated," and not conditioned. The message hammered home by scientific psychology was "that psychologists know how to use this motivation to control what people will do." However, there was misunderstanding regarding the word *control*, and psychologists contributed to this misunderstanding through "a myopic concentration on techniques of behavior." Control was "but one component in any program from personal improvement or social reform" – an instrument of neither powerful nor the expert.

It became a true profession of faith to define the social mission of psychology as "a better way to advertise psychology and to relate it to social problems": "Instead of repeating constantly that reinforcement leads to control, I would prefer to emphasize that reinforcement can lead to satisfaction and competence. And I would prefer to speak of understanding and prediction as our major scientific goals ... because they lead us to think, not in terms of coercion by a powerful elite, but in terms of the diagnosis of problems and the development of programs that can enrich the lives of every citizen."[107]

Between 1960 and 1969, scientific psychology abandoned the language of behaviourism to participate in the democratic shift to a new individualism that emerged throughout the decade, the "personal" revolution. Henceforth, it would be a question of providing tools to the individual who was freed from old constraints. Society would not improve by proposing reform programs that resembled "experimental protocols," but by allowing individuals to take psychology and practise it for themselves: "We must use psychology to give people skills that will satisfy their urge to feel more effective."[108] Freud certainly altered the idea of humankind, but it was up to scientific psychology to carve this change in stone, thanks to its methods. This was what psychology could become: not a science for mind engineers in the service of the powers that be, but a technique the laity could possess and utilize: it was no longer about imposing solutions on individuals, but involving them in the process by helping them formulate and achieve their own goals. Moral work should be done by the individual alone. Psychologists must "give psychology away," claimed Miller during an eloquent, spontaneous soliloquy, and the saying stuck.

The first behavioural therapies, beginning in 1960s Great Britain and America, due to their experimental nature, paired the patient with the therapist, thus relativizing the asymmetry between the one who treats and the one being treated. Cognitive and cognitive behavioural therapies pursued this approach.[109] Scientific psychology also participated broadly in the "triumph of the therapeutic," and in the destabilization of verticality, in much the same way that humanist psychology and personal development did.

These ethical changes affected the whole of society. At work, for example, new theories of organization appeared during the 1960s, showing that the external control of punishment/reward systems, as well as mechanical discipline of Fordism and Taylorism, were not the only ways to get results from workers. New methods were proposed to manage by objectives and get workers involved. "People will exercise self-direction and self-control in the service of objectives to which they are committed; their commitment is a function of the rewards associated with the achievement of their objectives."[110] Regulating behaviour through punishment/reward systems or with stimulus-response mechanisms was no longer suited to a society in which people were not only expressing new aspirations and demonstrating new intelligence, but one in which company management was favouring motivated behaviour, which it considered more productive than conditioned behaviour.

The democratic ideal is that psychology allows ordinary people to become experts of themselves: "The people at large will have to be their own psychologists, and make their own applications of the principles that we establish." The knowledge is available; now the expertise must be made available to all. The old competitive relationships of rugged individualism and supervision that relied on punishment/reward systems was to be replaced with cooperative relationships, mutual understanding, and individual capacities, since it was by making people competent that they became motivated. The environment was no longer a maze the psychologist observed with an intention to control behaviour, but as an anthropologist of *culture*, who must describe in order to understand behaviour: "The important thing is not to control the system, but to understand it."[111]

Albert Bandura stayed on the same path as Miller when, five years later in 1974, he gave a presidential address to the APA: "Reflecting the salient values of our society, reinforcement practices have traditionally favoured utilitarian forms of behavior. But conditions are changing. With growing reservations about materialistic life-styles, reinforcement practices are being increasingly used to cultivate personal potentialities and humanistic qualities." Reinforcement techniques must be geared toward people, and not experts. Psychologists made changes to their problem: "Interest began to shift from managing conduct to developing skills in self-regulation ... Control is vested to a large extent in the hands of individuals themselves."[112] Reinforcement practices became self-reinforcement practices making it possible to establish a positive dynamic of motivation and skill, allowing a capable individual to self-actualize with an expanded freedom to choose. In 1977, he presented his "theory of self-efficacy" as progress "toward a unifying theory of behavioral change": "The present theory is based on the principal [sic] assumption that psychological procedures, whatever their form, *serve as means of creating and strengthening expectations of personal efficacy.*"[113] The perception of personal efficacy led to the subject of behavioural change; it was imperative to help subjects help themselves, to be their own agents of change. To do so, we were to create a virtuous circle in which a feeling of accomplishment motivated the subject, a state that reinforced the feeling of accomplishment.

An Individualism of Capability

Scientific psychology was therefore changing behavioural control from social engineering to a control all could exert over their own lives. Henceforth, *control* would mean both "an increased freedom to choose" and "self-control." Self-regulation was the path to effectively self-actualize according to personal goals.

In no uncertain terms, Bandura recalled that the profession took little interest in how individuals constructed their own reinforcement plan according to their preferences: "To cite but one example, there exist countless demonstrations of how behavior varies under different schedules of reinforcement, but one looks in vain for studies of how people, either individually or by collective action, succeed in fashioning reinforcement schedules to their own liking."[114] This was the new paradigm of psychology. It was asserted when the profession was faced with new ways of living in society, in which choice and decision were no longer values of the economic individual – material values – but were renewed by a broadened lifestyle choice that each person had decided to adopt. The representation of the individual as a creator of values expanded considerably and had a positive reception by underrepresented groups. Every person should have access to positive individuality.

These ideals emphasized individuals' capacity to act as well as their creative and innovative behaviours. Choice, creativity, and individual initiative: these led us to what could be called an individualism of capability. Adopting a personal course of action now became fundamental, and the idea of hidden potential was one particularly key aspect.

Coming back to the famous Tom Wolfe article from 1976, the "'Me' decade" represented "the greatest age of individualism in American history," in which "all rules are broken!" This article was published when such individualism stirred conflict and recurring controversy about the fate of the American character. Essayists inspired by psychoanalysis presented pessimistic analyses. Philip Rieff thought the triumph of the therapeutic contributed to a loss of ethical direction, which was demonstrated with the generalization of the "adapted attitude" at the expense of the "analytic attitude."[115] The values of choice, essential to democratic freedom, dissipated into personal preference. In the 1970s, Richard Sennett and Christopher Lasch (among many other essayists) took up these themes and found that the primary symptom was the rise of narcissism at the expense of Oedipalism. Narcissistic and borderline pathologies are variations similar to the difficulty of self-regulation and self-reliance. The deterioration of democracy (the "emotional" that downgrades morals to individual preference, the federal centralization that generates dependency, the experts who control privacy, etc.) came through in the crisis of personal assertion that is narcissism.

The moment in which America was thrown into an examination of conscience, scientific psychology, a practice that does not usually ponder the meaning of existence, pulled out all the stops to equip individuals in the pursuit of their goals, in order to activate the divine spark. The idea of directing the individual from without by the "visible hand" cannot therefore be an adequate model of ordinary rational conduct. The picture of the scientist with limited rationality is not it either, since it is no longer a question of measuring an individual using a superior model. Scientific psychology intends to arm individuals for this new freedom, a positive freedom that allows them to use a skill set without which they cannot obtain personal autonomy: "Freedom is not conceived negatively as the absence of influences or simply the lack of external constraints. Rather, it is defined positively in terms of the skills at one's command and the exercise of self-influence that choice of action requires."[116] The issue is no longer control, but individual and societal change with a path to well-being. Competence and motivation form the virtuous circle of this dynamic of power to act on oneself and by oneself. Competence and motivation is the name given to practices transforming the spark within into "opinion, experience, and interest,"[117] to use Pocock's expression regarding Scottish theory of sociability, through cognitive exercises. Empowerment, which covers the aforementioned themes, became the subject of several articles and came to maturity in the 1980s.[118] Is giving away psychology not inspired by such an idea?

From Hume's principle of facilitation to Bandura's competence motivation, we have outlined a history of sociological ideas and values driven by scientific psychology and empowered with *cognitive* neuroscience. A naturalism that does not refer to the biological basis of the brain appeared within the jurisdiction of the moral authority acquired by neuroscience. The term *neuroscience* must be put in perspective by returning to its biological foundation: with what concepts and experimental results did biologists push the limits of knowing individuals through their brain, to the degree of thinking they would be able to build a "biology of the mind"? How and in what sense did they progressively demonstrate a necessary relationship between how a brain functions and an individual's behaviour?

3

The Brain-as-Individual

A Physiology of Autonomy

The new model postulated that, in a way, the brain informed, regulated, and controlled itself by sending itself messages. It does not
wait to receive instructions from higher or outside authorities, but
issues actions for which it anticipates the result and verifies that the
result has been achieved.

Marc Jeannerod, *La Fabrique des idèes*

In 1949 neuropsychologist Donald Hebb wrote in the introduction
of his influential book on the organization of behaviour, "Psychology
has an intimate relation with the other biological sciences, and may
also look for help there. There is a considerable overlap between the
problems of psychology and those of neurophysiology." To explore
these close relations, we must ask ourselves a serious question: What
is the neural basis of expectancy, or attention, or interest? To get past
the impression of "animism" that all of these notions evoke for the
scientific community, notions that "cannot be escaped if one is to
give a full account of behavior," the solution would be to develop a
theory of thought to show how thoughts "can be a physiologically
intelligible process."[1]

This chapter is dedicated to the history of this physiological treatment during the second half of the twentieth century. In it, we will
describe biologists' reasoning, the hypotheses on which their work
is based, and the conceptual and experimental leads used to grasp
cerebral mechanisms in a dynamic perspective that made plausible a
theory for a biology of the mind. The main conceptual achievement
was the brain's capacity to modify itself throughout the life of an
individual, thanks to neuronal growth, and a key biological concept

set forth by Hebb in 1949 known as synaptic plasticity. This concept allows us to understand the real biological mechanism that serves as a basis for expectation, interest, and attention – in a word, the mind – and at the same time shows us a brain capable of changing itself, a brain-as-individual. A social value fundamental to autonomy will be devoted to it: the infinite capacity of individuals to be agents of their own change. Synaptic plasticity is the concept where convergences are the most convincing achievements of biological research and the collective representations of the autonomous man of action.

A "RETURN" OF THE SUBJECT TO BIOLOGICAL FORM?

A 1960 conference on the unconscious brought together the cream of the crop in French psychiatry and philosophy. One psychiatrist presented a report on consciousness and the unconscious through a neurobiological context: "It is, I hope, with a grin that you, like myself, have taken the announcement ... of a report on the neurophysiology of the unconscious."[2] Further in his presentation, while considering the contributions made by the biggest neurobiological movements of the time, he reasoned that they "end up forming a 'neurometaphysics' of the organism ... they reintroduce the notion of the subject into the study of cerebral functioning."[3] This evokes the "surprising diversity of concepts and levels of reality from which we can tackle problems of the biological foundations of the mind."[4] The tone of the psychiatrist underlines the surprise concerning a neurobiology of the human subject considered in the totality of a thinking, feeling, and acting being. At that time, such a claim seemed manifestly incongruous, or at the very least unusual.[5] In fact, the disciplines grouped together today under the umbrella of "neuroscience" were divided between those that took an interest in motor and sensory disorders (vision, hearing, etc.) – neurology, and those that treated mental pathologies – psychiatry. There was also an important tradition of biological psychiatric research on these pathologies. Nevertheless, in 1960 neurobiology was concerned primarily with cerebral mechanics.

Twenty years later, the atmosphere had changed: the "subject," the "self," and "consciousness" were top of the list in neuroscientific research. In 1985 Michael Gazzaniga summarized twenty-five years of research and offered instruction in his book *Social Brain*: "What do not change are initial unanswered questions ... centered on how brain science might address problems of personal consciousness and through those [achieve] a wider understanding of social processes."[6] In 1988 Gerald Edelman, who received the 1972 Nobel Prize in Physiology or Medicine for his discoveries concerning the chemical structure of antibodies, affirmed that, "without an understanding of how the mind is based in matter, we will be left with a vast chasm between scientific knowledge and knowledge of ourselves."[7] Erik R. Kandel, who received the same Nobel Prize in 2000 for his work on procedural memory, thought most biologists were "convinced that the mind will be to the biology of the twenty-first century what the gene has been to the biology of the twentieth century."[8] A report from the French Academy of Sciences, published in 2003, highlights the extent to which "apprehending the brain is vital in order for us to understand ourselves."[9] Over the long term, many neuroscientists were hoping for a complete explanation of the mind on a cerebral basis. Although this goal was underscored in an appraisal on neuroscience in the twentieth century published in 2000 by the journal *Cell*, the article also acknowledged "enormously complex problems, more complex than any we have confronted previously in other areas of biology,"[10] like awareness, will, and subjectivity, reminding us of Edelman's contention that "[the brain] is the most complex object in the known universe."[11] Nancy Andreasen (former editor-in-chief of the *American Journal of Psychiatry*), in *Brave New Brain*, published in 2001, highlighted the fact that "the convergence of these two domains of knowledge [molecular biology and cerebral imaging] is one of the most exciting things that is happening in medicine and mental health at the moment. Their convergence has already changed how we think about both the causes and the treatment of mental illnesses." Over the short term, these advances, she stated, should find the causes of schizophrenia, mood disorders, and anxiety. Over the long term, the goal was to "find a 'penicillin for mental illness' ... [and] fight schizophrenia or dementia as effectively as we can currently fight infectious diseases."[12]

The neuroscientific community often brings us back to the end of the nineteenth century, to the time of "the great division" in which neuropathology and pychopathology diverged and separated. At this moment Freud also wrote his *Project for a Scientific Psychology* (1895), which he rightly presented as the psychology for neurologists, in which he was not yet able to cut psychoanalysis from its "biological basis." Indeed, many neuroscientists support Jean-Pierre

Changeux's call in 1983 on the opening pages of *Neuronal Man*: "Perhaps the time has come to rewrite Freud's *Project* and to lay the foundation for a modern biology of the mind."[13] Consequently, the Holy Grail was put into perspective, uniting the extreme finesse of psychoanalysis to account for human passion and credible science. Since then, tens of thousands of scholars have researched the "role of the subject in his own ontogeny."[14]

A half century after the conference on the unconscious, we have clearly witnessed, as neurophysiologist Marc Jeannerod reminded us in 2011, a "return to the forefront of a ghost who had long ago disappeared: the subject."[15] Treating the "subject" physiologically implies surmounting the division between neurology and psychiatry. How did biologists debate this point? This was witnessed during the second half of the twentieth century with the shift of a reactive brain into an agent brain. The new brain triggers itself proactively and can make hypotheses, simulate action, and conceptualize consequences. This shift in viewpoint corresponds in biology to what happened in scientific psychology when it shifted its concentration from the environmentalism of the other-directed individual to the mentalism of the inner-directed individual.

I propose to understand studies on the relationship between cerebral mechanisms and behaviour in the following way: a two-pronged complementary approach qualified as an individualization and a de-individualization of the brain. The first clarified the way researchers came to the central idea of the brain as an endogenous system that activates itself as well as the being to which it belongs. The second explored the changes that accompanied the innovation represented by cerebral imaging. This modified what is considered as the brain. With imaging, the new discipline of "cognitive neuroscience"[16] was established in the 1980s, and, at the end of the twentieth century, it developed into "social neuroscience" by extending toward the social. At the same time, it contributed to the brain entering the collective psyche, starting in the 1990s.

INDIVIDUALIZATION:
FROM THE REACTIVE BRAIN TO THE AGENT BRAIN

The brain that was constructed, starting in the 1950s, was progressively conceived as a *dynamic self-organizing system* that mobilizes itself independently from external stimuli (coming from outside the individual). The condition for independence regarding the outside world is at the heart of the anthropological aim for a biology of the mind: if it can be proven that the brain *itself* powers a being to act in the world, and not merely to react, then we will have greatly advanced the knowledge of humankind through the brain.

In order to understand this idea, we must have a look at neuropsychology.

Henri Hécaen, who played a major role in the development of neuropsychology in France, defined it in 1972 as "the discipline that treats higher mental functions in how they relate to cerebral structures."[17] Its subject comprised behavioural disorders caused by cerebral lesions, placing it "on the cusp"[18] of neural sciences and psychology. Modern neuropsychology explains psychological dysfunction, but it does not identify brain knowledge and self-knowledge, and therefore does not in any way claim to know humankind completely. Between modern neuropsychology, which elaborates on higher mental functions starting after World War II, and cognitive neuroscience as it strives to become a biology of the mind, the difference is due to the extension of a materialist philosophy on mental phenomena as a whole, and the material basis of the brain explaining mental superstructures.

The difference between a neuropsychological program and a cognitive neuroscientific one is well put by Michael Gazzaniga when he explained the choice of the term *cognitive* rather than *neuropsychology*: "Our objective was to emphasize that understanding normal cognition – not the determination of the brain areas subserving discrete cognitive activities – was the goal."[19] The project was to discover a biological basis of all mental functions. It is hard to mention this without bringing to mind Gall's phrenology around 1800. The originality of Gall's ambition is that "it [was] one of the first attempts to elaborate an understanding of the totality of man by examining one part of his body."[20] Gall was ridiculed because all that was remembered from his work was intelligence bumps. However, starting in the 1950s in the United States and Canada, many neurologists referenced him as the first anatomist to shed light on the cortex as an essential part of the brain and to have divided differentiated functions into zones.[21] The project for establishing a biology of the mind brings us to an important question raised by the representation of humankind underpinned by Gall. Georges Lantéri-Laura clarified this by using language from the second half of the twentieth century: "Knowing man is possible only from the moment we recognize what he knows of himself and, depending on circumstances, is not enough for interpreting his behaviour. The truth of man is beyond what he can know of himself. If such a rigorous knowledge of man is possible, it must first focus on that, and this can be done only by elaborating a semiology that makes it possible to understand fundamental tendencies without analyzing inner life."[22] Aside from what an individual's real behaviour shows and the words used to support it, there is sub-personal knowledge made up of biological movements affirming something of individuals in their entirety. Gall is both the model for a biology of the mind by attempting to understand humankind through the brain, and the counter-model, since his endeavour was discredited as the result of errors.

Concepts making it possible to conceive an agent brain started popping up between the 1950s and the end of the 1970s, when the first brain imaging machines made their way into labs and hospitals, but without the more central role they would play in the last twenty years of the century in the construction of the brain–mind matrix.

From Neurology to Neuropsychology

Neuropsychology was first a noun that replaced the neurological term *higher cortical functions*,[23] then it became the discipline through which cognitive neuroscience and neural sciences came together.

"Volition is at the heart of human reality; it is the manifestation of our inner being. How does the brain assure its implementation?" wondered Marc Jeannerod in 2009, for whom the journey of shifting from neuropsychology to cognitive neuroscience was exemplary.[24] The response by the return of the subject "in" the brain was metaphorical. To give substance to the "return of the subject," we must specify what the word means for those who use it in cognitive neuroscience. As a physiologist, the key issue here is how to account for volition as an elicitor of action.[25] In a physiological sense, this implies that action is a voluntary *movement*, and therefore its neurobiological foundation is motor: the premotor cortex appears at the intersection of how the human mind plans and executes actions.

This issue leads to the following question: Is action necessarily a motor response to an external sensory stimulus, or is there an internal activation system that corresponds to volition?

Modern neurology had started amid patients presenting primary function deficits, like speaking, hearing, and vision. A first set of theories came together in the 1860s with aphasia. These theories can be characterized by two traits: localization and association. Localization of motor aphasia in the left parietal lobe (close to the projection area for tongue and mouth movements), then localization of sensory aphasia in the left occipital lobe (close to the afferent area – input – auditory). If there are sensory areas of reception and areas of motor emission, there must be nerve connections driving one another. This is called conduction aphasia, an aphasia resulting from affected anatomic pathways going from the sensory area to the motor area.

For historians of neurology, the discipline was divided between localizers and globalists until after the Second World War. If, on a clinical level, this distinction has little impact – there are symptoms to which corresponding lesions must be sought – on the level of examining a cerebral centre of intelligence, sensibility, etc., there is a distinctive split.

The relationship between lesion and function are at the heart of neurology. Patients who are aphasic, apraxic, or agnosic are affected by deficits in a primary function, but their minds are healthy. Matters become more complicated insofar as psychiatric or psychological symptoms are often accompanied by neurological disorders (like with Parkinson's disease), whereas neurological disorders, like those of the frontal lobe from which Gage and Elliot suffered, give rise to personality disorders. As dysfunctions of the central nervous system are pathological, neurology had a tendency, for a long time, to set aside functional disorders with an unknown lesion or anatomic basis.

Neurologists contend with a brain that has suffered and reacted, and not with one that acts. It is the shift from reactive brain to agent brain that must be understood.

In 1947, Henri Hécaen (*the* face of French neuropsychology for three decades) and Julian de Ajuriaguerra expressed this complication in question form: "Must we separate focalized symptoms, those that result from the dissolution of a primary function, and global disorders, those that result from a general dissolution of nerve functions?"[26] In other words, must we separate neurology and psychology? For them, the two are indissociable, and separation is arbitrary: "Nerve functions are not static, but are coordinated amongst themselves, so much so that a lesion does not only disorganize an autonomous function that is dependent on the damaged zone, but the functioning as a whole: the localization of the lesion does not correspond to that of the function."[27] All of the neuropsychology that came after the war was built by going beyond the lesion/function pairing. There is no mechanical relationship between anatomic regions and function, but rather a "functional localization more evenly ... 'distributed' to account for nerve plasticity phenomena."[28]

The "subject" is introduced to neuropsychology as a reaction to globalist approaches. It will constitute the answer of localizers based on biology. Paradoxical? No, since the triumph of localizers over globalists is that the localizers integrated the systemic or structural aspect with the global approach: there is localization, but the local zones are not isolated, which means the affected function does not have a single localization in a single cerebral area. According to Hécaen, "In human cortical pathology, there is a tendency to reject the notion of a cerebral mosaic made up of limited centres that carry out specific functions, and to consider relatively large regions endowed with diverse potentialities, the different parts of which work on the same function."[29] There was triumph long before anyone started talking about cognitive neuroscience. So what happened?

Two things: the development of a *new neuroanatomy*, in which everything is connected to everything else, presenting a complete brain; and the emergence of a *new physiology*, which discovered mechanisms that act within the connections. They move together toward the orbitofrontal cortex, which seems to be the junction of anticipation and action.

Syndromes of Disconnection: An Anatomically Complete Brain

Since the beginning of modern neuroscience with the discovery that motor aphasia resulted from left frontal lobe lesions, neurologists took greater interest in the left hemisphere, sometimes called dominant; most pathologies were the result of lesions in this hemisphere. The right seemed to be "without any functions other than motor, sensibility, and sensory on the left side of the body."[30] Throughout the 1950s and 1960s, a new neuroanatomy developed around connections between the two hemispheres as well as intra-hemispheric connections. It transformed the brain into a network of networks.

The corpus collosum, or the callosal commissure, is the main anatomical part of the brain that links the two hemispheres. In the 1960s, work done on the split brain by Roger Sperry (awarded the Nobel Prize in Physiology or Medicine in 1981) and his team, a member of which was Michael Gazzaniga, empirically showed that there is no dominance of one hemisphere over the other, but a functional dissymmetry in each. This dissymmetry of the two hemispheres, also called lateralization, depends on a different biological organization. This organization is the very mark of humankind.[31] It means that mental capacities develop thanks to a division "between two functional spaces that must be considered synergetic and complementary, and not autonomous and independent, and that the acting subject can choose according to his needs."[32]

Following closely the work on the split brain, it was American neuroanatomist Norman Geschwind, whom Damasio collaborated with and studied under, who showed anatomically the multiplicity of connections, in a lengthy two-part article published by *Brain* in 1965 on "disconnection syndromes in animals and man." Neuropsychology has him to thank for establishing the importance of connectivity in the brain, which is to say the connective pathways observed as such. The article is considered "a manifesto for the neo-associationist school"[33] because it established in a very detailed manner that dysfunctions occur along connective pathways. The concept of disconnection applies to lesions in associative pathways, which link areas within one hemisphere or join the two together. It demonstrates that syndromes of "higher cortex functions," aphasia, apraxis, agnosia, are better described as perturbations produced by anatomic disconnections between motor and sensory centres. In other words, disconnection causes dysfunction. Therefore, neurology goes beyond the lesion/function mechanic perspective in favour of a relational approach that perceives the brain as a system.

The concept of disconnection starts from the idea that several combinations of lesions can set off the same syndrome. Work on aphasias had distinguished between those from motor or sensory areas (made up of grey matter) and those from affected conduction pathways between these two areas (made up of white matter). Returning to this work, Geschwind showed the pathways linking cerebral areas between each other (within each hemisphere and across hemispheres) not only transport information from one region to the next, but they also inhibit and activate. There are multiple, indirect connective pathways, and every area is connected to multiple others. These pathways are also called the association cortex, associative centres, etc., the important thing being that these nerve pathways serve as relays, which comprise white matter.

Comparing a patient incapable of reading (alexia, blind to words) but capable of writing (without agraphia) with a patient who has both syndromes allows us to understand reasoning. The difference is that the first patient kept the capacity to spell words, whereas the second no longer had, meaning the former "preserves the 'centre' which turns spoken into written language and also carries on the reverse operation."[34] The second patient is affected with disconnection syndrome. Here we have a clinical demonstration, but the article uses modern research methods in human and animal neuropsychology developed after the war.

At the end of this assessment, Geschwind examines the philosophical implications of the adopted method in order to establish this type of diagnosis: "We constantly found that many confusions about the patient in our minds as well as in those of others resulted from failure to do the exact opposite of what the rule to look at the patient as a whole demanded, i.e., from our failure to regard the patient as made of connected parts rather than as an indissoluble whole."[35] The part of this patient who *knew* (non-verbally) what he was holding in his left hand was not the same as the one that would have allowed him to *say* it. For the clinician to be able to accurately describe the patient's pathology and to be attentive to his needs, he must be treated not as a whole, but in parts. He specifies, and the point he makes is decisive: "I am not advancing 'the atomistic approach' as a basic philosophical postulate to replace 'the holistic approach,' but am rather suggesting that failure to consider the applicability of *either* type of analysis will ... lead to errors."[36] He is perfectly correct, as neurological research will show: parts connected to each other by multiple connection pathways form a system. Here, we have an authentic neurological perspective that allows us to account for the infinite subtleties of neurological symptoms by going beyond the debates between atomistic and holistic approaches.

Geschwind coined the expression "behavioural neurology" around 1970. He founded an association with the same name in 1982, and it quickly became the Society for Behavioral and Cognitive Neurology.[37]

Now we will be able to understand the role of motor areas and get closer to Gage and Elliot, and by that I mean the orbitofrontal (ventromedial) premotor cortex.

The motor cortex (called primary), which distributes commands to muscles, is connected to the sensory cortex (parietal), which receives stimuli from the outside world, to subcortical structures and to the *pre*motor cortex. It is considered premotor since it is found just anterior to the motor cortex and occupies most of the frontal lobe. In this region, sensory information, coming from the outside world, comes together with information derived from subcortical regions relating to memory and affectivity. "This synthesis between the two types of information is possibly what best characterizes the prefrontal cortex's function: abstract immediate goals, make longer-term plans and possibly refrain from executing them."[38] Here we can recognize the flip side of Gage and Elliot, both of whom suffered lesions in the orbitofrontal region. "This group supplies the motor cortex with information of endogenous origin, detached from actual execution, intervening in the elaboration of goals, plans, intentions, and motivations which possibly lead to action."[39] The prefrontal cortex is the "brain in action."

The concept of disconnection, first used for neuropathology, was absolutely central to cognitive neuroscience, which defines most pathologies as disconnection syndromes, but extending it to psychiatric pathologies, like schizophrenia,[40] remains hypothetical. A review published in *Brain* in 2005, which pays tribute to Geschwind forty years after his publication in the same journal, states it plainly: "Today, the disconnection paradigm is still to be found within the neurology clinic and outside it within 'functional' disorders as diverse as schizophrenia ... autism ... and dyslexia ... where disconnection 'lesions' remain inferred rather than demonstrable."[41]

In order to go from cerebral to dynamic mechanics, first there needed to be a complete brain. This has been done: at our disposal is an anatomical system of connections between the different parts of the brain. As biologist Francisco Varela wrote some twenty years after Geschwhind's publication, "The brain is therefore a highly cooperative system: the dense network of interconnections between constituent components implies that all that goes on there will eventually be a function of *all* its components."[42] We have a system of connections, but we do not yet have the mechanisms allowing the brain to elaborate goals, which would transform the brain that reacts into one that acts, that moves on its own, a condition for human autonomy. This is the new physiology. It allows the brain to become the expression of a self that generates its own activity – anticipating, comparing, deciding.

Corollary Discharge: A Brain That Triggers Action Physiologically

The debate can be presented as follows. Must there be an outside stimulus for the brain to trigger an action? In this case, the origin of the action is external. This is the "peripheralist" theory, which indicates a sensorimotor path of action. On the contrary, are there purely endogenous mechanisms, implying human action possesses an origin independent of the outside world? In this case, the origin of the action is internal; it needs only brain and body. This is the "centralist" theory, which represents a motor-sensorial axis. If the peripheralist theory is correct, the brain is a system that reacts to information from the outside world. For a biology of the mind to be possible, centralist theory must be correct because it considers the brain as a self-activating entity.

The starting point of the hypothesis is the existence of internal stimulation mechanisms, distinct from external sensory stimulation. This hypothesis is physiologically necessary in order to understand the stability-insuring mechanisms for perceiving the world, and supplying a spatial and temporal framework that the individual can draw on to act in this world. Neurobiologists illustrated this idea with the notion of "corollary discharge," which can also be called "efference copy," which shed some light on frontal lobe disorders.

This notion gained momentum with studies of vision problems in animals. The question was how the nervous system distinguishes between the image that scrolls across the immobile retina and the eye movement that follows the movements of the outside world. If the nervous system does not have "central coordination" making it possible to make this distinction, the visual system is unstable. In 1950, Erich von Holst demonstrated central coordination within the nervous systems of insects and fish that regulates visuomotor behaviour: "Each time that the motor centres send a command to the effectors, they send at the same time a sort of copy, the 'efference' copy, of this command to other regions of the nervous system."[43] The command for eye movement simultaneously sends an efference copy to the retina's sensory message. The same year, Roger Sperry showed a "corollary discharge" of central origin in fish that goes toward visual centres, allowing the animal to distinguish between the shifting of an object due to the retina's movement and a mobile object.

A famous experimental device designated the "awake monkey" was developed in the late 1960s. It demonstrated this capability on a neural level: the animal is coached to do a certain task (touch different-coloured balls in a certain order, for example) for which it receives a reward for carrying it out correctly; when the task appears, it must wait for an execution signal (go) or a non-execution signal (no go) sent by the experimenter. A discharge of premotor neurons was thus observed between the moment in which the task appears and when the signal is given. Not only were neuronal activity and behaviour associated, but the device also allowed for an "entry into the cognitive process that precedes action."[44]

Hans-Lukas Teuber, a giant of neuropsychology from the second half of the twentieth century, on par with Geschwind (who in 1961 overhauled the psychology department at Harvard University by breaking away from the department of economy and social sciences), broadened the concept beyond vision, making it a general feature of the nervous system. "Specifically, we postulate that when we make deliberate voluntary movements (e.g., shift our eyes across the room), *two* streams of signals are initiated within our nervous system, and not only one. One of these two is of course the classical motor outflow to the effector organs. The other set of signals is sent, directly and centrally, to the sensory systems, so that the consequences of the intended action can be taken into account. We call these discharges 'corollary' when they are essentially derivations of momentary motor commands, and 'anticipatory' when more remote consequences of the impending action are being computed. In either case, these signals ... involve an information flow that is the reverse of the classical Sherrington one: not from sensory to motor, from back to front, so to speak, but in the opposite direction, from motor and premotor to sensory and therefore from front to back."[45] The corollary discharge reveals a brain that acts on its own. As we just saw, the triggering of the discharge, which happens in the prefrontal cortex, is *the* physiological criterion of voluntary action. From there, reafferent chains or discharges are triggered, according to the necessities of the action, through interconnected cerebral areas. The different areas are integrated into a conception of the brain as a comparator of movement types and an anticipator of their consequences.

Patients with frontal lobe injuries like Gage and Elliot are characterized as having difficulties in planning voluntary actions. The study of such patients highlighted "what is at the heart of prefrontal cortex functioning: determining a goal and making a plan of action."[46] The prefrontal cortex is not involved in the action itself, but in its conditions, because it lies at the crossroads of motor and emotional regulation, and it is precisely the orbitofrontal (or ventromedial), in the premotor cortex, that is particularly connected to subcortical zones where emotions are treated, and which are involved in anticipating actions.

Neural systems therefore have an *independent* activity of impulses coming from the outside to which the brain reacts, a purely endogenous activity. From here, the mechanist explanation becomes dynamic.[47] "Whereas autoregulation systems, such as those producing reflex activities, are energetically closed systems, in the sense that the energy required for the response is present in the stimulus, or a disturbance that induces a deviation from the reference, voluntary movement proceeds from an open system whose energy comes from within. It is as such that its endogenous origin confers upon it a new, affirmative character. It proceeds from an intention constructed by the subject, and from a representation of the goal to be achieved, which are triggering elements in the process."[48] This endogenous activity is the veritable biological basis from which we can identify an understanding of individual subjectivity to brain knowledge: "The notion of central state is merely the biological counterpart to that of interiority and subjectivity, both of which deeply penetrate toward the action's origin, the mystery of the being."[49]

Here emerges the issue of a brain system: at the beginning, there is action, but at the beginning of the beginning, there is motor. By delving into the depths of this motor, the dynamic conception of the brain is introduced. "We went from a feedback model to a feedforward method. This turn reveals the difference between the classic homeostatic mechanism, based on the maintenance of a pre-established reference, and the mechanism of the internal model based on achieving an exterior goal":[50] the homeostatic mechanism is, precisely, too static, and does not take into account biological complexity. The "internal model" is the mechanism leading to the discharge of prefrontal neurons. This model represents the goal of an action, biological in nature, making it possible to execute actions directed toward said goal.[51] Human action, having become movement, needs representation in order to find its human character. This representation, as we saw in the previous chapter, is supplied through cognitive psychology: these are internal models.

Jeannerod proposes that "the principle function of the cognitive system ... is to manufacture representations by using data supplied by sense organs or by data stocked in the memory and which constitutes our knowledge and beliefs. The notion of naturalization postulates that representations are natural objects, and that as such they possess not only physical properties, like any other object, but also semantic properties."[52]

There were alternatives to the representational conception, like that of biologist Francisco Varela. He inverted the child model and that of the expert who solves problems: "The deepest intelligence is that of the baby who acquires language from a daily stream of dispersed scraps, or which reconstitutes meaningful objects from a shapeless flow of light."[53] We are faced with the infinite complexity of a being thrown into the world; therefore, we are dealing with a more authentic human reality. It is to this reality that we must adjust cognitive science.

This approach refers to a series of concepts that circulated in the 1970s and 1980s: "Connectionism, self-organization, association, dynamic networks," wrote Varela.[54] This brings into question representation as a relationship between a subject and a predefined world, and substitutes it with an intertwining of subject and world. At the same time, it weakens belief in the brain as a command centre. Where machine intelligence concerns problem-solving, human intelligence concerns accomplishing actions within inseparably interconnected contexts: "Since representation does not play a key role, intelligence is defined more as a problem-solving faculty, but one that *penetrates* a shared world."[55] The replacement solution is the concept of emergence. The cognitive system is constructed out of very densely linked components, which function locally, instead of from a centre that coordinates a sequential series of actions. This connectionist model is analogous to that of biologists, and inspired by them, treating information according to parallel pathways. It is therefore more attuned to biological concepts, like corollary discharge. Such links express "the configurational nature of the system," indicating the interdependence of elements that constitute it, and for this reason, "a *global* cooperation *emerges* spontaneously." The main advantage of this perspective is that it "does not require a central processing unit to control its functioning."[56]

Because the environment considers the matter in terms of representations (this is the case for a majority of researchers) or penetration of a world, it does not have as much importance biologically speaking. Research would soon show that neuronal populations "have one property in common: the dynamic properties of the action of integrated neuron populations cannot be deduced from knowledge of the action of the single neurons within them. Instead, the population properties are emergent."[57] With emergent properties of dynamic neuronal networks, we are finally able to speak of self-organization. These properties were explained by evolution, which replaced the idea of a functional system,[58] and by the unique complexity of the brain. Self-organization indicates a being capable not only of driving itself, but also of modifying itself.

Synaptic Transmission and Cerebral Plasticity: Is the Brain (Like) an Individual?

The living animal organism, be it larva or human, is characterized by the fact that it drives itself – it is the criterion that distinguishes the living from the mechanical. For a global biological theory to account for this as biology, the brain must not only be sensory, but must also be an entity that acts on its own, that develops a purely endogenous motor activity. However, another element is missing to illustrate how the brain self-organizes: the way in which it integrates the individual's temporal experience, or in other words, learning and memory.

For individual intelligence to be mobilized, the brain must keep traces permanently, in such a way that learning itself must be fixed into the cerebral matter. There needs to be a physiological counterpart to these psychological processes. This issue concerns the relationship between cerebral mechanisms and behavioural responses, between biology and physiology, in short, between the sub-personal and personal levels.

The biological key resides in the concept of plasticity, which explains how the brain modifies itself in relation to an experience.[59] Its biological mechanism is synaptic transmission; therefore, it is a connection issue. At a molecular level, the conceptual loop of a biology of the mind is closed. Not only does transmission and synaptic plasticity establish the capacity of the brain to transform itself (to transform its organization) according to the needs of the individual, but the modular and distributed functions of the brain do as well.

Synaptic *transmission* "has created the most important generalizing propositions in neuroscience," wrote neurobiologist Vernon Mountcastle, in the introduction to a 1998 instalment from *Dædalus* (the journal from the American Academy of Arts and Sciences). The installment was dedicated to a half-century survey of research on the brain – Mountcastle had discovered shortly before that neurons from the posterior parietal cortex possessed visuomotor properties. From the first elements of its description in the 1940s, "perhaps the most important is the discovery of synaptic plasticity and descriptions of its candidate mechanisms."

"Synaptic transmission has emerged as an important generalizing proposition in neuroscience."[60] It is on the synaptic transmission level where learning about the world occurs biologically, in the brain. This is key to explaining the relationship between the cerebral level and the psychological or cognitive level, that of true individual behaviour: it is the basis of the "cellular learning paradigm."[61] Why? Because synaptic connections between two neurons, through which the chemical transmission passes, increase when regularly mobilized. The increase in connection density is an expression of cerebral memory. Transmission and plasticity join together to form the molecular base of global cerebral plasticity. First confined to critical periods (during which the development of the human being was at stake), since the end of the twentieth century plasticity has been viewed as a general continuous property of the brain at work throughout life. It allows for the creation of a cellular base for all brain function: learning, memory, and perception.

The best-known expression of this connectivist concept comes from Hebb in 1949, in his *Organization of Behavior*. It is based on a hypothesis formulated in two stages. For the experience to be observed biologically there must be a temporal arrangement, a trace. Nevertheless, for this trace to transform into something permanent, a structure must fix it in the memory. That is the hypothesis of the dual trace mechanism, which "would comprise ... an initial transient, *dynamic* storage which would give way to a permanent *structural* form of storage."[62] From this duality, he introduced a neurophysiological premise that has been cited numerous times: "The general idea is an old one, that any two cells or systems of cells that are repeatedly active at the same time will tend to become 'associated,' so that activity in one facilitates activity in the other."[63] Reinforced connections between cells occur when synapses increase.

Biologists refer to synaptic plasticity as "Hebb's rule" or "Hebbian plasticity" – the coinciding activity of the two cells leads to structural changes, in other words, to permanent traces in the brain. The neurons assembled from a rise in synaptic activity were coined "cell assembly theory" – which biologist Gerald Edelman used with his theory of "neuronal groups." They rely on learning, which increases the intensity of synaptic transmission (its dynamic) and distributes it into multiple cerebral areas linked extensively by nerve fibres.

Hebb's rule is omnipresent in neuroscience because biologists and psychologists found, within this idea, a neural foundation for learning and memory. Another element put forward by Hebb provided extra traction to his idea: the rule works in the absence of any real stimulus, by a representation of something, for example. ("You need not have an elephant present to think about elephants," he used to say.) "The Hebbian principle was not only catchy because of its clear-cut and experimentally testable formulation; it also rendered synaptic plasticity immediately and intuitively meaningful by positioning it in the context of neuronal assemblies. Hebb's postulate was also particularly powerful because it gave a possible neural explanation to two notions held by early philosophers and psychologists: that information enters the brain and reverberates, thus leaving persistent traces; and that information flow in the brain must change for learning and memory to occur."[64] The appeal of this rule is such that researchers did not hesitate to raise the stakes to metaphysical heights: "The nature of this connectivity may finally resolve the nature-versus-nurture debate that set the path for synaptic plasticity research and that has persistently remained unresolved for more than 2000 years."[65] Philosophers and anthropologists share this idea and say it should drive us to revisit our social concepts.[66]

At the same time, for biological psychiatry, most chemical molecules (neurotransmitters and neuromodulators), transmitted from cell to cell, had been discovered thanks to neuroleptics and antidepressants starting in the 1950s. These medicines conferred neurochemical transmission to a broader public because they solidified the link between an action in the brain and a change in mood or in delusional ideas.[67] From a neurological standpoint, studies in the 1960s started to show that, following a lesion, "a reactional synaptic sprouting"[68] occurred, thus filling in the damage caused by the lesion. That was an explanation for functional rehabilitation phenomena in neurology and a decisive result that made progress in understanding the power of the brain: synapses modify themselves in response to lesions and can proceed to a *restitution* of the damaged function. However, functional recuperation could also be the result of a *substitution* of other neuronal networks to those damaged, thus reorganizing connections in various zones of the brain. Synaptic plasticity elegantly explains both mechanisms.

Gerald Edelman said the most significant word for understanding the brain was *neuroanatomy*: connections and the way they are formed, maintained, reinforced, or weakened that allows for the understanding of brain function,[69] namely its physiology, its mechanisms. In order to account for the mainly endogenous activity of the brain, biologists refer to a system capable of self-organization thanks to the development and interconnection of an increasing number of neurons, which form what Edelman called "experiential selection" – continuous synaptic selection increasing the neural density to form a "neuronal group" while it weakens elsewhere.

Synaptic connections also make it possible to demonstrate empirically that they are the foundation of brain self-organization, the basis of its architecture: "It is dynamic morphology all the way down."[70] However, something must be added to synaptic transmission to get to this level: re-entrant signalling. Thanks to it, certain signal functions (vision, for example), distributed into different areas and interconnected through nerve pathways, are integrated. Re-entrant signalling is the keystone allowing for a biological explanation for how the brain self-organizes through its own architecture and morphology, and therefore without the need to resort to central coordination: "Nervous system behaviour is to some extent self-generated in loops; brain activity leads to movement, which leads to further sensation and perception and still further movement. The layers and the loops between them are the most intricate of any object we know, and they are dynamic; they continually change."[71] The system works without central management, through its pure "dynamic morphology." The re-entry loop "offers the key to resolving the problem of integrating the functionally segregated properties of brain areas despite the lack of a central or superordinate area."[72] This concept explains the dynamic continuous signals that simultaneously generate within the cerebral areas, linked in both space and time. The opposition between specialized modules and distributed knowledge is dated: the brain functions on the mode of both relative specialization and functional integration – Mountcastle spoke of "modular nodes."

The individualization of the brain via cerebral plasticity mechanisms covers that of the human being itself – maintaining an ambiguity between its sub-personal status as *part of a being* and its new personal status as *a being*. A proposition that flows from this property has garnered support in the neuroscientific community: "*No two brains are identical and any single brain is continually changed by its experience.*"[73] Can the existence of individual variations in cerebral functional organization be the subject of harmful and discriminatory political applications? "We understand that such a proposition could be met with reticence," wrote neurologist Jean-Louis Signoret in 1987, but "in no way does it prejudge possible qualities of mental capacities."[74] Infinite individualization of the brain does not mean that there are biological inequalities among individuals, nor does it refer to a hierarchical theory. It speaks more to the very complexity of human beings in that they are "an essential element governing the ability of the brain to match unforeseeable patterns that might arise in the future of a behaving animal."[75]

Each brain, like each human being, is unique: development of both is shaped by individual experience. It is difficult to know whether the "individual" in question is the brain or the human being, to the extent that the register of the description suitable for the brain is analogous to what is required to describe the human being. Thus the neuroscientific community wonders how it categorizes the world, recognizes situations, etc. It is thought of as "an organ that constructs worlds rather than reflects on them," answers Varela.[76]

At the end of the twentieth century, cognitive neuroscience was able to reach a remarkable degree of biological individualization: the brain became the most fundamental level of explanation, thanks to the infinite dynamic modifications and therefore individualization, all within a structure characterized by relative specialization and functional integration. In this way, the brain is elevated to a status of quasi-being or quasi-individual; however, it is not a matter from which to glean any moral judgment for members of the neuroscientific community: the differences between brains do not imply any hierarchy among individuals. They are the way, as the biologist would say, to account for the infinite diversity of humans from the infinite diversity of cerebral anatomy. The brain of the individual is as variable as the individuals themselves; it is characterized by an infinite individualization that distinguishes members of the only human species – what Edelman calls the "specialness" of the brain.[77]

The cerebral subject is the endogenous system, self-driven, formed as a network and not as a central behavioural regulator.

The problem of pertinent differences in anatomical variations of the brain is found in questions raised by cerebral imaging. With it, we truly enter the era of a biology of the mind, one that builds a bridge between brain and mind. Its construction passes, unlike what we just saw, by the de-individualization of the brain.

DE-INDIVIDUALIZATION OF THE BRAIN IN THE MATRIX SPACE OF NEUROSCIENCE

Starting in the 1980s, an academic alliance was established between biologists and psychologists, along with a partnership of brain and cognitive science, around cerebral imaging technology. A rapid expansion of imaging dominated this sphere, culminating in the creation of the Human Brain Project in the early 1990s. This was when the expression "cognitive neuroscience" was instituted. A first edition of the *Handbook of Cognitive Science* was published in 1984, and the first instalment of the *Journal of Cognitive Neuroscience* came out in 1989.

The brain won a decisive battle when it demonstrated, thanks to biologists before the 1980s, its permanent endogenous activity: the capacity to decide and act is not the result of a command centre, it is "seen as linked to perception and as articulations between the individual's projective expectations and his permanent endogenous activity."[78] Yet victory was not truly claimed until the 1980s, when consciousness, emotions, judgment, memory, etc. were developed with the introduction of the normal subject, the traditional subject of experimental psychology, in neuroscience laboratories. It gained a foothold thanks to cognitive psychologists, who made a rather forceful entrance into the domain, and to cerebral imaging, which allowed for the recording and measuring of cerebral data alongside behavioural data.[79] The scientific and metaphysical excitement reached laboratories. "It may well have been," writes Marcus Raichle in 1998, "the combination of cognitive science and systems neuroscience with brain imaging that lifted this work from a state of indifference and obscurity in the neuroscience community in the 1970s to its current role of prominence in cognitive neuroscience."[80] Cerebral imaging confirmed correlations between mental and cerebral activities. This operation increased the value of the brain as a candidate for understanding humankind anthropologically: if mental activities reside in the brain, it is because the brain has the highest value for explaining humankind. It cannot be integrated into a superior whole, but itself makes up the totality. For this idea to become credible, it was necessary to modify what imaging showed *as* the brain.

From the Anatomical Brain to Digitized Space: Brain Activity of the Mind

Cerebral imaging has become the preferred tool for those in "cognitive neuroscience." Why? In order to get an authentic biology of the mind, the indispensable condition is to match the anatomical information of "where does this happen?" with the physiological information of "how does this happen?" We had to find a synthesis of structure – the "where" question – by carrying out bottom-up research, and the function – the "how" question – using top-down methods. Cognitive neuroscience had been fully dedicated for the last thirty years to establishing a structure-function synthesis. For that, a "functional neuroanatomy" was elaborated by mapping the brain. Such a conception of neuroanatomy is tightly linked to concepts like "neuronal groups" and "re-entrant loops." Functional neuroanatomy refers to a brain put in motion thanks to its own internal architecture. The project moved forward by *abandoning the reference to an empirical individual*.

For some time neurologists and neurosurgeons have had an anatomical atlas of the brain, mapping tools that are requisite for research and clinical practices in order to identify the location of damaged structures in an individual compared to a normal brain. The first cerebral imaging machines were used in the following neuroanatomical perspective: seeing the lesion made it possible to establish a diagnosis or to carry out a more precise neurosurgery. Their aim was individual cases: localization was part of a clinical goal, and the scans produced optical images analyzed by observers. This knowledge referred to what was typical, to what characterized a given individual. Likewise, the brain atlas at that time was developed from supposedly normal brains to compare them to patients' brains, in other words, to serve as a reference to neuroanatomical localization. Here, we are clearly in clinical neurology and neuropathology, and for these disciplines, it is the "where" that counts.

The *Lancet* published the first article using cerebral imaging for mental illness in 1974 ("Abnormalities of Cerebral Blood Flow Distribution in Patients with Chronic Schizophrenia"). An editorial from the 1996 *American Journal of Psychiatry* with a charming title – "Imaging for the Clinical Psychiatrist: Facts, Fantasies, and Other Musings" – considers that, at that time, the hope for distinguishing, for example, schizophrenia from dementia did not bear fruit. "Many isolated but seemingly attractive findings have resulted in speculative musings, rather than the construction of a significant, testable hypothesis and validation with an independent sample."[81] In 1994, the first article on MRI imaging was published in the same journal. It started by affirming that this tool "will probably be of importance in assessing brain abnormalities in psychiatric disorders,"[82] However, fifteen years later, in September 2011, another editorial from the same journal considers that "the value of what has been learned has often seemed elusive."[83] Forty years after the first cerebral imaging machine, judgments on the capacity of imaging to diagnose mental pathologies all led in the same direction: no solid correspondence was established between a psychiatric syndrome and a set of cerebral areas and circuits. And by solid correspondence, I mean to say having conclusively demonstrated the mechanism by which a certain set produces a syndrome.

Imaging went in a direction different from that of the diagnostic instrument: it became the aid and framework for a general science of human behaviour, sound or sick, by transforming it into *functional* imaging. By introducing this adjective, it meant that imaging had now become cartography, the aim of which was to build a bridge between cerebral and mental activities. This was not the objective in the 1970s. Yet, it was by building this bridge that neuroscience had hoped to succeed in diagnosing illness, but illness, as we will see shortly, was no longer formulated in reference to a syndrome category.

Starting in the 1980s, there was a clear reorientation in the clinical approach. Psychologists practising experimental psychology introduced a new research object: higher brain functions, like perception, consciousness, memory, intelligence, and thought, which dealt as much with the healthy person as it did the unwell. The work of these psychologists was to study tasks carried out by sound subjects. It did not aim to single out individual cases, but to shed light on shared mental functions in normal individuals.

Psychologists studying the mind and biologists studying the brain were brought together to introduce mental functions into cerebral anatomy, thanks to two innovations. The first was of a techno-scientific order, with the positron emission tomography scan, then with functional magnetic resonance imaging scans, which allowed for the observation of cerebral activity.[84] The second innovation was conventional and from it came a conceptual change in how the brain was understood: in place of neuroanatomical references that go through a visualization of individual brains – real brains – there was a system of coordinates measured in a digital space. This innovation was itself the result of a double dynamic that took shape that started during the last decade: digitization of information, automatization of the production and treatment of data, and work in networks of multidisciplinary teams. The first phase of cerebral imaging was optic (the image is observed), the second was digital (we assess the data).[85]

At the beginning of the 1960s, a change of blood flow was directly demonstrated in healthy subjects as they carried out a task. The variation of blood flow is a function of the activity, implying the brain is in action.

The first cerebral imaging machine, the CT (computerized tomography) scan was realized in 1972: "Overnight," writes Marcus Raichle, understandably enthused, "the way in which we looked at the human brain changed."[86] However, the technique did not allow for a distinction between grey and white matter, neurons and connections.[87] Positron emission tomography was constructed from the limits of the CT, making it possible to measure blood flow on the same subject repetitively, thanks to an injection of a radio-pharmaceutical product. The reasoning was as follows: "This rationale for the use of PET was based on the assumption that metabolic fluctuation might indicate changing physiology and that such changes precede anatomical alterations detectable by structural imaging technologies."[88] Flows produce alterations in cerebral regions – this is what functional anatomy shows. The technique was limited by the need to record the activity for several seconds in order to produce an image with a correct spatial resolution, one that was observable. The functional MRI uses another technique for measurement: the amount of oxygen transported in the blood inversely proportional to the degree by which it is affected by a magnetic field – this point was demonstrated at the end of the 1980s. Functional MRIs are today the most widely used technique for measuring cerebral activity.[89]

These techniques are considered functional anatomy since they provide information on regional functions of the human brain. Metabolic variations are both functional, since they indicate activity, and structural, since this activity takes place in an anatomical location. But how could we be certain that the data from structural and functional anatomy were equivalent? In other words, how could we standardize it in order to compare data of different nature?

To match these two types of data, to be able to determine the location in which the process takes place, we had to be able to compare and standardize images. At the beginning of the 1980s, imaging machines had variable modalities of function and were used in labs with a diverse range of research programs. This made it difficult to determine, for example, if the subjects had held their heads still or in the same position, or whether the person formatting the image did so consistently (removing "noise," for example, or in other words, the irrelevant information). Brains themselves differ in shape and size. On all levels, there reigned a certain heterogeneity. The solution for constructing a template was in transforming the cerebral image by taking it from an optic system examined by an observer to a digital space that could be treated automatically. It came in the form of a matrix, transforming representations of the brain.

Brains have been kept in neuropathology laboratories at hospitals for research purposes for a very long time.[90] Starting in the 1970s, brain banks were developed. Unlike neuropathology labs, these banks had to standardize in order to establish accurate classification protocols. Moreover, they received brains from people who were not diagnosed and could be used as control brains to compare against brains whose tissues were damaged or destroyed. During the 1980s, with the development of cerebral imaging, brain scans were being collected.

If the brain is a real and rare entity, the scan is an abundant, virtual object. Technological advancements in the 1980s quickly raised the issue of an overabundance of data, which needed to be classified. This proved to be a real challenge.

With cerebral imaging, brain banks were transformed into *databases*. The brain, anatomically studied, became an informational research subject. Scans hold no meaning in and of themselves; they hold interest if we are able to compare them using databases in order to shed light on pertinent differences. This is the reason to construct a normal, average, healthy brain model able to serve as a measurement standard.

The solution for these comparisons came about through the construction of a three-dimensional (x, y, z) reference space, each point of which can be identified digitally in a matrix, allowing heterogeneous data to be treated. They are collected with computers and are mathematically reconstructed using an algorithm, organized using boxes that correspond to a "functional brain region." This represents "the average amount of brain activation in that box of the brain over the period of time of the scan."[91] At the same time we have the brain *region*, the anatomical "where," and the brain *activity*, the function: this is functional anatomy. Digital data coming from scan collections can thus be organized into a kind of brain atlas. Traditional brain anatomy was a landscape that the observer deciphered; now it is a Euclidean space operated digitally. It is clear that in order to understand humans, for there to be true understanding, they cannot not be put through just any examination: "The ideals to which these tools strive consist in removing the individual, both as idiosyncratically ill ... and as subjectively (inconsistently) interpreting or manipulating data."[92]

Following George Bush's 17 July 1990 proclamation heralding the Decade of the Brain, federal agencies in the United States began to initiate policy incentives for the development of neuroinformatics. This eventually led to the establishment of the Human Brain Project.[93] Neuroinformatics is a tool that allows for the handling of vast numbers of heterogeneous datasets (psychological, neurophysiological, sociodemographic, etc.) by translating them into a common digital language. In the early 1990s, several American universities and the Montreal Neurological Institute formed a consortium to develop an atlas of the average brain based on brains from 450 healthy subjects. They were then put into multiple databases: DNA samples from each subject, as well as sociodemographic, clinical, and historical data. This new brain atlas could serve as a reference for identifying parts of the brain that were activated during a certain task. The most difficult part was finding a normal brain from a healthy subject. This is essential if the atlas is to be used as a reference tool. The normality of the selected subjects was that of control subjects in experimental psychology systems. It was defined by what it was not: "Subjects are normal if they are untraumatized, unmedicated, unaddicted, non-diabetic, not pregnant, and not having had neurosurgery, psychiatric or neurological disorders."[94] They do not represent an average slice of the population, but an ideal, healthy, or normal one. Algorithms were developed to homogenize the heterogeneous data by giving them a numeric value.

From that moment, to the extent that the imaging community thought it had constructed an objective brain that could actually serve as a cerebral template, it truly became possible to study the brain empirically in terms of variability, to locate pertinent and irrelevant anatomical differences, or in other words to distinguish behaviours – like the brains of Gage and Elliot – but also *forms* of intelligence – like the brains of high-functioning autistics. The dataset, an accumulation of scans, made it possible to research normal variations in brain structure in terms of probability.[95] These databases therefore have a normative dimension: "They can be used to indicate normal variation and pathological deviation. They are even being developed to trace individuals 'at risk.'"[96] Neuroanatomy was the key to cognitive neuroscience. As Anne Beaulieu sums up the dynamic, "What had begun as a better tool for localization of PET activity (a better target brain based on a larger, normal sample) became an exploration of the normal brain, and of its variability."[97]

Cognitive psychologists, who worked within the general population to characterize representative behaviour rather than pathologies, had undertaken the search for a normal brain model.[98] It was also achieved through an abundance of heterogeneous data and increased collaborations among professions having different research supports (molecular blood analysis is not required in all questionnaires). Brain imaging thus progressively broadened its scope to the whole of human behaviour. But this broadening clearly implied that there was a new conception of the brain, one in which functional anatomical localizations were those of populations, and not individuals, and in which the relationship between behaviour (a task) and an anatomical structure were measured in a probabilistic manner, and not viewed by an observer. To sum up, in order to establish a bridge between brain (anatomy) and mind (functional), cognitive neuroscience developed a strategy to associate the two adjectives, *anatomical* and *functional*. The idea was to circumvent the individual level by both the infra-individual (brain circuitry) and the populational (their normal statistical distribution).

The Neuroanatomical "Where,"
but What of the Neurophysiological "How"?

Does neuroimaging, as a technical support for anatomical and functional cartography, allow, neurophysiologically, for a better understanding of a subject's intentionality? Most theorists think so. For example, in 1997 Jeannerod's team published a study showing that when a subject is asked to memorize an action in order to reproduce it, and then is asked to recognize it among other actions, the same regions of the brain are not activated. "In this experiment, it was the subject's intentionality to carry out one task or another that became 'visible,' which no other technique could have shown us."[99] The traditional neuropsychologist would have mentioned two anatomical correlates.

To answer the question, "What are the basic functions of the cerebral cortex?" Vernon Mountcastle responded in the introduction of *Dædalus*, "No one knows." What he meant was that the large amount of knowledge, despite its impressive character, "is phenomenological, with few explanations at the level of mechanism. What exists in profundity is knowledge of the geography of the brain and the connectivity within it – answers of twentieth-century neuroscience to *where* questions."[100] Enumerating the main results of cognitive neuroscience, he maintained that "the functions of the cortex of the frontal lobe in working memory, in planning, and in willing action have been confirmed, and some defects in frontal-lobe activation observed in some psychotic states. Taken together, these results sustain the related concepts of functional segregation of certain processes in local cortical regions and their functional integration into distributed system action of the several, sometimes many, local regions active during the execution of perceptual or cognitive tasks."[101] In other words, imaging confirms the hypothesis of distributed knowledge – there is no hierarchy in the human brain. Nevertheless, he issued a warning: the results obtained are "geographic in nature ... They do not yet reveal the dynamic neuronal operations that generate the recorded changes in local blood flow."[102] *Geographic* means "neuroanatomical," and only physiology considers mechanisms, and only it can show the "how" of biological processes. Blood flows are secondary signs of neuronal activity; they are not the activity itself. How are they linked to neuronal activity? Gerald Edelman, in the same issue of *Dædalus*, observes, "The distributed property of different, segregated functions raises extraordinary difficulties for attempts to understand how brain anatomy relates to brain physiology,"[103] whereas Mountcastle goes one further by asking, "What are the neuronal operations within the distributed systems of the cortex?"[104] Anatomy, even functional anatomy, is ... anatomy.[105] What remains is the mystery of "how," which is to say the pathophysiological mechanisms by which a pathology is triggered. The next step will be to describe the *how*, or the *real* causal relationship between brain activity and "behaviour," in other words, to use the widely known metaphor, how the brain "decides" one way or another. Even though multiple correlations have been discovered, correlation is not causality, and the discovery of mechanisms implies finding biomarkers. So, do we need to approach the "how" differently?

Breaking Down the Individual Brain in Big Data: Towards a Pathology of Brain Circuits?

Today, we have entered a new stage brought about by concern for going beyond the geographic character of functional cartography: realizing the program for a biology of the mind necessitates that we leave behind pathologies themselves, and syndromes (depression, schizophrenia), such as they were defined by classical psychiatry or, starting in the 1980s, with the publishing of the third edition of the *Diagnostic and Statistical Manual* (the DSM-III) in the United States, by stats and epidemiology. It should be specified straightaway that leaving the idea of pathological entities is not done in order to use any particular treatment concerning the patient. It is more a question of envisioning multiple and heterogeneous direct actions on the brain. One neurologist, a staunch proponent of fusing neurology and psychiatry, underscores the point that "this emerging knowledge offers possibilities that should eventually give us the unprecedented ability to engineer changes in the brain by means of psychosocial intervention, environmental manipulation, psychopharmacology, molecular biology, cell transportation, or neurosurgical procedures."[106] Therapy gains no advantage from the new knowledge, only the cerebral goal is of import. But how do we intervene in the brain?

Syndromes, like depression or schizophrenia, unlike cancer or cardiovascular disease, are not natural entities and make it difficult to advance matters of pathophysiology, which is a key to progress in most medical specializations. Over the last twenty years, all biomedical research has been digitized. It was done translationally, from bench to bedside. The psychiatric exception is, in the end, an insult to science and the well-being of the patient.

In October 2003, directors from five of America's main health agencies (the National Institutes of Health), including the National Institute of Mental Health (the NIMH), published an article online in PLOS *Biology* entitled "Neuroscience Networks: Data-sharing in an Information Age," in which they write, "As we emerge from the 'decade of the brain,' we are entering a decade from which data-sharing will be the currency for progress in neuroscience." Studies from the decade of the brain also brought about research in human genome sequencing, which had largely contributed to digitizing biology. In this context, the authors of the article write, "Here we describe some of the recent progress in efforts to map the brain as an example of the potential and the challenge of sharing data in an era when neurobiology, like genomics, is becoming an information science." What is the issue? Always the same: "to integrate this information into a coherent, accessible form that permits hierarchical analysis from RNA to protein to morphology to connectivity to function in a universal language while preserving fidelity." The idea of integration that was proposed accelerates the dynamic initiated by recommending a "*collaboration* of scientists who add value to the enterprise by working in multidisciplinary teams; *coordination* of efforts to attain a goal; and *computation* through the use of informatics, models, and simulations."[107] Translational research, this is what the NIMH would now fund.

Biomedical research in psychiatry worked by referring to the American classification of mental disorders, the *DSM-III* (and its successors, the *DSM-III-R* in 1987, *DSM-IV* in 1994, and *DSM 5* in 2013), which was elaborated in order to end actual diagnostic chaos.[108] Its advocates had established "research diagnostic criteria" (RDC) on a statistical and epidemiological basis. The goal was to avoid having to resort to the clinician's subjectivity by finding a way to objectify mental disorders by a standardized interview built from the classification. This objectifying research was also based on the idea, or the hope rather, that the symptoms described by the statistical tool corresponded to natural species, which would one day discover pathophysiological mechanisms. The *DSM* model resolved the issue of reliability, which is to say that two or more clinicians would independently make the same diagnosis, given the reality of the pathology, the absence of the constant physiological corollary representing a continuous limit. Syndromes remained syndromes, or systematic associations of symptoms (clusters, to use the lexicon of a statistician), no underlying organic basis having been discovered since 1980. However, comorbidity between different syndromes (like having both anxiety and depression at the same time) appeared as an absolutely general phenomenon. Consequently, instead of allowing for a descent toward a biological foundation, classification multiplied, between the third in 1980 and the fifth in 2013, not only comorbidities between syndromes, but also the syndromes themselves.

The underlying problem was cruelly clear: the system for classifying pathologies made it possible to establish reliable diagnoses, but not to exploit the results of the research on the brain, whereas, in all medical disciplines, progress on the biological basis of illnesses was translated using clinical results. The issue with "data" was to break the impasse by getting rid of the DSM, at least as far as research was concerned, and going for a new system of classification, a new diagnostics directed entirely by neuroscientists. The solution was presented as follows.

The NIMH, after much preparation and having mobilized several work groups, came out in 2010 with a strategic research plan centred on what the DSM was missing: validity.[109] "Our expectation," wrote NIMH director Thomas Insel a few years later, "based on experience in cancer, heart disease, and infectious diseases, is that identifying syndromes based on pathophysiology will eventually be able to improve outcomes."[110] Devised as a program for a pathophysiology of mental illness, he proposed a paradigm shift in research, which was based not on *diagnosed* syndromes, but on *observable* dimensions of behaviour, like fear or attention, as they correspond to natural entities and would facilitate the research of causality. These dimensions were called "transnosographic" because they can be found in several syndromes. They are units that are finer than a syndrome, in the sense that they are directly observable, and they have specific functions. Fear or attention is the object of analysis, not schizophrenia or bipolar disorder. Dimensions have a location, and they are grouped into "constructs" that can be described by the fact that they correspond to known perturbations in neuronal circuits, which are themselves located in one of five "domains" of selected function. The choice of domain is a reflection of the contemporary thinking on aspects of motivation, cognition, and social behaviour,[111] – the "social," it has been noted, is always a principle domain of neuroscience. For example, in the domain of cognitive systems, the construct of "perception" is broken down into dimensions of "visual perception," "auditory perception," etc.

Research on domain criteria starts with neural systems responsible for important behavioural functions, which have a robustness steeped in evolution, whereas research on diagnostic criteria started from syndromes.

The integration of these data takes the form of a matrix in which the rows denote dimension, construct, and domain, and the columns represent the levels of analysis, making it possible to work on the constructs. There are seven: genes, molecules, cells, neuronal circuits, physiology, behaviour, and self-reports (questionnaires, interview scales, etc.). They go from the most fundamental, the gene, to behaviour – we are in the brain-mind matrix. Circuitry possesses the highest value, because it allows for the linking of "different levels of biological and behavioural analysis." Moreover, dimensions are understood in a longitudinal perspective as common risk factors that trigger many pathologies. Therefore, they open possibilities for early intervention to reduce the risks of triggering pathologies and modify the relationship between prevention and treatment.

Today, there is a research program worthy of its name, which integrates biological and psychological levels by including molecular genetics, neuroanatomy, and neurophysiology. It also gets its support from disciplines as varied as epidemiology and experimental psychology. This matrix program produced a new understanding of psychopathology, the aims of which are domains, laying the foundation for a future classification, which, as its advocates would tell you, would be "agnostic" in terms of syndromes. The new acronym RDOC (research domain criteria) replaced the insufficient RDC (research diagnostic criteria). Academic research the world over was mobilized around this new model.

The general hypothesis of the RDOC matrix was that dysfunction in the neuronal circuits, the basis of these dimensions, would be identified using neuroimaging tools and molecular biology, thanks in particular to new methods that allow the quantification of connections in vivo. It had another hypothesis that was even more general: mental disorders are brain disorders. Are they like neurological disorders, even though no lesion for whatever mental illness has been found? The response from the NIMH was, "In contrast to neuro-logical disorders with identifiable lesions, mental disorders can be addressed as disorders of brain circuits"[112] – circuits being the most important domain level. There is no pretention to discovering brain lesions in psychopathology. The cleverness of the argument stems from the fact that it invents (discovers?) a concept (brain circuit disorder) that makes it possible to distinguish everything between neuropathology and psychopathology all while keeping it within the brain. Mental disorders are the result of affected brain circuits rela-tive to specific domains of cognition, emotion, and behaviour.

The Obama administration's initiative on the brain was launched in April 2013 (BRAIN, Brain Research through Advancing Innovative Neurotechnologies) on the model of unlocking the human genome, and the goal was to build a detailed map of brain activity (Brain Activity Map Project). It brought together teams from neuroscience and nanotechnology. The Human Connectome Project, supported by the NIHs, consisted of two consortiums under the leadership of psychologist Deanna Barch, one dedicated to the amelioration of MRIs, and the other to establishing a database (from genetics to personality traits to cognitive abilities, on 1,200 volunteers) and an interactive map of a healthy three-dimensional brain showing its structure and functions. It was part of a growing number of collabo-rative projects. The key question that the map and the database must answer, according to Deanna Barch, is, "How do the differences between you and me, and how our brains are wired up, relate to dif-ferences in our behaviors, our thoughts, our emotions, our feelings, our experiences?"[113] These are projects in functional anatomy. They hold a conception of mental pathologies in terms of disconnection syndromes. The "connectome" is central to all of these projects.

How should the contribution of this new classification be pre-sented to the patient? Steven Hyman, director of the NIMH from 1996 to 2001, characterizes it by referring to a review article on genetics applied to psychiatry: "Underlying common genetic and environmental factors appear to explain the overlap between mem-bers of major groups of illnesses. Individual differences, not shared in the family upbringing, reflect differences in circumstance that may change over time and are responsible for the expression of ill-ness at any particular stage of life. Thus, as an individual matures and experiences life for himself, or herself, the manifestation of any behavioral trait, including mental illness, reflects the unfolding of

that person's individuality and unique life story."[114] Here we have
a matrix description of the causes of illness. If the diagnosis of the
neurological patient is marked by the existence of a lesion, the illness
by which the psychiatric patient is affected is diagnosed by entering
the heterogeneous domain data (from genes to questionnaires) that
characterize it into the matrix.

Neuronal groups and re-entrant loops, these concepts devised
thirty years ago have their corresponding pathology in the new
pathophysiological concept of brain circuit disorders of the RDOC.
By undertaking the establishment of direct connections between
behavioural dimensions and brain circuits, this new approach closes
the gap between the biological, the psychological, and the social.
"Clearly," Insel wrote in 2010, "this is a vision for the future, given
the rudimentary nature of data relating measures of brain function
to clinically relevant individual differences in genomics, pathophysiology, and behavior. In the near-term, RDOC may be most useful for
researchers mapping brain–behavior relationships."[115] The decisive
test for diagnostic validity of domain criteria will be to establish to
what extent they will allow for prognostics or revisions in response
to treatment. We will then know if they are authentic biomarkers
for more personalized treatments: there are many "ifs," and "we are
still a long way from knowing if this approach will succeed," states
Insel.[116] Diagnostic and prognostic, dimensions/risk factors common
to syndromes, personalizing care thanks to treatments from heterogeneous data (from DNA to psychosociological questionnaires)
coming from very large samples – these elements are interdependent.
Empirically testing its validity, as Insel recalls, lies in an indetermin-
able future.

The Brain Becomes an Individual

The model of a causal relationship between brain and behaviour,
represented by our exemplary brains, has been extended to psychopathological patients, without reducing them to neurological
patients, but by considerably enriching the approach to the brain.
Let us sum up the dynamic.

We have read how this perspective was displayed in the two-fold
movement of individualization and de-individualization of the brain.
The line from neuropsychology to synaptic plasticity individualized the brain on the basis of a model of every human's uniqueness

and, by doing so, modified its epistemological status, raising it to a personal quasi-entity. The brain is, as has been noted, personified, but more specifically it is personified according to the most valued social models in society: the scientist or researcher (who verify their results), or of the entrepreneur or people of action (who must continuously make decisions). Each individual is "wired" differently, has a different brain, because each possesses a combination of different life experiences: the human brain is truly ... human.

The line of the brain–mind matrix has, on the contrary, de-individualized it by devising a populational brain, probabilistic and digitized, and by positing the theory that there are more direct links between behaviour and brain circuits than can exist in a syndrome, thanks to substituting domain criteria with diagnostic criteria. The model is agnostic in both treatment and syndromes. It can thus aggregate and catch the interest of all professions involved in the care of psychopathologies.

This is how the brain was credited in two ways with having the highest value. First, by elevating it from a sub-personal status to a personal one. It is the modifiable material basis on which everything else is elaborated: it is the entity that counts the most. Second, by taking the form of a matrix in which the whole of human reality can be held in a factorial perspective that aggregates all domains. Consequently, it allows us to explain everything.

By positing the general hypothesis of a necessary relationship between brain and behaviour, cognitive neuroscience raised the question for the many that phrenology could put only to scholars: the truth of individuals cannot be discovered by analyzing their behaviour, but by a new semiology, sub-personal and populational in which the brain now occupies the former place of the individual – the personal level. Yet no determinism can be drawn from this necessary relationship between brain and behaviour. So what lesson can be taken from it?

Using the words of the great storyteller of the heroism of hidden potential, Oliver Sacks, "This sense of the brain's remarkable plasticity ... has come to dominate my own perception ... So much so, indeed, that I am sometimes moved to wonder whether it may not be necessary to redefine the very concepts of 'health' and 'disease,' to see these in terms of the ability of the organism to create a new organization and order, one that fits its special, altered disposition and needs, rather than in the terms of a rigidly defined 'norm.'"[117] The lesson given to us by biological research is that individuals can find a solution – creative – to their problems and that we must not despair nature, which we can always truly count on to rebound. Nature shows that the human brain possesses such a level of functional versatility (distributed knowledge, re-entrant loops, synaptic plasticity) that the individual should be capable of overcoming whatever normative assumptions caused by illness, thanks to a creativity that corresponds to the individual's needs. It is a call for tolerance of diversity in the polar narrowness of normal/pathological – it is the brain of a new individualism illustrated through autism. The biological concept of cerebral plasticity is based in the collective representation of autonomy; it transfigures the capacity of the individual to change, thus activating one of the most ordinary and valued ideals, affirming that somewhere deep within the self there still are resources for coping.[118] The brain has become an individual.

Metaphors personifying the brain, founded on models of the autonomous individual and on biological mechanisms as a foundation for behaviour, occur within empirical experimental research. More specifically, the moral authority of neuroscience is built on the combination of collective representations and scientific concepts. This is how the scientific idea of "cerebral plasticity" was transformed into a social value, as we will see in chapter 5. However, neuroscience will first have had to take on the "social."

4

Social Neuroscience, or
How the Individual Acts with Others

Quite often we lose the fact that the developmental trend in the clearly more complex ... societies of our day demands a higher degree of differentiated self-restraint from individuals.

Norbert Elias, "The Civilizing of Parents"

Character capabilities are crucial ingredients in enabling people to pursue and achieve their own individual wellbeing.

Building Character, DEMOS

The agent brain took shape. With the ever-growing power of cerebral imaging tools, the capacity to process massive datasets with bioinformatics, and the development of a matrix-based approach to the brain–mind relationship, the use of new concepts, like the endogenous activation system, allowed for a prodigious expansion of research. In experimental settings, this research closely correlated diverse mental functions and localized neuronal circuits in a specific cerebral area, as well as other areas of interconnectivity. Therefore, it is not surprising to hear neuroscientists affirm that understanding cerebral machinery could contribute to a better functioning society by facilitating both cooperative relationships and well-being among individuals. Relevantly, scientific psychology, under which brain science falls, has, since its outset in the early 1900s, piloted engineering or social reform projects, and has done so through useful practices that have become commonplace (selection tests, etc.). From environmental advocacy by behaviourists to the mentalism of the cognitive school (chapter 2), there are old underlying interests and stakes, the changes to which we have attempted to pinpoint. Starting in the

1980s, these changes, along with the broadening research of higher brain functions (chapter 3), garnered increased interest for cooperation among individuals that persists in society today.

This new area of investigation has developed into a variety of designations: social neuroscience, cognitive social neuroscience, neurobiology of social cognition, cognitive neuroscience of social behaviour, etc. Studies have since multiplied and now constitute their own domain. They are divided into many topics, with at least two specialized reviews in English, and include manuals, special issues, and journals of psychiatry, psychology, and neuroscience.[1]

THE NECESSITY OF SOCIAL

What are the "social" stakes for these disciplines? To what extent is it necessary for them to make such an emphatic reference to it? What does it indicate?

"As social neuroscience develops, it will certainly challenge our ways of thinking about responsibility and blame, and have an impact on social policies,"[2] the editorial of the new 2006 journal *Social Neuroscience* boldly stated. Do new neuroscientific concepts push us to change our notions of responsibility and blame? This question is phrased in a very allusive way. Does neuroscience provide new possibilities to influence behaviours to make them more regular and reliable? The answer was given by one of the main proponents of behavioural economics, a new branch of scientific psychology that links cognitive psychology with social behaviour through human passions. It expanded into neuroscience under the name of neuroeconomy,[3] with an array of subcategories (like neuromarketing). Economist Richard Thaler, a leading figure of social neuroscience who was awarded the Nobel Prize in Economics in 2017, wrote in 2013 in the *New York Times*, "It makes sense for *social scientists* to become more involved in policy, because many of society's most challenging problems are, in essence, behavioral."[4] The scientific idea is to extend the power of cognitive neuroscience beyond perception (of colours, for example) to behaviour (choice and decision-making), which ipso facto includes motivation and intentionality. The social and political position is to extend possible applications into practical domains. However, their nature is not different from that of scientific psychology since 1900, which relied on a scale of our understanding of the brain that is entirely different from today's.

The challenge touches less upon renewing the categories of responsibility or blame than it does upon the credibility of the scientific
method to deal with moral and social questions. The complexity of
this challenge is maximal by nature, with methods centred on practical control of individual behaviour.

This chapter, first and foremost, establishes how social neuroscience is the expression of a change in our ways of acting, in a society
preoccupied with individuals and their relationships. It reveals new
contingencies marked by the question of trust in others and, at the
same time, an increased worry about self-regulation of behaviour
– a worry upon which neuroscience has seized. It also attempts to
specify all that neuroscientists attribute to the term *social* and the
issues faced by their disciplines concerning social behaviour. Next,
we will return to our exemplary brains, those of Gage and Elliot, as
well as the high-functioning autistic. The focus on these brains will
be to show two complementary ways of elaborating social relations,
in addition to serving as a backdrop to research demonstrating how
the cognitive (or psychological) mechanism and the neurobiological
mechanism are combined. On a cognitive level, each of these brains
offers the paradigmatic illustration of two major concepts that make
it possible to consider relationships starting with the individual:
empathy and theory of mind. This chapter will also examine the
proposed biological basis for these mechanisms, the essential virtue
of which is to connect cerebral functioning and the outside world in
the form of an "internal model" or "shared representations." We will
thus have three principle categories on the subject of neuroscience:
emotional, cognitive, and biological, which form as many compart-
ments. In short, we will have at our disposal the tools and theory
allowing neuroscience to connect nature and culture.

For which applications is this useful? What are its uses in social
life? What practices are entailed?

The sciences observed here are part of a rich tradition that essentially views action according to two major modalities. One is to
mechanically obtain cooperative behaviours, using the watch spring
model from Adam Smith (see chapter 2), and the other is to acquire
habits through exercises. The first is at the centre of behavioural
economics, the specificity of which focuses on "changing behaviour
without changing [the] minds"[5] of individuals. This will close out
the chapter. The second, which is the topic of the following chapter,
will be dedicated to neurocognitive versions of autonomy exercises

that were developed in the mental health field starting in the 1980s, under the name of rehabilitation and recovery. Unlike the former, it is organized around practices that change the mind in order to change behaviour.

Reconfiguring Character within the Concept of "Social Competence"

The shift in collective representations from the visible hand of organizations and experts toward autonomous ideals of new individualism is manifest through broadening the value of creation geared toward lifestyles. Through this shift, the inventory of possible choices for everyone was enriched considerably. As a result, diversity and creativity or innovation was encouraged; it then moved our societies increasingly toward ways of behaving in work (or as a couple) that valued individual initiative, competition, and cooperation. Thus, we are witnessing a shift from vertical relationships toward horizontal ones and the ascension of trust at the expense of obedience. Increasing one's value is no longer a solitary adventure analogous to a rat in a maze using its intelligence to find the cheese. Value is about establishing cooperative relationships and "prosocial" behaviour, in a context where each person is to create a unique lifestyle.

Relationships. This theme began its ascension when consumer society was at its peak. In the United States in 1967, futurists Herman Kahn and Anthony Weiner considered that one "of the characteristics of many of these new movements, among the most interesting, is a worry regarding personality and connections with others ... that is relatively new in American intellectual life of the last hundred years."[6] A few years later in France, sociologist Michel Crozier noticed that "all human phenomena that we record in all domains have something in common: the multiplication of partners and the increased complexity of the game." But the question regarding relationships, he specifies, is not quantitative: "Each of us interacts with a larger number of people and does so more freely in choosing a partner and in the interaction's quality than was done in the past."[7] With the reference to individuals and relationships comes the idea of complexity.

The issue of relationships points to a more profound change in collective representations that would conjure up an apparent paradox of our modernity.

The increase in moral liberties, especially sexually, under the banner of valuing choice and emancipation, softening the codes of conduct between parent and child, man and woman, and the social acceptance of a sexual life outside marriage eases these traditional controls. However, this enhanced freedom in conduct requires at the same time an increase in emotional and motivational self-control. Norbert Elias lucidly formulated the reason for this: "The increased equality between man and woman as well as a more equitable distribution of access to power made the two groups exercise more restraint toward one another."[8] Because they are more free and egalitarian, these social relationships are therefore more demanding as well; they come in two interdependent forms of a loosening *and* a strengthening in social controls. This two-pronged movement (more freedom and more self-control) raises new questions and new contingencies.

At the same time, in the workplace, going from divided to flexible work led to a change in how discipline is defined: discipline is subordinated to the obtention of individual autonomy and therefore the capacity to *self*-motivate, be it working or finding work. It tends toward *self*-discipline. This change brings to the fore agents' responsibility for their actions: dependency between agent and action is more essential than during the disciplinary moment of Taylorism or Fordism. This global change came into our societies with the spread of behavioural regulation models, which was to autonomy what mechanical obedience was to discipline: at that time, it was about making individuals useful because they were docile. Today, it is about developing the capacities for individuals to self-activate and self-control, capacities for which our contemporary vocabulary has been enriched by a new concept: being "proactive." If there must be discipline, it is not primarily for obedience, but for developing empathy and self-reliance. Discipline under the idea of mechanical obedience (other-directed) slackens, and self-discipline (inner-directed), which is the discipline of autonomy, increases.

Generally, the connection of our societies to time is radically geared toward the future. Again, Norbert Elias foresaw the link between time and the question of self-control nearly forty years ago: "In order to claim to be an adult in societies with such a structure ... it is necessary to have a very high degree of foresight, restraint of momentary impulses, for the sake of long-term goals and gratifications. It requires, in other words, a high degree of self-regulating restraint of drives and affects"[9] The more social complexity increases, especially with the incertitude of the future and the length of interdependent bonds that the globalization of society represents, which implies an increased inter-affectation of actions from each other, the more we feel concern for the capacity to self-activate and self-control. In this context, the intelligence on human relationships acquired a new practical value, a necessary quality of populations recently entered in the game of choice and self-propriety, who are faced with new ways of working or living as couples.

The theme of trust that was sought in this way brings to the fore a category at the crossroads of lifestyle: emotion. It is not that emotion was not taken into account in moral reflections, nor was it left out of psychological writings, but "emotion" as a unifying category started its quick ascent in the 1970s and went to the heart of the social and scientific psyche in the 1980s. And there it would remain. Neuroscience is credited with having rescued emotion from obscurity. Emotion's place in cognitive neuroscience, as we saw with the brains of Gage and Elliot, unites cognition and behaviour.

This subject has exploded since the 1970s in the social sciences, philosophy, and, of course, psychology. For example, a review article on the anthropology of emotions published in 1986 highlights this in the opening sentence: "Interest in 'the emotional' has burgeoned in the last decade ... A concern to understand the role of the emotional in personal and social life has developed in response to a number of factors, including dissatisfaction with the dominant cognitive view of humans as mechanical 'information processors.'" It was a recurring theme throughout the article containing over two hundred references, some of which would become emblematic of the "emotional turn." Emotions are not simply opposed to reason, they are essential to its functioning: "Emotions are treated as evaluative 'judgments,' and more emphasis is placed on their voluntary and cognitive aspects."[10] In the workplace as well, work started changing with the ascension of client pressure. Sociologist Arlie Russell Hochschild[11] published *Managed Heart* in 1983. It was a resounding success and put forward the idea of *emotional labour*, essential to organizing a space in which workers had to cooperate, take initiative, and therefore decide and choose. In short, they had to adopt a personal line of conduct.

As a result, a new description of character emerged, which is everywhere today and incorporates these complexities by making emotions of decisive importance: namely, social competence.

Behaviourism probed how the world acted on the individual, cognitive psychology how the individual acted on the world, and social neuroscience how individuals interact with each other. Relationships were at the centre of these disciplines, so formulating an improved neurobiology of relationships that allows us to understand the mechanisms making humans reliable represents a major stake. These social neurosciences complexify the motives for action by broadening the idea of personal interest beyond just egoism, which is a notion that it too simplistic to account totally for individual behaviour being that the individual has become so relational.

In this trend, the concept of character was reconfigured by the ideals of self-actualization and cooperation with others, the intricacy of which has been manifest for a half century. Let us sum up the dynamics examined in chapter 2. In the eighteenth century, human nature emerged from the transformation of passions pushing individuals to be concerned with their own character. It was a *moral* concept during the second half of the nineteenth century with the rise of the altruism/egoism polarity, which placed emphasis entirely on the will and the capacity to act according to good or bad criteria. At the beginning of the twentieth century, it became a *psychological* concept, progressively considered in terms of personality and determined by unconscious conflicts or guided externally by the environment (behaviourism, but also Leninism and Taylorism). The good/bad moral criteria were reconfigured into normal/pathological criteria around health. From character, which is supposedly self-sustained morally through education, to personality, which needs to be guided by conscience, conditions in society represented new complexities, which made the visible hand of the expert necessary. One such expert was the psychotherapist. In the last quarter of the twentieth century, character became a social concept, a life skill referring to the idea that, if people want to succeed in life and feel good about themselves, it is better to be open to others than egoistical. However, the openness in question is less an abnegation of altruism, which has an element of self-sacrifice, than it is of having the *skill to be empathetic*, the ability to take into account the perspective of others.

The new character is presented using multiple and novel expressions found everywhere: "emotional" competence, "interpersonal skills," "relational," "non-cognitive," "social," etc. Inserted in our ordinary uses, social competence can be thought of as a largely accepted moral code, a societal institution of which the cardinal value is autonomy. Social neuroscience is perfectly situated in the Scottish moral tradition of the sociable individual as it inseparably links biological human nature, the idea of self-actualization and cooperation, and individual and societal well-being. The equalization of cooperation and well-being is accomplished through self-regulation, which is emotional control. To be able to cooperate is to be well socialized, and to be well socialized is a sign of well-being. Starting at the end of the twentieth century, empathy, which is *the* social skill, was to the motive for action what altruism had been at the end of the nineteenth century in Great Britain. But the morals of duty and the "implicit Kantism" of the former was substituted by the morals of purpose of the latter, which is why it is thought of as a social competence.

The Three Meanings of Social in Neuroscience

In a world guided by the values of autonomy, characterized by permanent change and profound transformation in the workplace, the family, and religion, with opportunities and contingencies on every level, the possibility of discovering the psychological foundations or correlates in cerebral structures and being able to act on them, from a perspective of behavioural regulation, in no way lacks appeal.

These disciplines are often suspected of being "neuro-essentialist" because by establishing the existence of a social brain, they replace the "social" with the "brain," and they naturalize the first with the second. There is, however, some insight to be taken from the idea of a "social brain." They have every reason to attribute the term *social* to individuals, so why not to their brain? We could not see how "society" forms a system of forces acting on the individual, as is asserted in sociology, if society were not so deeply embedded in the individual one way or another, if society did not permeate it down to the nucleus of each cell. Society's action cannot be only outside the individual, like a physical constraint, since that would imply there is the individual on one hand, and society on the other, even though the individual is plunged, before birth, into a world of social expectations. If social obligation, as Marcel Mauss wrote in 1924, were truly an obligation, it must govern even our "physiological reactions."[12] We now know, to restate what was recently published in *Nature Neuroscience*, "The social and emotional circuitry of the brain is continuously being shaped by forces that impinge on the nervous system during prenatal development and throughout life."[13] It should therefore be possible to understand scientifically the mechanisms by which the brain "imprints" the "social" and, maybe one day, to act directly on certain neuronal mechanisms. The big question is, How does the brain imprint these behaviours?

Cognitive neuroscience starts with the brain, and therefore from the infra-individual, and not from the actual relationships in which individuals are immersed. This is less a question of oversight or denial than it is an essential point of method: it would be difficult to achieve an understanding of the cerebral mechanisms that make individuals cooperate (or not) unless they are stripped of their real relationships, isolated from their own context and therefore any concrete connections, putting their social life between parentheses, in order to create an experimental device in which relationships can be simulated. The "social" is thus found in an apparently paradoxical fix: it is on the most superficial level from an explanans standpoint, but on the most fundamental from the explanandum standpoint; it counts secondarily as a basis for behaviour, but it is of the utmost importance to explain it through cerebral mechanisms. It represents the final piece of the connection between brain and behaviour because social behaviours are the most complex: they bring the highest level of cognitive processes into play, and so they are difficult to study in animals and require sophisticated analyses. That these behaviours are "the most complex" means also that they are of the highest value.

Needless to say, numerous scientists think that possessing such knowledge would ameliorate both prosocial behaviour and individual well-being. For Antonio Damasio, "neurobiology not only can assist us with the comprehension and compassion of the human condition, but ... it can help us understand social conflict and contribute to its alleviation." This discipline would allow us precisely to "protect reason from the weakness that abnormal feelings or the manipulation of normal feelings can introduce in the process of planning and deciding."[14] An appraisal published in 2007 by a team of established psychologists and neuroscientists recalled, "The ability to understand, interact, and connect with others is essential for mental and physical well-being. So essential is this ability that social impairments have serious consequences both for individuals and for society. Given the critical importance of adaptive social functioning, it is essential that social neuroscience research address relevant psychological and neural mechanisms."[15] Another appraisal was published in the same year: "Several exciting lines of social cognitive neuroscience research are providing new discoveries, generating original ideas, and challenging longstanding conceptions of existing social science perspectives."[16] What discoveries? What original ideas? Before answering these questions, we must specify the way in which neuroscientists use the word *social*.

The term is used mainly to designate behaviour *between congeners*, human or non-human primates. "Social cognition refers to the processes that subserve behavior in response to conspecifics."[17] These responses are social behaviours. There is no complete approach to psychopathologies that can set aside social behaviours because with them, meaning without the others, we cannot understand that "diagnostically, social dysfunction is either a core feature of a disorder (e.g., autism, social phobia, schizophrenia, any of the personality disorders) or serves as a marker of the functional impairment required to meet diagnostic threshold."[18]

The theoretical foundation is taken from evolutionary biology, for which humans are the most social of all the primates. From this viewpoint, the social very clearly deals with the *human species* in general and not any particular society or civilization. That humans are the most social of the primates[19] is the leitmotif of social neuroscience and the primary reason put forward by social neuroscientists to justify their research programs. No other species besides ours possesses such a "high level of social organization, none share our capacity for stable large-scale cooperation between genetically unrelated individuals."[20] This biological capacity to cooperate allowed humans to dominate the planet. "We have unequivocally won the cross-species competition for global domination. What allowed us, as physical underdogs, to claim this unlikely victory?... [I]t is our interpersonal faculties, especially our ability to cooperate with and understand others."[21] Ontologically, we are a social species. Our superiority lies in our relational capacities, which themselves result from the fact that our brain, via its architecture, morphology, and size, has produced a unique mind among the primates, a mind of the *self*.

We are the most social species, since it is with others that our individual experience is moulded and imprinted on the brain. "The brain is constantly being shaped, wittingly and unwittingly, by environmental forces that impinge on organisms. The circuitry that has been implicated in social and emotional behavior appears to be importantly shaped by experience, and early experience in these domains is likely involved in governing differences among individuals in their vulnerability or resilience to future adversity."[22] They condition normal as much as pathological behaviour.

Yet the adjective *social* has another use that complements the biological criteria of the species. It is psychological, or, more precisely, it is a product of social psychology.

The neurobiology of social cognition has to do with knowing the neuronal systems that favour responses addressed to conspecifics. The research focuses on "the specific mechanisms through which social norms act to induce prosociality."[23] It can be broken down into three levels, as specified by the editors of a work on the neuroscience of social interaction, the subhead of which sums the mind up neatly: "Decoding, imitating, and influencing the actions of others": "the social level, which is concerned with the motivational and social factors that influence behaviour and experience; the cognitive level, which is concerned with the information-processing mechanisms that give rise to social-level phenomena; and the neural level, which is concerned with the brain mechanisms that instantiate cognitive-level processes."[24] The three levels fit together in layers, the most fundamental of which, in the sense that it serves as the basis for the two others, is the neural. The part of the sentence that defines the social level, it should be noted, is vague and obscure: the social is made up of social and motivational factors. Here we find ourselves deep in tautology. But is there a way out of it?

The aforementioned editorial from *Social Neuroscience* defines the discipline as "the exploration of the neurological underpinnings of the processes traditionally examined by, but not limited to, social psychology,"[25] such as moral dilemmas, empathy, or self-regulation. This second use of the adjective *social* is found in behavioural social science. Biological and psychological concepts do not match up because they are complex constructions that are "difficult to map directly onto neural processes," and therefore must be broken down into simple elements. One of the major issues facing this new discipline that uses a "systemic approach" is the development of multilevel analyses with retroactive loops linking these levels together. "We strongly believe," the editorial continues, "that the social and biological approaches when they are bridged can achieve a more accurate understanding of human behavior."[26]

Ralph Adolphs, an American neurologist who was part of Damasio's team, considers that social neuroscience "might offer a reconciliation between biological and psychological approaches to social behaviour." This reconciliation would occur "in the realization that its neural regulation reflects both innate, automatic and cognitively impenetrable mechanisms, as well as acquired, contextual and volitional aspects that include self-regulation."[27] We share the first with other primates, whereas the second is specific to the human species. The adjective *social* is therefore defined on two levels, innate and unconscious, on the one hand, and acquired and conscious on the other, each referring to a distinct set of disciplines: the first is biology, and the second psychology. The role of neurobiology is to discover neuronal networks or neural structures that connect the inner-human to the outside world, thereby shedding light on cerebral mechanisms that trigger behaviour: the notion of decision is thus at the centre of all research. The capacity to understand others and to cooperate with them is the essential trait of the social human as a species.

On the third level, much less apparent but nonetheless decisive, the characterization of the social, throughout all this literature, is sociability – in other words, smoothing the edges with civility to make us *reliable*. Ontologically speaking, if the social is evolutionary it is a species-specific social. As we have just seen, on the sociological level, it continues to refer to the sociability of the individual of action as defined by Scottish philosophers. Neuroscience added the adjective *social* when it incorporated biological mechanisms into its research through which individuals establish trusting relationships with each other.

The few neuroscientific references on the social that were just mentioned leave the reader, at least the sociologist reader, with the strange impression that in these definitions vagueness reigns and as a consequence, everything is social. "The social is ubiquitous," writes Adolphs;[28] we can include anything that affects individuals in their decision-making. Nevertheless, there is an obvious weakness, a sign of simplism, at least if it remains unconnected to the tradition of Humean argumentation: morals are a matter of feelings and impressions. We must turn inward, to our own heart, thinks Hume, and "find a sentiment of disapprobation, which arises in you, towards this action. Here is a matter of fact; but 'tis the object of feeling, not of reason."[29] Humean (or Scottish) liberty does not refer to free will, nor does it refer to cultivating interior freedom in the solitary being (in German style), but to appetite, passion, sociability, and exchange. Individuals barely possess the self; they convert their passions by associating ideas according to observation and experience. In other words, by learning to fulfill their social role. Contrary to the elusive self, the role is itself very real. Converting passions into "opinion, experience, and interest"[30] (to use Pocock's terms) is the key element in moral discipline. A neuroscientist who reads that would be extremely surprised: it all seems to be objectively indisputable in the system of human action, generally speaking (of their species, and primates, particular as they are), and coincides step for step with the philosophical conception of humankind as formulated by the Scottish moralists in the eighteenth century. This is precisely what gives weight and authority to scientific research in social neuroscience and allows it to give an answer to the functional needs of our societies, yet does not explain the social individual.

In sum, the sociology of social neuroscience is centred on decision-making. Yet it is driven by passion because decisions depend mainly on what subjectively affects the individual, which is first and foremost perception. For this discipline, we must break things down: a human perceives, then evaluates, which involves feeling, and finally decides. Perceive, evaluate-feel, decide – this is how the neuroscientific subject is presented, as a person of action who adapts a means to an end in relation to time, centred on an uncertainty for the future and imbued with ideals of reliance.

Empathy: Emotional Compartment and Cognitive Compartment

It should be restated that the philosophy of cognitive science is situated, to again use the words of Daniel Andler, on an axis "seen as a relationship between independent reality and a subject in search of an accurate image of this reality" (see chapter 2). The main problem is therefore surmounting the solipsism of representation, or in other words, to establish how communication occurs between the subjective biological mechanisms within the individual and the external objective mechanisms from the world and other individuals. For the neuroscientific community, questions are raised concerning others, an issue first conveyed through problems of perception. There is the question of knowing what makes us capable of differentiating between our self and others (self-perception); then there is understanding the mental state of others, such as intentions, desires, and beliefs, a capacity based mainly on making inferences about the relationship between visible behaviour and underlying mental state; and lastly, the issues of self-regulation that necessarily bring emotions into the fold. Empathy, a rather broad concept present in collective representations and scientific concepts, provides a possible avenue to describe the mechanisms involved when one individual enters into a relationship with another.

To avoid getting into the nitty gritty details of debates among the neuroscientific and cognitive communities, it should simply be stated that there are three types, or modalities, of empathy. *Cognitive* empathy, also well known as the "theory of mind," is the capacity to attribute mental states to oneself and others (intentions, desires, and beliefs), and depending on the situation, be able to perceive or infer them. Experts distinguish between two approaches: the theory-theory, which asserts that in order to account for a belief, there must be a theory of beliefs; and simulation theory, in which the capacity to perceive the relationship between visible behaviour and the underlying mental states of others implies a simulation mechanism for those states. *Emotional* empathy is the capacity to put oneself in someone else's shoes; this is the most widespread use of the term. This type of empathy gives rise to the question of self-control. These two uses of *empathy* allow us to imagine an emotional and cognitive compartment where relationships are susceptible to being the subject of experimental observation. However, with it, we remain in the realm of psychology: there is no biological basis. Emotional empathy implies a motor basis, in other words, an idea of the affective-motor connected to emotional expression. They are supplied by the third type, *motor* empathy: it is a "neural resonance" that automatically and unconsciously activates neuronal networks and conditions certain aspects of cognitive and emotional functioning – we will return to this later with the neurobiology of relationships.

Through role play exercises, empathy is the simulation of one's own mental state, in order to envisage what one would do in varying circumstances in which others find themselves, as well as understanding the mental state of others by putting oneself in their place (desires, interests, etc.). Empathy implies both the self and the other; it comprises the relationship. Perceiving and understanding what others are thinking through inference or simulation is like being an onlooker viewing the self and others from the outside. In neuroscience, social individuals are presented in the form of a causal sequence: they are first spectators, then actors. Humans are excellent at mirroring one another.

Our two exemplary brains each shed light on obstacles that social cooperation may encounter: disorders of the frontal lobe, a part of the brain responsible for executive functions, like planning an action or controlling behaviour,[31] diminishes the capacity to cooperate, for want of *emotional* empathy; and disorders linked to the autism spectrum reach the same impasse, but due to a lack of theory of mind, or *cognitive* empathy. The autism model was broadened to schizophrenia in order to account for relational difficulties that are typical of the illness. People suffering from lesions in the prefrontal cortex and high-functioning autistics represent two ways of foundering in social roles. The first is negatively, by embodying irregular, inconsistent behaviour, denying others because of the lesion, and by extension, because of the egoistic, narcissistic self or the insensitive psychopath. Those affected lack the qualities that would allow them to be considered reliable. The second is positively, by questioning the hypocrisy that accompanies social relations and acknowledging that apparent behaviour and real motives can be totally opposed. They unmask the social comedy. Some lack character, and therefore lack social competency, while others, through the negative, show they possess this competency and make excellent candidates for having a place among the heroes of modern life. Disorders in executive function put a negative face on individualism, whereas being on the autistic spectrum invokes a positive impression through hidden potential. These two categories are complementary in that they shed light on our moral ideas: they were, and still are, the object of multiple studies whose aim is to understand the neurobiological mechanisms through which we respond to our conspecifics.

The perturbed social behaviour of a patient affected with frontal lobe lesions suffers anomalies in decision-making, difficulties in self-regulating, and problems in social interactions resulting from damaged emotional circuits. The same goes for individuals suffering from borderline personality disorder who therefore lack emotional self-control.

In order to expand knowledge regarding neurological patients to psychopathological patients with borderline personality disorder, narcissistic pathologies, or psychopathy, an entire series of experimental studies was carried out in which affected subjects were

put into repetitive stressful situations that involved constant decision-making. The idea was to understand if the affected individuals
experienced a reduction of activity in the same regions. The trials
were therefore conceived in order to test the hypothesis, which
asserts that the ventromedial prefrontal cortex and other associated
regions would fail to activate during a task that triggered negative
emotions and required motor inhibition. It was thus possible to
study the relationship between emotions and inhibitor systems and
demonstrate "a plausible neural basis for the difficulty borderline
patients have in modulating their behavior during negative emotional states and a potential marker for treatment interventions."[32]
Having serious difficulty controlling their impulses, they have a tendency to make unwise decisions. People with borderline personality
disorder "exhibited distinctive responses in the anterior insulae associated with failure to recognize social norms and to cooperate."[33]
Chronic difficulties concerning the self and interpersonal relationships was explained through concepts that are as neuroscientific as
they are social: these subjects lack empathy, which may have been
the result of negligence or abuse during childhood, thereby impeding
their ability to mentalize. Other test subjects had ventromedial prefrontal cortex activity that was relatively inferior to that in healthy
subjects. There continue to be articles referring to a neuropeptide
theory or an endogenous opioid insufficiency. Neuropsychological
studies comparing patients with personality disorders to those having suffered prefrontal lesions suggest that impulsivity and negative
affectivity present in both groups could be linked to dysfunction in
the orbitofrontal cortex.[34] Over the long term, the issue is to build
a "causal theory" showing "a deficit in recruitment of brain mechanisms of emotion regulation."[35] All this research suggests that the
capacity to accomplish one's own goals and the capacity to cooperate are intrinsically linked, that in the end it is more difficult to live
an accomplished life without empathy.

Gage and Elliot did not possess empathy and demonstrated antisocial behaviour because they lacked emotion. Their brains were
incapable of simulating the mental state of others and they could not
imagine putting themselves in someone else's place. Without emotion,
there is no possible appropriate relationship: "Such a disorder keeps
patients from learning to associate their harmful action with the pain
and distress of others."[36] However, they also lack reason because their
behaviour is irrational when considering their own interests: they fail

systematically because the lesion in the prefrontal cortex perturbs their executive functions. "This ... is an area in which inputs from internal sources conjoin with information received from the outside world." The region is "responsible for subjective reactions to the outside world and for allowing efficient navigation in the social environment."[37] An individual's anatomical compass, this region is considered responsible for social handicaps accompanying several psychopathologies. It is a compass because executive functions manage global cognitive abilities. Their importance is indicative of an individual's capacity to adapt to new situations – thanks to cognitive flexibility, working memory, capacity to plan, etc. They are also essential to non-routine behaviour, which requires such capabilities (known as top-down). According to cognitive neuroscience, these elements are concentrated in the test of decision-making. The scientific hypothesis of a cerebral basis for social behaviour recycles the moral and social questions raised by new individualism's central figure, the narcissistic individual, unreliable for lack of empathy, and they now have been reoriented toward the mechanics of neuronal networks.

The discussion around high-functioning autism centres on the other major basis for relationships: cognitive empathy or theory of mind.

The lack of empathy in the autistic person is much different on a moral and social level because, unlike Gage and Elliot, it is cognitive before it is emotional. The autistic struggles to understand the mental state of others (desires, intentions, affections) and therefore to feel emotions toward them; the person is disinterested in socio-affective relationships and very often feels alone (to the point, as we saw, that it feels like being an anthropologist on Mars). Their handicap with empathy is linked to their lack of theory of mind: they do not detect lies, trickery, manipulation, which are capacities that have given a decisive evolutionary advantage to the human species. They can be awkward and do not manipulate others. The perversion on one side opposes the innocence on the other. One is without morals, the other is very moral – the autistic individual sometimes makes "heroic efforts ... to make sense of the social world."[38] Both shed light on antagonistic aspects of social life.

The theory of mind was first put forward by an ethologist and a psychologist in an article from 1978 entitled "Does the Chimpanzee Have a Theory of Mind?"[39] It then had phenomenal success in its capacity to account for the social handicaps of autistics, regardless of their IQ, a symptom that is considered central to autism, starting with the article published in 1985, written by Simon Baron-Cohen, Alan M. Leslie, and Uta Frith, "Does the Autistic Child Have a Theory of Mind?"[40] To have such a theory requires the capacity to build second-order representations, by embracing the subjective perspective of others. It is the capacity to infer, and consequently foresee, what the other will do – for the man of action according to the Scottish moralists, knowing what the other would do if he were in my place and what I would do if I were in his is the primary criterion for making decisions.

This idea made it possible to test a hypothesis on special types of competence: *conceptual* competence used to understand others' perspective. Psychologists had just shown that it was present in four-year-old children, thanks to an ingenious test, the Sally-Anne test. A situation was imagined in which one child's belief was different from another's. The criterion for carrying out the task was that the child understand that people can have different beliefs about a situation. Three categories of children of the same age were tested: children affected with trisomy 21, autistic children (whose IQ was not inferior to the first category), and normal children. Sally places a marble in a basket, and then walks out of the room; Anne then enters, takes the marble and puts it in a box. Sally returns, wanting to play with her marble. The children are asked where Sally will look to find her marble. Nearly all those in the first and third categories answered correctly, whereas 80 per cent of autistic children failed the test. Thus, the test isolated a comprehension criterion that is purely social, in the sense that the subject does not understand the social act of feigning, and this lack of understanding is independent from mental deficiency. The subject did not perceive the meaning of the situation. There is something worth examining here concerning the brain–behaviour relationship.

This problem with cognitive empathy accounts for the incapacity of autistics to feign or lie and, conversely, to understand that others feign and lie. It keeps them from perceiving the intentionality of others' actions in many everyday circumstances. Autism is today seen as a pathology of social interaction – what psychiatrists and neuroscientists call the "social phenotype of autism."[41]

Scientific theory, empiricist social doctrines from the Scottish school, and our own social concepts mix to such an extent that it is difficult to distinguish them. But that is not because the social neuroscience of empathy had discovered a better, more scientific way to establish the simple intuitions of Scottish moralists. On the contrary, the social concepts and values the Scots held evident, and the characteristics of humankind after which behaviour was modelled, deeply structure neuroscientific theory and guide research, which gives their results a socially exceptional "resonance."

Neurobiological Support of Relationships: A Neural Resonance

We are at a most delicate point for neuroscience: explaining how the brain links the outside world and the individual's inner world.

In 1990, Leslie Brothers came up with the hypothesis for the social brain:[42] *social* refers to the neural structures involved in the capacity to respond to any kind of signal emitted by conspecifics and characterizes a particular domain of the mind, a specific module, social cognition. Even though they could be used in cognitive tasks, these structures were clearly activated in response to an outside stimulus, and therefore were of a social nature, like facial expressions or emotions.

"One of the key problems ... is to uncover the biological mechanisms underlying mentalizing and to show how these mechanisms evolved. To solve this problem we need to do experiments in which people (or animals) interact with one another rather than behaving in isolation."[43] These are the conditions for which we hope to locate the mechanisms allowing every person to decode, imitate, and influence the actions of others. Formulating the key issue to the social, as such, is a clear approach in terms of the contingency of human relationships.

Although studies undertaken on neural systems involving empathy could be interpreted in various, even contradictory, ways, there seems to be consensus on the idea that such systems exist.

Cognitive empathy "crucially depends upon self-awareness and self/other distinction, in other words, on our ability to distinguish between whether the source of our affective experience lies within ourselves or was triggered by the other."[44] This ability depends biologically on what neuroscientists call shared neuronal networks, which allow individuals to recognize the mental state of others thanks to a simulation conducted in their own brain. These networks are "neural representations" that condition the possibility to mentally project oneself into another's perspective. To see others or to picture them in a certain emotional state automatically activates "neural representations" corresponding to those actions, sensations, or emotions. They are shared between the perceiver and the target (to use the diction of this group), and this sharing is the mechanism that makes it possible to understand the mental state of others. It is a *simulation* mechanism: to understand what others are doing, we simulate their movements; to understand what they are feeling, we simulate their feelings and emotions. Activation is generally initiated automatically, without the subject being aware of it.

Shared neural representations are a key concept of the neurobiology of relationships. It comes from social psychology and "was taken up by cognitive science to account for the similarity in the processes for treating information and the neuronal networks that underpin them and which are activated when we mentally simulate an action, when we produce and observe this action executed by another person."[45] In 1995, the discovery of mirror neurons largely bolstered the credibility of this concept.

Mirror neurons were a neuronal system first found in the premotor cortex of macaques, then in the Broca area of humans: because these neurons are motor *and* sensory, they fire when subjects observe a direct action in another and when they themselves carry out the same action. The neurons also fire when they simply imagine themselves performing the action. The same goes for mouth movements and sounds (in this case, the auditory system is activated). The conclusion drawn from this discovery was that perception and action had the same biological substrate. From there, researchers and philosophers came up with the fascinating hypothesis that within these circuits lies the biological basis for social cognition, because these neurons allowed people to simulate, in their own brain, what was happening in the head of someone else. This type of neuron ranks highly as a possible biological explanation for the principles of communication between humans. It is through them that social relations, intersubjectively, have become a critical biological subject.

These neurons opened the gates to a domain called "motor cognition": "The discovery of neurons with visual properties, the most complete type of which are mirror neurons found in the motor cortex, had a profound influence on several domains, currently referred to as 'motor cognition'... As such, they make up the neuronal basis for representing an action."[46] To see someone else carry out an action and carry it out yourself involves the same system. Perceiving and acting, at least as far as motor function is concerned, falls under the same neuronal system. From this we can conclude the neural mechanism provides the basis for understanding an action. After 1996, neurological discoveries started to accumulate: a class of mirror neurons was responsible not only for observing an action, but also for the sound produced by the action, and another was linked to the observation/execution of mouth movements.[47]

This communication is unconscious (the subject is not aware of it) and infra-personal (it takes place in the brain, thanks to motor and sensory neurons) and is triggered automatically. Mirror neurons offer a possible biological mechanism to explain the "principle of communication" (Hume) that is empathy, making it possible to show that simulation is automatic, unconscious. It is a bottom-up process. Conscious activation is triggered depending on the context and according to the reverse process, which is top-down.

With internal models, neuronal representations, mirror neurons, empathy, and the theory of mind we have the relevant biological and psychological tools to scientifically describe the regularities and irregularities of cooperation between individuals, by basing them in experience. Regularity of experience and anticipation of the future are decisive criteria when deciding to act one way or another.

BEHAVIOURAL ECONOMICS: COGNITIVE PSYCHOPATHOLOGY OF EVERYDAY LIFE

Social neuroscience was built as a complexification of the motives for action, broadening the idea of personal interest well beyond egoism, which economics locked in. Yet it always used a perspective in which individuals were the final arbiter, even if that meant searching their brain for the mechanisms of this arbitration, the means nature has given them. Behavioural economics enables us to raise key questions regarding these disciplines: how and under what conditions are social order and behavioural regularity produced by the individual, without being constrained by a higher authority? How are cerebral mechanisms, put into motion by the "multitude of minuscule architects," our neuronal networks, likely to be used wisely in order to obtain prosocial effects? The answer is found in two social mechanisms: "cognitive bias" and "the nudge." The first is caused by the failing of an action, and the second its success.

The new alliance between economy and psychology was presented as a reform of social science – behavioural – the problem of which was to better grasp the regularities of the experience, and therefore better anticipate the future and have control over contingencies. Two sets of studies provide a clue for answers concerning this alliance's potential. The first set shed light on the criteria that best insure this regularity by focusing on the conditions for trust in situations of exchange. The second focused on the recent discovery of a fundamental mechanism of regularity, that of systematic error, which psychologists Daniel Kahneman and Amos Tversky called "cognitive bias" (today, the most used concept in behavioural science). It also involved updating another mechanism to help deal with it, brought to the fore by economist Richard Thaler and lawyer Cass Sunstein: the "nudge." Their regularity is such that we should rely upon them as traits of human nature in order to make public policy more efficient.

Conditions of Regularity: Equity for Meeting the Requirements of Trust

Behavioural economists and neuro-economists devote a good part of their work to situations involving monetary exchanges, which is indeed fertile ground for exploring the fundamental element to cooperation in the domain of passion (appetites): trust,[48] the reliability of each partner. All of the research showed that equity and justice are more powerful *biological* motives for action than personal interest, where gain is involved.

In cognitive neuroscience, the moral qualities required for cooperation between individuals follows the criterion of radical negative freedom borrowed from behavioural social science: an individual is not forced to cooperate. However, we must wonder which cerebral and cognitive mechanisms favour or disfavour cooperation, and how we can get the human brain to increase its interest in or its appetite for cooperation, its sense of equity, altruism, or trust in the exchange – even more so since moral feelings and emotions have a biological basis (which lesions in the prefrontal cortex and autism enable us to explore), introducing the prospect of accessing mechanisms directly.

In order to grasp the reasoning behind this, let us use the example of altruistic punishment, one of the best-known case studies in behavioural economics, carried out by Ernst Fehr and his team at the University of Zurich.

Large-scale cooperation between individuals who are not genetically related is a social characteristic that is uniquely human. To punish others for violating social norms means there is a cost for those who dole out this type of "altruistic" punishment, in the sense that "they involve costly acts that confer economic benefits on other individuals."[49] Insofar as punishment does not give any advantage to the person who punishes – the egoistical hypothesis – this person "derives satisfaction from punishing norm violators" – the altruistic hypothesis. This hypothesis takes root in the theory of evolution. It suggests that punishment is not a direct biological mechanism, like digestion, but it is a reflexive activity, meaning there must exist mechanisms for satisfaction by proxy. Such experiments reproduce situations that can be likened to the "prisoner's dilemma" in game theory, in which it is in the players' (two prisoners) interest not to denounce each other (to cooperate) in order to avoid conviction, a decision that involves trusting the other party. However, without any way for the two to communicate, eventually they give each other up. These games were enhanced with the scope of uncovering the moral conditions under which cooperation would be favoured. Here, biology and morality are linked tightly together.

One common experiment involved two players, both with the same amount of money in their possession. They can both win by trusting each other: if A trusts B and sends him ten units, B will receive four times that amount, or forty units; B now has fifty units at his disposal and can choose either to send nothing or half (twenty-five units) to A. If A does not trust B and does not trigger the action, each one keeps ten units. If B behaves unfairly, A can punish B by penalizing him up to twenty punishment points (there is one minute to decide, during which the brain is scanned).

The experiment lays out four opposing conditions for measuring the activation of reward circuitry at the time of punishment: intentional and costly (if B keeps the money, B intentionally takes advantage of A's trust, and the punishment is not costly for A, but is for B); intentional and free (the punishment is not costly for A, but is for B); intentional and symbolic (punishment has no cost for player B since there is no opportunity to punish him); unintentional and costly (the sum is distributed haphazardly). In this last case, punishment cannot be satisfying for A since B does not enter into it at all. When the intent is to punish, or the opportunity to do so is lacking (two situations), punishment cannot bring satisfaction, which is contrary to the other two cases. All these situations contrast, and therefore can be measured using brain imaging and questionnaires. These four possibilities were tested on players in the A role, each having been put in a setting with several players in the B role. The idea was to empirically show the existence of certain cerebral activity and the decision to punish, so as to come up with hypotheses on the participation of cerebral architects in decision-making (here, the caudate nucleus), and "in processing rewards associated with the satisfaction of the desire to punish the intentional abuse of trust."[50]

The key to the experiment is to examine activity in the caudate nucleus of those players who doled out the most punishment in the intentional/free situation. The hypothesis is that the higher the activity is, the more the subject will have a tendency to punish, even when it is costly to him. The results show that this is the case: there is thus a correlation between an entity's cerebral activity and his behaviour. In the case where punishment is costly, player A "has to weigh the emotional satisfaction of punishing against the monetary cost of punishing, which requires integration of separate cognitive operations in the pursuit of a behavioral goal. Much evidence indicates that the prefrontal and the orbitofrontal cortex are involved in integrating separate cognitive operations and decision-making." To conclude, "Altruistic punishment provides relief or satisfaction to the punisher and activates, therefore, reward-related brain regions."[51] Equity is a question of pleasure/displeasure, or using today's diction, a question of happiness and well-being that is established in affective and emotional detail.

Exploring conditions for regularity consists of multiplying experimental situations in order to highlight the affective effects in the widest variety of situations. For example, a situation in which the offer is truly unfair, yet remains financially attractive, allows us to examine the neuronal correlates of the tendency to accept unfair offers – an increase in activity in the prefrontal cortex, and a simultaneous decrease in the anterior insula. The prefrontal cortex and the amygdala, notably, are particularly reactive to cooperative behaviour and therefore are equitable with partners. Another distinction can be introduced – the rate of rejection is higher when the player knows that a more amicable offer could have been extended. Players are sensitive to equity when it comes to the distribution of money, but also regarding one another's intentions. There are other studies on the application of norms with not only two players or parties, which is the simplest (you hurt me, I hurt you), but with three: within this shift, the element of impartiality is introduced, which is entirely essential. A third party applying norms is specifically human: it is one way to name institutions using an individualist language.[52]

The first result found that humans are more sensitive to equity, and therefore being treated with dignity and respect, and less interested in monetary or economic gain. If empathy is *the* condition for prosocial behaviour, equity is its guarantor: order and regularity, controlling future eventualities are better assured when moral criteria, like equity, are referred to rather than material criteria, like gain. Equity is more predictable than monetary value, and so moral motivation is *statistically* more powerful than material motivation. The motive for these morals is "the self-interest that is served by accruing a good reputation through altruistic behavior ... Reputational enhancement clearly has a role in human cooperation."[53] Its foundation is the invisible hand of social relations that fosters reputation, a mirror humans hold in front of others as much as they gaze into it themselves.

The second result found that the "minuscule architects" (amygdala, striatum, etc.) are propelled into action, like the watch example proposed by Adam Smith, "by a spring [neural distribution] which intends the effect it produces as little as they do," to build the order of social relations – an order without reference to higher entities, like laws or contracts. All of the circuitry involved in reward is activated by the partners' cooperative behaviour. The activation of this circuitry itself shows "that fairness processing is relatively automatic and intuitive."[54] This trait is absolutely central, since it demonstrated the existence of a biological foothold in the feeling of fairness – "fair treatment can be rewarding in itself"[55] – resulting in an evolutionary mechanism that upholds its foundation. In conclusion, "Altruistic punishment provides relief or satisfaction to the punisher and activates, therefore, reward-related brain regions."[56]

These two results show that social relations totally innervate the human biological tissue and that it should be possible to advance understanding of the biological mechanisms of prosocial behaviour.

From there, the debate in neuroscience is between two theories: one supporting the idea that information is treated by specialized cognitive modules, and the other, favouring fundamental domains of general cognitive processes – the capacity to have capacities – both resulting from evolution. The majority of the neuroscientific community leans toward the second, the argument for which can be stated thus: "The ability of human culture to create modern institutions of justice ... is enabled by the evolutionary elaboration of domain general cognitive processes for value learning, decision-making and perspective taking."[57]

Cognitive Bias and the Politics of Nudging: A Mechanism for "Changing Behaviour without Having to Change the Mind"

Initially, the main idea of scientific psychology employed a metaphor of choosing a path according to limited rationality (see chapter 2). The question was answered by introducing a solitary action for which each sequence was presented as a 0/1 option that occurs according to the sequences of a decision tree, between which either the rat in the maze or the savant must make a choice utilizing the logic of discovery. Currently in behavioural science, individuals know what they want, but they undergo multiple distortions. A list of these distortions can be compiled, as Freud did with forgetting names, the slip of the tongue, misunderstandings, and other awkwardness. In *Psychopathology of Everyday Life* he stressed the extent to which these revealing blunders are caused by the determinist mechanics of the unconscious: "Certain inadequacies of our psychic capacities ... and certain performances which are apparently unintentional prove to be well motivated when subjected to the psychoanalytic investigation, and are determined through the consciousness of unknown motives."[58] Whereas Freud thought in terms of revealing blunders, indicating an unconscious intention, the behavioural scientists thought in terms of error in judgment and choice: our preferences and interests (be they egoistic or altruistic) differ because we perceive poorly, we give in to cognitive bias and that keeps us from understanding where our true interests lie. Behaviourists are less preoccupied with the ambivalence of human intentionality than by distortions of perception, and more precisely, by recurring distortions. Therefore, individuals of today constantly make choices and decisions – to such an extent that there is an abundance of literature to help them fight against decision fatigue and favour willpower.[59]

Do we have mechanisms to avoid distorting our judgment, which poisons our everyday life, makes us act against our own self-interest, and keeps us from self-actualizing with the choices we make? That is the new question asked by scientific psychologists. In a society of generalized autonomy, if it were still possible to place an expert whose visible hand can guide the individual down the right path, we would nevertheless rather employ styles of behavioural regulation that put the individual in the situation to make the right decision.

Daniel Kahneman and Amos Tversky, both psychologists, are strong proponents of this type of psychology. They reintegrated motivation and psychology into the economy – giving us the term *behavioural* economics, for which Kahneman received the Nobel Prize in 2002 (Tversky had already passed away).

The aura of Daniel Kahneman is so phenomenal that he already has a place in the pantheon of the great masters of the human mind. In 2011 he published *Thinking, Fast and Slow*, which is a memoir of his life's work, which the *New York Times* ranked in the top five works of the year. The *New York Review of Books* presents him as one of the top three explorers of the psyche, alongside Freud and James, asserting that if the first two are interested in our "deeper emotions," he is the explorer of our "more humdrum cognitive processes." "His great achievement was to turn psychology into a quantitative science. He made our mental processes subject to precise measurement and exact calculation, by studying in detail how we deal with dollars and cents."[60] The *New York Times* wrote, "Kahneman and his research partner, the late Amos Tversky, will be remembered hundreds of years from now, and how their work helped instigate a cultural shift that is already producing astounding results." What kind of shift? "They proved that actual human behavior often deviates from the old models and that the flaws are not just in the passions (which oppose reason) but in the machinery of cognition." Their work represents "a crucial pivot point in the way we see ourselves."[61] Economist Richard Thaler, co-author of the famous *Nudge*, which we will come back to, talked about the work: "We overestimate the importance of all we think about. We are wrong about the past and misjudge what makes us happy. In this in-depth presentation of a life's work, one of the most influential psychologists in the world demonstrates that irrationality is bone deep, but it is in no way necessary that we think worse of ourselves."[62] And so there is a solution on scale with the problem, a mechanism that avoids individual decisions.

Kahneman's question is, Why do humans not reason statistically? Why do they make errors systematically and recurrently, which go against their own self-interest, whatever that be? The starting point is utilitarian, because it posits the principle that "each individual is the best judge of his own welfare," but it is made more realistic by considering that the judge is not very good. Or, that he is a partial spectator. How does one turn him into an impartial spectator? The question is asked in these terms because the sequential character of the action (perceive, evaluate affect, decide/act) implies the subject of the decision/action be a spectator who first observes in order to evaluate, then becomes an actor who decides.

The reason humans do not reason as they should is due to the fact that they are constantly victims of what Kahneman calls "cognitive bias." This is the new major concept added to the edifice of the mechanics of passions. Kahneman is to cognitive bias what Freud was to the unconscious. You cannot mention one without the other.

Kahneman and Tversky's claim to fame came from an article published by *Science* in 1974, "Judgment under Uncertainty: Heuristics and Biases." It is one of the most cited articles in "social science" (Google Scholar showed 52,000 citations as of August 2019) and has "been used productively in many fields, including medical diagnosis, legal judgment, intelligence analysis, philosophy, finance, statistics, and military strategy." According to Kahneman, this article questioned two in-vogue ideas of human nature espoused by "social science": one, individuals are rational and their reasoning is generally solid; two, emotions (fear, anger, etc.) could explain irrational behaviour. A second article, just as important, was dedicated to decision-making when the future was uncertain, therefore the problem of choice. One of the most important developments in their theory, the author tells us, was "that we now understand the marvels as well as the flaws of intuitive thought."[63] The relationship between intuition and competence (or a successful action) is at the heart of this reflection.

The work explores the biases of intuitive thinking in order to "improve the ability to identify and understand errors of judgment and choice."[64] The human mind functions according to two main types of coordinates: the first is fast thinking, which is intuitive and related to the automatic mental activity of perception and memory; the second is slow and deliberative thinking, which involves mental activity made up of effort and close attention. Kahneman calls intuitive thinking "System 1" and deliberative thinking "System 2." They represent two fictional characters who make it possible to metaphorize what the human mind is doing. Recent empirical research established a table on which the "System 1 is more influential than your experience tells you, and it is the secret author of many of the choices and judgments you make."[65] Automatic operations of the first system function by association, whereas the controlled operations of the second are analytical and need rational calculation to weigh the elements. S1 is an associative machine, and S2 an analytical machine. These are fictitious characters and not systems in the proper sense of the term, which are located in the brain. Like the three agents of Freud – the id, ego, and superego – they must not be viewed in a realistic way, but as metaphoric tools used to highlight mechanisms.

The interactions between S1 and S2 are the common thread of the book: S2's task is to control the impulses of S1; its mission is self-control. It is not emotions that keep us from making good judgments, choices, etc., but an excess of confidence, major cognitive bias, generated by S1, which makes each person a partial spectator, and is shown through the confusion between preference and actual interests, the symptoms of which are systematic errors of judgment and choice.

Lawyer Cass Sunstein and economist Richard Thaler provided the response to the mechanism of cognitive bias in the book *Nudge*, published in 2008.

The book is built around the opposition of the engineer, who imposes what he has decided to be "good choices," and the choice architect. A choice architect "has the responsibility for organizing the context in which people make decisions."[66] How do you influence behaviour in such a way so that it does not make people feel constrained? How do you push people to opt for the good choice without imposing it? Today, the most efficient practices for obtaining a desired behaviour is not found in directing, as a conductor would an orchestra, or a supervisor would the workforce. Individuals require more tact, and it is better to use little things from their environment to warn, remind, or alert them, just like giving a neighbour a light nudge saying, "Be careful." If you think that is how it should be done today, then you are, as the authors write, "welcome to our new movement: *libertarian paternalism*." Yet these two concepts are opposed to each other; either you are paternalistic, or you are libertarian. But it does work if used absolutely, dogmatically. There is a libertarian aspect because the starting point is "people should be free to do what they like" and consequently we should endeavour to design policies that "maintain or increase freedom of choice." There is a paternalistic aspect because this conception affirms "that it is legitimate for choice architects to try to influence people's behavior in order to make their lives longer, healthier, and better." Not only does libertarian paternalism not ban people from smoking, but more subtly, it does not keep them from doing it by making life difficult. No, a nudge is "any aspect of the choice architecture that alters people's behavior in a predictable way without forbidding any option or significantly changing their economic incentives."[67] How does it work?

The basic political principle of the nudge is quite simple. When you buy a phone, it has several options. The manufacturer chooses to equip all phones using a standard option that by default involves a decision to decline that option. We are able to see that in general people do not modify the proposed option. They keep it. The default choice illustrates a fundamental trait put forward by psychology: the inertia factor, or the tendency for people to reproduce their habits. Consequently, "by properly deploying both incentives and nudges, we can improve our ability to improve people's lives, and help solve many of society's major problems."[68] Individual well-being, resulting from right behaviour, and societal well-being are linked.

The default option contains two main ideas. The first is that small changes (put in place by choice architects) can lead to big changes in behaviour, according to the logic of effect. The second is that public policy adopting this mechanism is based on the principle that it is about "changing behaviour without changing minds." Health policy has a tendency to act on the mind ("Smoking Kills" printed in bold on packs of cigarettes) so as to modify behaviour – it targets System 2. Those who are inspired by behavioural economics are centred on going with the "grain of behaviour" by acting on automatisms. Instead of informing to influence, by addressing System 2, you modify the context in which people act, which is a modification whose effects go through System 1. For example, in the United Kingdom, where government authorities recently reformed the pension system with a law requiring employers to automatically enrol their employees for a retirement savings plan by giving them the choice to pull out of it if they so desire, the data collected over a three-year period showed that enrolment went from ten million salaried workers in 2012 to close to sixteen million in 2015.[69]

If the default option is the best-known incentivizing device in behavioural economics, it must certainly be because it functions as a purely social mechanism, with the central idea being to influence behaviour by "leaving as much choice in the hands of citizens as possible."[70] The other modes of action that refer to nudging are less automatic, but they are still conceived to diminish the burden of individual decisions. "Our goal is to allow people to go their own way at the lowest possible cost."[71] The lowest cost would be "facilitating things for them." The idea is perfectly clear: to encourage individuals to make the best choices *for themselves*, it is better to act on their behaviour without prescribing or constraining, indirectly, as if they themselves were deciding. "Behavioural approaches embody a line of thinking that moves from the idea of an autonomous individual making rational decisions to a 'situated' decision-maker, much of whose behaviour is automatic and influenced by their 'choice environment.'"[72] Choice architecture is the mechanics of passions in the age of autonomy-as-condition, meaning that we do not look to guide individuals' conscience by constraining their freedom to choose, but to incentivize them through mechanisms that preserve this freedom.

Public policy inspired by behavioural economics was introduced to the United Kingdom, which is manifestly the land of election. Behavioural economics deals with more varied subjects and goes well beyond the field of finance: child education, health-care policy, crime prevention, etc. Yet these questions are always probed with the facilitation of an action in mind, and lowering the cost of making a decision. In 2009 David Cameron's government published MINDSPACE: *Influencing Behaviour through Public Policy*, which sets out a program for changing behavioural habits that consists of "harnessing the same automatic effects to nudge people onto a different, self-sustaining, track, without always explicitly stating the need to pursue a particular goal."[73] The report was followed by the creation of a public laboratory for social innovation, the Behavioural Insights Team, nicknamed the Nudge Unit, whose goal is to find innovative ways to encourage, empower, and support people so that they make the best choices for themselves. It quickly diversified. Their work has to do exclusively with behavioural psychology, neuroscience, and economics.

Policy that employs behavioural economics, a new science of choice, aims to make the individual more reliable in a context where freedom of choice is the highest value – it is all about modifying behaviour by giving the individual the final say, much the same as the default option. In this context, behavioural economics is a practice placing people in a situation of having to avoid making choices by using a mechanism that automatically produces a positive effect, the default option of which is a paradigm. As a result, it avoids decision-making and, at the very least, makes it as easy as possible by economizing on invoking willpower. It appears that willpower is under severe strain in a society of choice and individual initiative, one in which decision-making is unrelenting and, consequently, cognitive bias constant.

On the other hand, exercises of autonomy, which are the object of the next chapter, aim to facilitate autonomy by increasing the social competence of people who submit to it.

Let us sum up the dynamic before examining these exercises. To cooperate implies having empathy toward others, the capacity to put oneself in another's shoes, keeping the other's point of view in mind, the capacity to be self-reliant and to express oneself. Cognitive neuroscience provides answers to these moral and social expectations, which spread throughout our societies largely during the last third of the twentieth century. Its authority does not come from original ideas (they are widespread in the public sphere) or major discoveries for the treatment of patients (as we will see in the following chapter), but rather a crystallization of our most valued and therefore most common ideas concerning autonomy within neurobiology and through experimental evidence-based methods. It is less the originality of the idea at stake than it is the coming together of a social idea and a scientific theory. They nourish one another, mixing the idea in a somewhat confused way, which a sociological description nevertheless has hopefully highlighted.

5

Exercises in Autonomy

Individualist Rituals to Reconstruct One's Moral Being?

Each Self requires what was once a king's privilege, to have a distinctive Self, and plan a world in the form of some utopic project or theatrical production of its idiosyncrasy.

Pierre-Yves Pétillon,
La Grand-Route. Espace et écriture en Amérique

After a session of cognitive remediation therapy, a patient suffering from schizophrenia tells the psychologist providing the treatment, "Before I was handicapped, but thanks to our work, I hope to become handicapable."[1] What a profoundly lucid way of expressing a *sociological* definition, not only of the new viewpoint on the mentally ill, but also, going beyond psychiatry and mental health, on the establishment of a new individual with the generalization of the ideals of autonomy over the last half century.

"Cognitive remediation" describes a neuroscientific method of caring for and providing support to those with mental illness, which started its rise to prominence in the 1980s, as patients with serious psychiatric issues were essentially treated as outpatients. It originally articulates two cardinal notions in mental health, *rehabilitation* and *recovery*. The first term designates practices, and the second, a new idea for healing, but they are used interchangeably because their meanings are interdependent. They are central to this chapter's subject, "exercises in autonomy."

In this chapter and the following one, the emphasis will shift a bit. Up to this point, cognitive neuroscience was viewed through the lens of moral authority based on an aspect of individualist modernity.

Now it is time to tackle the epistemological question brought up in the introduction: How far can we take the understanding of humans simply by knowing their brain and organism? Or, to use Mauss's words, In what way can there be no interval between the biological and the social? In order to answer that, these two chapters outline the way in which cognitive neuroscience is entirely involved with the individual's existence, at the same time necessitating a reflection on the two main ways of reconstructing one's moral being in a mass individualist society embodied by psychoanalysis and cognitive neuroscience – or at least their practices.

In the past, handicap and ability were opposed (ability being aligned with autonomy); today, these two terms are associated by the *degree* of autonomy and the *diversity* of its forms. Autonomy is a relative concept. "Handicapped" is a state, "handicapable" is a journey and, more precisely, has less to do with a cure than with *personal transformation in the face of negativity*, the difficulties of which are no doubt more intense, dramatic, and painful than those of the ordinary person, but not of another nature.

Recovery is the system of caring on which the ideal of hidden potential relies, hidden potential being this fundamental attitude in the face of adversity, contingency, or negativity. It is the institution of it. The guiding line of this system of action is, by casting the widest net possible, to develop individuals' ability using exercises that will lead them on a path to personal transformation by being the agent of their own change.

More specifically, a set of ideals progressively came together to form a system that can be described using four characteristics: the ideal of hidden potential, the definition of ailment through the polarity of handicap/asset, the shift in status of the mentally or cerebrally ill toward that of moral partner, and the therapist taking on the role of coach, or even peer-helper. This system presents the diversity of the available means to transform a diminishing handicap, deviancy, or pathology into a strengthening asset with a personal solution or, to use the language of David Hume, with our ability to convert a negative passion into a positive one. It dramatizes multiple hardships, dilemmas, and limits, which individuals are confronted with in order to reconstruct their moral being.

The interest for tackling hidden potential using schizophrenia is to extend the high-functioning autistic's brain to psychopathology, to the mental illness, *the* symbol of psychiatric confinement, embodying the "other" of reason. Using the model of autism, this approach to schizophrenia allows us to considerably broaden the concept of human capability by reformulating it according to a typical/atypical pairing, and therefore to consider potential incapability as a different capability, a neurodivergence.

After presenting the context in which ideals of "capability" are developed, by examining the case of schizophrenia in great detail, we will describe rehabilitation and recovery. We will follow them up to the decisive reorientation brought by cognitive remediation, in which exercises used for adopting better habits had broadened its intended target, to the point it deals henceforth with increasing insight. The chapter will then take on the meeting of cognitive neuroscience and artificial intelligence, illustrating a new World Wide Brain. This meeting brings the machine-as-partner (automated therapy, social robots, etc.) into the fold through the contemporary mechanics of converting passions. It strengthens the two trends. On the one hand, there is an automation in the education of positive habit acquisition, and on the other, the progressive extension of the field of action of these sciences toward insight. Lastly, after showing how there is "no interval between the social and the biological," we will tackle the question of the role played by cognitive neuroscience in these exercises, and what it specifically brings to the ideal of hidden potential.

SOCIAL COGNITION: THE FOCUS OF BECOMING AN INDIVIDUAL FOR SCHIZOPHRENICS

In 2006, introducing a new French psychiatric journal dedicated to psychosocial rehabilitation, a psychiatrist emphasizes that it is a way to take into account "important advances in patient aspirations, whether they are able to accept them as such or not. New generations of users and those close to them accept being marginalized less and less ... The desire to best value a maintained potential has become the most profound corollary of self-esteem."[2] This highlights clearly that persons affected by ailments are individuals just like anyone else. Moreover, to treat them as such has therapeutic action. What kind of action? It consists precisely of valuing the "maintained potential" and "self-esteem." Introducing Yale University's guide for recovery and community health, *Getting in the Driver's Seat of Your Treatment*, a well-known "survivor" of American psychiatry specifies recovery values:

To me recovery means I try to stay in the driver's seat of my life. I don't let my illness run me. Over the years I have worked hard to become an expert in my own self-care. Being in recovery means I don't just take medications ... Rather I use medications as part of my recovery process ... Over the years I have learned different ways of helping myself. Sometimes I use medications, therapy, self-help and mutual support groups, friends, my relationship with God, work, exercise, spending time in nature – all these measures help me remain whole and healthy, even though I have a disability.[3]

Being able to consider yourself in good health despite handicap or illness: this idea of recovery puts us right at the heart of a paradigm shift, namely considering oneself *as the actor* of one's own good health.

Choice, courageous and tenacious work, creativity (the different ways of helping oneself, from medicine to spirituality): it is all there. The ideal of hidden potential associates traditional, heroic virtues of courage, tenacity, and audacity with new ideals of creativity, innovation, and diversity, which started making their way into the collective mindset in the 1960s.

What happened? The handicapable was unthinkable without a transformation in the values of equality and freedom, in terms of the generalized ideals of autonomy that made their way to new populations, providing the possibility to enter the arena of democratic individualism. In the mid-1970s Tom Wolfe published his article on the Me Decade,[4] in which he positions the self in the light of the "divine spark" each one of us is capable of awakening. The first hero of hidden potential appears in a patient afflicted with Tourette syndrome, followed ten years later by autism (see chapter 1). If the high-functioning autistic is the embodiment of this ideal, rising from the depths of mental retardation to the status of super-individual, then those "with schizophrenia," to use the current terminology, or those affected by psychotic disorders have undergone a similar transformation. In just a few decades, hidden potential, this unperceived and decisive dimension of the new collective representation of autonomy, has totally revamped the social basis that prevailed in the treatment of psychotic people. A place was made for them, albeit fragile and precarious, but it was, nevertheless, a place in the world.

This new mindset became widespread in the sociological context of a twofold change within psychiatry: the health-care system, on one hand, started concentrating on the social life of the affected subject, and, on the other, epidemiology and bio-psychiatric research opened therapeutic hope to people afflicted with schizophrenia.

Starting in the 1970s, there was a mass exodus from psychiatric hospitals initiating what experts called "deinstitutionalization," and at the same time the emergence of the proper viewpoint of the patient in psychiatry and in neurology.[5] The shift from in-patient to outpatient treatment of people affected with serious psychiatric and neuropsychiatric pathologies represented a new situation. It led to a necessity to help those being cared for to equip themselves with the ability to live in society, a concern that would be marked by the rise of the idea of *social* disabilities, and the correlative *relative* capabilities.[6] For outpatients, their symptoms are not only at the forefront, but there are also new "deficits" in the ability to live among others. Even patients whose negative and positive symptoms have decreased continue to be at a disadvantage in social interactions. Therefore, a "functional evaluation" is necessarily added to the psychiatric diagnosis, in other words an evaluation that centres on functioning *in society*. Through "social cognition," relationships (or their disorders) become a central label of schizophrenia.

At the same time, one side of schizophrenia that a long hospital stay may have lost sight of reappeared. Conversely, it demonstrated some creativity in the social skills favoured by the new social and moral context of autonomy-as-condition. It resulted in a mechanism that classic psychiatry and practising psychoanalysts had been using since the beginning of the twentieth century: a "restitution mechanism."[7] Therapists noted that a substantial number of people affected by these pathologies found their own solutions for restoring equilibrium, making it possible for them to live in society. The "restitution mechanism" is a creation of an acceptable self despite the illness. Stability and creation are indissociable when the therapist works with the psychosis.[8]

In 1974, three psychiatrists, phenomenologists, and/or psychoanalysts practising psychotherapy with patients afflicted with schizophrenia published *Schizophrenia as a Lifestyle* in the United States. They paint a picture of people who are far beyond that of the chronically committed: they are alive, alert, intelligent, and able to make it through life thanks to their own personal inventiveness.

They are the subject of a "way of life, a mode of existence – that is, the behaviors have meaning in terms of person experience."[9] The main distinction between symptoms and experience, which is at the heart of recovery practices, is clearly affirmed herein. Not only does practising psychotherapy make "the person behind the schizophrenia" visible, as the authors write, but furthermore, "*mirabile dictum*, his disease doesn't seem ultimately pernicious and deteriorative." The book brings patients closer to ordinary people, "ill or not," by showing that schizophrenia is like "a way of being-in-the-world."[10] One of the authors notes that such people become visible because society started receiving the mentally ill as outpatients, as deinstitutionalization began in the mid-1960s.

Personal accounts published by American psychiatric journals from the 1970s show the wide diversity of people affected and the solutions they find. The *Schizophrenia Bulletin*, one of the most prestigious international journals in the field, was the first to create a "Personal Accounts" column, which had clear testimony as a condition of publication. The editorial requirement was that "such contributions be clearly written and organised." The journal requested that "clinicians who see articulate patients, with experiences they believe should be shared, might encourage these patients to submit their articles."[11] *Psychiatric Services* followed in 1993, and *Transcultural Psychiatry* has recently launched its own column. Today, there is no lack of articles in British and American journals retracing the paths of mentally ill patients "who succeed." However, here the phenomenon is both perplexing and interesting, because schizophrenia is a pathology supposedly characterized by a disorganized thought process. It should be noted that in France, by contrast, no psychiatric journal has published articles in which the author was afflicted by mental illness.

De-institutionalization played a part in revealing the lack of social skills in people affected by psychotic disorders as much as it showed the diversity of solutions all could bring to their own problems. This two-sided trend is central to the practices examined here.

As these institutional changes were happening, scientific research brought new elements to the table that allowed for a shift in the pessimistic apprehension of the illness. First, longitudinal epidemiological studies developed during the 1970s showed a systematicity of favourable trends in a large swath of people affected by schizophrenia. Insanity is no longer the unavoidable outcome of madness.

In 2013, a meta-analysis that appeared in the *Schizophrenia Bulletin* estimated that one patient in seven recovered.[12] Next, on the biomedical level, the neurodegenerative illness that was schizophrenia was relabelled as a cerebral developmental disorder. So the term *neurodevelopmental* opened a therapeutic perspective: neuronal connections were not established in the brain during childhood development. These connections are therefore not innate, as shown through "soft signs," and they prevent the acquisition of abilities to evaluate context, to take into account another's perspective, inferences, etc. In short, all that is specifically understood by the term *social cognition*. In sum, "Mental illnesses can be broadly viewed as resulting from inefficient, maladaptive, or biased distributed neuronal representations underlying critical cognitive and emotional processes that are necessary for successful community functioning."[13] The hypothesis of dysfunction during development opens pathways to studies on the pathophysiology of mental illnesses, based on the concept of cerebral plasticity, the aim of which is the discovery of, on the one hand, potential predictable "biomarkers," and, on the other, potential therapeutic actions on the dysfunctional cerebral circuitry. And a shift in criteria for funding given by the NIMH for research projects and putting diagnoses into "domains" (see chapter 3) moves entirely in that direction.

The word *hope* enters into the lexicon of schizophrenia. At the same time, a slight shift in the 1980s was the most spectacular change regarding insanity.

In 1989, the *Schizophrenia Bulletin* published its first article on voice hearers, written by a psychiatrist and a psychologist who started the movement in the Netherlands, Marius Romme and Sandra Escher,[14] in a sort of dossier that highlighted an oversight in the research that had given rise to the *DSM-III*: the self in schizophrenics.[15] "The reduction of 'hearing voices' to being viewed merely as a pathological phenomenon is not very fruitful in helping patients to deal with these experiences," wrote the authors. The movement, which started after the first congress in 1987, opened a space so that personal accounts of those affected by psychoses could be heard, not as some manic delusion devoid of meaning, but as a narrative full of significations, which could be useful in the care of these individuals. It was an emancipatory movement for individuals suffering from the paradigmatic symptoms of psychosis (hearing voices), but it would become the occasion to help better their condition. Therefore it is necessary to "demedicalize" to better treat, and it is necessary because the patient must be able to live within society, not in some hospital or socio-medical institution. The basis for this movement was to help control the voices through groups of patients helping each other, possibly with the support of a professional therapist. This could go far toward an understanding that hearing voices is not necessarily a symptom of psychosis, but simply a different capacity. The reality of delusions and hallucinations is less important than the intensity of their positive or negative consequences on individuals, and the difference made in their lives.

People affected by schizophrenia triggered a dynamic similar to that of high-functioning autistics, because through hidden potential, it became possible for them to self-actualize in social life. The individualist turning point was, to use the key phrase of the movement, turning patients with an illness into people with problems[16] – and who does not have problems? – which ipso facto implies that those problems can be converted into advantages, especially when they manifest a particular spiritual or artistic sensibility. Approaching symptoms in this way makes it possible to go beyond questioning, to which only a therapist holds the key, and moves toward treatment based on consequences in terms of experience, to which the patient holds the key.

Two evolutionary lines are drawn: one leans toward a "different" lifestyle bringing patients out of their pathology, and the other, which favours the idea of patient-as-partner or patient-as-individual. This creative power is revealed in several ways, thanks to which a handicap is converted into an asset, and through which subjects *grow*, increase their value by discovering the possibility of *recognition* along the path of personal transformation, however limited it may be.

RE-ESTABLISHING SOCIAL COGNITION, OR HOW TO MAKE INDIVIDUALS AGENTS OF THEIR OWN CHANGE

An article on "the cognitive trail" (*la piste cognitive*) published in 2006 by *L'Information psychiatrique*, declared rather straightforwardly, "Studies on schizophrenic disorders have been affected over the past years by the development of clinics for cognitive disorders," which are concerned mainly with memory, attention, and executive functions. The authors add that there is a necessity to go beyond "the collective resistance, inherited from a time when it was not possible to note a symptomology without attributing some relational meaning to it."[17] The cognitive issue is how to act on the faltering functionality. The target is practical subjects who must be able to act in society. The cognitive issue conditions their social skills.[18]

In the old school of psychiatry, when patients' symptoms stabilized and they could leave the hospital, they entered an adaptation phase of life on the outside, which consisted of work centred *on* them. In the same article on the cognitive trail, another psychiatrist notes, "When, in 1997, we started psychoeducating patients, we were a long way from understanding the neurocognitive difficulties in their everyday lives ... We had to go from a situation in which the doctor ordered treatment to one in which doctor and patient together elaborate a shared model of the illness and decide on how to care for it."[19] In the new school of psychiatry, patients engage in exercises performed *with* them. Therapeutic ideas therefore go from adaptation to capability – a tectonic shift.

To be part of society, one must be capable of doing and being. Recovery (as an achievable objective) and rehabilitation (as a set of practical means) are the global institutional responses to problems raised by bringing psychiatric patients into the community. Their philosophy is clear and bright, as one of its American proponents recalled in 1994: "The central goal is to enable such individuals to develop their capacities to the fullest extent possible."[20] Such an ideal involves social organization centred on individuals, not only on their needs, but also, and this is newer, on *their values*. It pursues individualist strategies adopted by scientific psychologists in the early 1970s, whose aim was to place control in the hands of individuals (Miller, Bandura, etc.) by motivating them to develop these "dispositions to act," otherwise known as skills. Recovery also falls within the change of approach to disabilities that substitutes the handicapped individual with a handicapable situation, a change that was ratified by the UN in 2006 with the Convention of the Rights of Persons with Disabilities. This established that, instead of putting emphasis on compensating for deficits, it would be better to provide support for the people in need, allowing them to make decisions concerning themselves and to develop the capacities to do so.

Recovery is a system of action that implements the abilities to do and to be, which makes it possible to fulfill the individualist contract of autonomy, and without which the subjects cannot be part of society. It is an offer of support to the individuals, who, on the one hand favours "acting *with* them" over "acting *on* them," and, on the other hand, shifts emphasis away from *compensating* for the deficit to *increasing* potential. Regulating behaviour is thought of less in the classic terms of directing consciousness, which consists of compensating for the defective will of the unhealthy individuals. More recently, it has become about supporting the individuals so they are capable of adopting a personal course of action when faced with a multiplicity of contingencies; in other words, in the contemporary idiom, to make good decisions.

Recovery is both the key concept in offering support to the mentally ill subjects in public and the concept by which they are emancipated as individuals, the reference by which they become moral and social partners. Recovered patients are capable patients, in the sense that, even with symptoms and depending on varying aspects, they must be able to assume responsibility for their lives to a certain degree.

In the 1970s, around the same time that Albert Bandura espoused his ideas on self-efficacy, the United States witnessed an expansion of social skills training. The first method, Personal Effectiveness for Successful Living, was built "on the motto of the National Association of Social Workers, 'helping people help themselves.'... [S]ocial skills training aims more specifically to teach people to help themselves." The objective of this method was to "enable clients to learn how to get their own needs met with less involvement of ... clinicians."[21] In other words, it was about getting subjects to a point of minimal self-understanding in order to value their own goals. The aim of social skills training was formulated with George A. Miller's idea of giving psychology away: "What better way to empower a mentally disabled person than to equip that person with the know-how and skills to meet his or her own needs without direct assistance from a clinician?"[22] This program was brought to France starting in the 1980s, mostly in the form of role-playing, helping exercise "target skills," offering aspects of socialization with professional guidance.[23]

Looking to develop individual capacities, rehabilitation practices employed a key idea from psychodynamic therapy: individuals, and not the therapist, are the principal agents of their own change.

To grasp what is at play here,[24] we must go back to the foundation of this guided exercise, also known as psychotherapy. At its outset, psychotherapy was a guidance of consciousness that compensated for a lack of will in subjects afflicted with an illness, in order for the subjects to make changes. It was therefore an action. In behavioural therapy or traditional cognitive therapy, the end of the activity is already determined in the mind of the agent (therapist), the subjects being treated as students, as patients. However, in an action, there is not only an agent and patients, since the subjects undergoing therapy are also doing something (a cognitive exercise, for example). They are acting on their own, but in a subordinate way. It is therefore important to specify degrees of acting, which allows us to distinguish between a principal agent (here, the therapist) and immediate agents (the subjects in treatment). The main role is held by the therapist, who is the principal agent of change. The support shifts from being a relationship in which the clinician is the principal agent of the patients' change (she trains the students) to one in which the patients assume this role, are treated as partners, and therefore are in a situation to be the principal agents of their own change. This practice of acting on what the individual is going through involves a reading grid that mobilizes three couplets: handicap-asset, symptomatic healing/functional amelioration, and symptom/life experience. This grid makes it possible to dig deeper into the different modalities of capacity.

Rehabilitation practices are generally cognitive and behavioural. Philosophically, they are an institution of Humean essence: they consider individuals as practical subjects, engaged in the action, associating means and ends; they offer support to individuals through exercises that allow them to take on new behavioural habits and thought processes. Epistemologically, these practices are situated in a tradition of scientific psychology, the keyword for which is *learning*. Sociologically, they act, engrained with the ideals of hidden potential.

The Neurocognitive Version of Recovery

The major change in the *idées-forces* of cognitive and behavioural approaches went from the idea of patients as students, whom the therapist teaches solutions and trains to take on other behavioural habits or ways of thinking, to that of expert partners, who must develop skills to find solutions to their problems. At the same time, the attention of professionals went from evident cognitive distortions that need correcting toward underlying cognitive processes that need modifying and that treat information. However, the concept of exercise is sharply complexified when exercises in autonomy are involved. It goes from being static to dynamic, *developmental*, meaning it has a concrete application in real life.[25] For those who side with cognitive neuroscience, this change depends on a conception of schizophrenia as a neurocognitive developmental disorder with, in most cases, neuropsychological deficits. One article from the *Schizophrenia Bulletin* in 2006 provides the reason for it: "Cognitive function in schizophrenia is one of the most critical determinants of quality of life in schizophrenia, potentially more so than the severity of other aspects/symptoms of schizophrenia such as hallucinations, delusions, or even negative symptoms."[26] There is consensus on this point.

In a journal on the "social brain," published in 2004, Thomas Insel, then director of the National Institute of Mental Health, shed light on the neurodevelopmental side of disorders like "autism and schizophrenia," which "are characterized by abnormal social cognition and corresponding deficits in social behavior." Within the framework of this new viewpoint, "social neuroscience offers an important opportunity for translational research with an impact on public health."[27]

In cognitive psychology, a distinction is made between conscious cognitive processes, which are controlled, and unconscious, which are automatic. In schizophrenic patients, the former are affected. These processes affect secondary socialization – attention span, memory, learning, conceptualization, the ability to plan, controlling one's own behaviour, flexibility of thought. These deficits create cognitive bias and systematic error. They affect the intelligence of human relationships, and therefore social functioning. Particularly affected are the perception of emotions (like facial expression and tone of voice), the perception of intentions (theory of mind), and attributional style, which describes how the subject attributes causes to events. These derangements of secondary socialization result in neuronal connections that should not have been established as the brain was developing during infancy and adolescence.

Multiple variations of cognitive exercises were developed around the idea of recovery. Behavioural and cognitive therapies were being practised at the same time, but were supposed to be particularly committed to the contents of thought. The term *cognitive remediation* is the most widely used, but remains an issue of cognitive training systematically referring to the biological foundations of thought and emotion. Further ahead, we will see the neurobiological explanations of the social and therapeutic effects, or in other words, that the bench should be brought to the bedside.

In cognitive enhancement therapy, patients are given "enriched cognitive experiences through computer training and secondary socialization opportunities ... In this respect, the program incorporates an individual neurocognitive training program involving cognitive exercises designed to enhance attention, memory, and problem-solving abilities and a social-cognitive group that focuses on improving the social-cognitive abilities ... such as taking the perspective of others, reading nonverbal cues, and adjusting knowledge about the rules and norms of behavior based on the social context."[28] The general dynamic of cognitive exercises goes beyond habit-making and toward reflexive exercise, like evaluating context or attributing intent.[29] A meta-analysis published in 2007 by an American team strongly concluded, "Cognitive remediation programs that included strategy coaching had stronger effects on functioning than programs that focused only on drill and practice."[30]

Let us take a case study from a French team renowned in the theory of mind.[31] Schizophrenia comes in many forms, but its common thread is a difficulty to communicate and therefore act appropriately in given situations. Thus, research and care are aimed at communication difficulties. It can be broken down into difficulties in attributing intentions of others and in treating "social cues" or "social keys": "Difficulty of contextual treatment seen in schizophrenic subjects does not affect all contexts, but only semantic ones, and more than a 'deficit' of contextual treatments, we must talk about an impairment of contextualisation processes in patients who express themselves in the dynamics of the situation and how they interact with the elements that constitute it." Therefore, we must go beyond the very notion of deficit found in the lesion model of neurology. "It is not enough to show that schizophrenics do not establish, in any given task, a cognitive function similar to that of a normal subject, what matters is knowing what they use as a response strategy."[32] It would thus be better to move away from a neuropathology and toward a "cognitive neuro-psychopathology" that does not start from the lesion, as if there were an organic cause to the mental illness, but that adopts "an actual 'cognitive' point of view that underlies most studies completed on normal subjects. According to this point of view, cognitive processes and the representations on which they act happen in the brain."

Cognitive neuroscience does not postulate that "behaviour possesses a direct cerebral inscription."[33] Nevertheless, the cognitive operations underlying it would have, for their part, such an inscription. In this framework, it is no longer about learning how to behave, but "rehabilitating" the strategy of the deficient operation. In rehabilitation, there is the idea of empowerment, a notion involved in making one capable. The team from Versailles thus devised an application for trust games, where the subject matches the intentions of others. We are in a mechanism that puts into practice subjects' theory of mind and their ability to recognize emotions: they "interpret emotional displays from a female virtual agent, and decipher her helping intentions."[34] A helping intention is considered as a mode of a "cooperative intention." The goal is to better the subject's theory of mind by working on "generating hypotheses on the intention of others and selecting the most plausible hypothesis."[35] Training extends to reflexive capacities, those that are more complex, to integrate them as a part of the individual, so they go hand-in-hand with the individual, much the same as breathing.

In the CogRemed program, the patient is "an actor … in the interactive construction of this re-education, and is quickly engaged in a dynamic of success that makes him aware of the crucial cognitive dimensions like problem solving, the ability to plan, elaborate, memorize, that he can mobilize his attention and cognitive resources to solve a complex cognitive problem. The care team realizes from this to what extent these difficulties constituted a taboo for the patient. The patient discovers that a positive dynamic can be engaged, bringing a possible integration into society,"[36] a dynamic in which skill and motivation feed one another in a virtuous circle, in order to increase social capacities.

Strategies recommended by the *Encyclopédie medico-chirugicale* (psychiatry) in 2012 were based entirely on repetitive exercise: "Learning without error, extensive repetition of the task, doing exercises that gradually increase in complexity, support, positive reinforcement, verbalization."[37] These exercises can be used for schizophrenia as well as eating disorders or Asperger's.

They can all be accompanied by neurofeedback, which allows for the measurement of brain activity during the exercise. Visualization offers feedback to the subjects who can then adjust their training. "The aim of the neurofeedback training is to teach the brain to attain an appropriate state and to be able to maintain that state.

When we succeed, we can say that we have enhanced the brain's capacity for self-regulation, and that we have done this with the help of neurofeedback."[38] These techniques to train the brain are aimed at teaching individuals to modulate certain parts of their brain's activity by visualizing it in real time. Such techniques can thus be used for cases in which voice-hearing patients resist conventional forms of treatment.[39] Neurofeedback is a compilation of mental training exercises (based on neurophysiology, synaptic plasticity) derived from concepts in cognitive behavioural therapies (CBT) and coaching. "NF [neurofeedback] is a non-invasive technique that enables an individual to learn the cognitive strategies required to change neurophysiological activity (i.e., EEG), for the purposes of improving health and performance. The originality of NF is that it gives patients a more active role in their own health care and comprises a holistic conception in which cognitive and brain activities are modified together ... NF facilitates an on-line self-regulation of brain activity and as such may be considered as an adaptive and interactive brain therapy."[40] Whatever practices the professionals reference, they are all presented with the same approach.

CBT also took a resolutely individualist turn. The first CBT applied to psychosis aimed at correcting symptoms, but starting in the 1990s, they were extended to the patient's "cognitive restructuring."[41] One article published in 2006 by the *American Journal of Psychiatry* insists that therapy must take an interest in the meaning of the symptoms for the patient, that CBT "explores and develops the patient's own understanding of his or her symptoms," or that it helps patients "gradually learn to engage more constructively with their voices." Such therapy would be "perhaps more acceptable – or less demoralizing – for patients struggling with the personal meaning of what is happening to them."[42]

So now, there was a new wave of CBT.[43] As we saw, the keyword for scientific psychology from the beginning of behaviourism is *learning*. However, over the past thirty years, psychology has evolved with the new label of *clinical psychology*, by giving itself goals that go beyond correcting negative or faulty thoughts, like "Socratic dialogues, guided discovery, behavioural experiments, exposures to the feared and avoided, psycho-education and teaching the skills of self-monitoring, self-reflection and self-change. CBT ... is about helping people understand how they have become trapped by their attention, reasoning and safety-seeking strategies and how to find ways to develop out of those traps."[44] New approaches were introduced, like mindfulness, dialectical behaviour therapy, acceptance and commitment therapy, etc. Beyond traditional CBT, there was a development of "sophisticated models of mind, combining various aspects of psychodynamic theory with a better understanding of non-conscious process, attachment theory, somatic memory (i.e., conditioning)."[45] There is also a trend that uses patients' narratives in cognitive behavioural therapy for treating psychosis.[46] The exercises go toward augmenting reflexive capacities that were the prerogative of "psychodynamic theory."

AFFECTIVE COMPUTING AND MACHINE PARTNERS

A new day dawned when cognitive neuroscience and artificial intelligence met. During the 1950s, the association between information technology and psychology had reintroduced human intelligence using a scientific model, embodying human reason and carrying a knowledge ordinary individuals did not have at their disposal. Their second meeting, at the turn of the twenty-first century, involved the digital and the cerebral. It took place in a moral context of questioning the authority of experts to prescribe what correct behaviour the individual needed to adopt. This problem is less about having limited rationality than being systematically subjected to cognitive bias in a society where people must continuously make choices, and the general population suffers this new curse, known as decision fatigue. By allying digital and cerebral, the machine makes a huge shift away from being a mediator to being a partner, and increases the possibilities for exploring the diversity of our competencies, our most complex ones in particular, which are our social skills, our ability to establish and maintain relationships while being as comfortable as possible with their contingencies.

Toward a Digital Coach

In the past, automatism and quantification were synonymous with standardization, an antonym of creativity; they were worlds apart from anything related to individuality. Today, they evoke creativity and relational intelligence.

For people lacking relational and social skills, like schizophrenics or autistics, virtual reality and social robots offer perspective. Some such devices can be extended to treat people suffering from depression and anxiety, using therapeutic computer programs, thereby achieving a generalized distribution of psychology. What does this new technology bring to the table?

These programs enable people to train in situations similar to the real world. Here it is possible to simultaneously utilize different modes of action, be they sensory, visual, etc., also called a multimodal approach, all while conserving the advantages of the experimental apparatus used to measure cognitive (psychological) and brain activity. They represent a rapidly growing field: affective computing.

Programs with virtual agents whose function is to simulate interactions are being used more and more frequently.[47] By placing the subject into a simulated reality, emotions corresponding to real-life situations are triggered, unlike classic devices, which were more passive and of poorer quality. Virtual reality was created to play on the senses, to manipulate sensory impressions. These programs can be used in cognitive remediation therapy, which trains subjects in processes of increasing difficulty. By immersing the subject in a world made up of interactions between individuals involving emotional engagements, these exercises make it possible to surmount the "spectator gap." The aim is to study all of the *inferential* processes involved in natural interactions. Returning to the comments made by the university team from Lyon, the issue is "the lack of a real-world environment where patients are confronted with complex social interactions that take all components of social cognition into account."[48]

These practices help patients by breaking down complex situations and social interaction into simple elements. The RC2S program from the Lyonnais team, for subjects in remediation, guides a protagonist (Tom[49]) in predefined social interactions (ten scenes). The action takes place in steps. The first step analyzes the situation and interactions in which the subjects will be placed. For this, the therapist helps subjects to break down the situation, so that they work on specific elements. For the second step, patients are put in front of a computer to familiarize themselves with the social interactions into which they will be placed by virtual reality, situations where they will be able to experiment with a wide variety of skills (recognizing emotions, attributing intentions, etc.), one by one, and social relations described by all sorts of eventualities. The third step decomposes the patients' behaviour, interaction after interaction, so that they can work on the situation as a whole in each of its elements. The fourth step of this cognitive training is the review of exercises "to promote the transfer of strategies to daily life and their subsequent automation." When the final step is reached, the therapist and the patients go over the completed work, examine the difficulties that were encountered, and patients are pushed to give themselves two or three concrete objectives to reinforce the adopted strategies.

Patients are treated using criteria in parts, and each part comprises an exercise in the form of a training module, in order to adopt new habits, acquire Humean style automatisms, or to think much like one breathes. In its conclusion, "patients need to have ample opportunity for practice of skills until they become fully integrated and [at] least somewhat automatic."[50] New emotional computer technology raises hope for each person to develop the capabilities he or she is lacking in order to self-actualize, and conceivably this technology will go well beyond what we know today. Therapy is essentially relearning to socialize.

These recovery practices can very well be the object of a psychodynamic study in which patients work out "the clinical material ... in order to ... reappropriate it and give meaning to those places in which division and dislocation of the self-create risk."[51] They could also be used in psychodynamic and psychoanalytical approaches to psychodrama.[52] Cognitive, phenomenological, and psychoanalytical approaches are combined, creating behavioural habits and thought patterns that confer meaning to the ailment. This feeds a two-sided *complementary* psychodynamic, even psychoanalytical, and cognitive/behavioural movement – we will come back to this point in chapter 6. Supporting subjects by using behavioural and cognitive style practices, which facilitate habit-making through exercises, finds its psychodynamic complement in working out the meaning of relationships. The first engages individuals in parts and the second as a whole. In parts, because as a practical subject, their treatment includes specialized knowledge within different domains and skills (motivation-competency and learning through observation/imitation promoted by Albert Bandura are fundamental references).

At the same time virtual reality was being developed, new actors were making their way onto the scene of exercises in autonomy: robots. One function of robots is of particular interest to us: social, and therefore affective, robotics. Allistene, a French commission set up to reflect on research ethics in digital science and technology, considers that equipping a robot with affective capacities amounts to a three-pronged operation: "The ability a robot has to manifest what would correspond to humans as emotion (and what we would unjustly call language expressing emotions), to recognize emotional expressions in humans, and to reason by taking into account information relative to emotions. A robot with these capacities qualifies as 'affective.' A robot fitted with such abilities has a different way of interacting with each individual."[53] It is precisely this "different way" that makes it an excellent coach for training an infinite diversity of social skills to people manifestly lacking judgment for the social situations in which they are living.

Robot Assisted Therapy and Socially Assistive Robots are a component of the ALIZ-E project, part of the European Union's 7th Framework Programme for Research and Technological Development (FP7), which helps children who are on the autism spectrum.[54] Social robots "occupy a special niche between inanimate toys (which do not elicit novel social behaviors [only repetitive]) and animated social beings (which can be a source of confusion and distress to children with autism)."[55] They are designed as interfaces, which employ keys for social communication based on a range of modalities: they can direct their gaze using both their eyes and head, express emotions (thanks to the Facial Action Coding System), make facial expressions, and communicate verbally – they even have a motor that moves their mouth when talking. They are controlled using a technology called WoZ, the Wizard of Oz. They can be designed for any role: getting and keeping someone's attention, facilitating imitation (critical for learning), stimulate joint attention (for an activity with another person), etc. They help children learn to express their emotions and recognize emotions in others. The robot "reassures the [autistic] child thanks to its clear and predictable reactions, which are less susceptible to misinterpretation by the child, but which are nonetheless capable of offering an important support in the child's particular process in developing social skills"[56] – since it is the contingency of social relations that bothers the autistic individual. The social robot is a coach; it is a kind of teammate with the therapist, who does not replace her but can help to reduce her workload and, perhaps, allow the therapist to refocus on her primary task, the specific needs of the child.[57]

In their enlightening work, *Vivre avec les robots* (Living with robots), Paul Dumouchel and Luisa Damiano describe how empathy and artificial emotions come about in relationships between robots and humans, giving "rise to an affective dynamic that leads to pertinent social responses ... [and] enables an affective coordination with human subjects who experience difficulties with interaction, and this dynamic facilitates their entering into a social ecology centred on relations with other humans."[58] This perfectly highlights the interest for having non-humans to, in some way, positively engage people in society who would otherwise have no place in it. Using this point of view, robots function as substitutes or as interlocutors (and not, for example, as executive agents, like drones) and are potentially social actors, which means they will be found in all kinds of fields in which it is appropriate to create affective reactions, empathy, or theory of mind.

Associating cognitive neuroscience and artificial intelligence is expected to have a bright future not only for serious psychiatric pathologies, but also for all sorts of emotional difficulties and cognitive biases that modern life confronts us with. A recent event that took place in the United States illustrates this new situation.

The World Wide Brain: A Utopia for a Generalized Distribution of Psychology

On 31 August 2015, the director of the National Institute of Mental Health (the biggest public funder for research in "behavioural health" in the United States), Thomas Insel, published a blog post: "In the future, when we think of the private sector and health research, we may be thinking of Apple and IBM more than Lilly and Pfizer."[59] He estimates that two factors will lead technology firms toward biomedical and mental health research: big data ("companies that know how to extract knowledge from data have become essential partners for progress towards new diagnostics and therapeutics") and continuity of patient support made possible by digital technology ("the promise of technology to change health care, shifting it from episodic to continuous, from reactive to proactive, from physician-centered to patient-centered"). Two weeks later, it was announced in the press that Thomas Insel was leaving his current position for one at Google Life Science, in which he would explore pathways enabling the expansion of its missions to detect and prevent illness through digital technology and bring it to "mental illness."[60] Insel is an emblematic figure of the World Wide Brain.

What domains will be targeted? Two major themes of scientific psychology: prediction of behaviour and training. For the first theme, a proactive approach is in play, like detecting risks likely to trigger psychosis. The NIMH, Insel recalls, is "developing algorithms to identify and analyze speech as an early window into the disorganization of thought."[61] For individuals who are at high risk of psychosis, these algorithms have already been used to detect those risks that will trigger one.[62] Regarding treatments, many of them "are psychosocial interventions, and those can be done through a smartphone. And most importantly, it can affect the quality of care, which is a big issue, especially for psychosocial interventions … One of the best treatments for depression is cognitive behavior therapy. It's building a set of skills for managing your mood. You can do it with a phone as well as face to face. A lot of people with severe depression or social phobia or PTSD don't want to go in to see someone. This lowers the bar."[63] Today, automating psychotherapy is an important step, be it to treat pathologies, like anxiety or depression, or to practise better control over one's emotions before a job interview.

A set of partnered technology has set in motion the dream of giving psychology away in such a way that all can become experts on their own lives. Therapy and support are not only becoming accessible everywhere, at any time, and in a variety of forms, but they can now take place without any human reference whatsoever. By going from an intermediary status to that of partner, the machine has found its niche as a digital peer support, embodying, through technological devices, our collective representations for regulating behaviour.

The World Wide Brain can be defined as a set of practices using digital technology that allows for, on the one hand, an increase in individual capacities, be it making habits or developing perspicacity (*augmentation*, to use a keyword from the digital world), and, on the other hand, relationships (*connections*, to use another key word). An increase in cooperation and exchange goes through a technosocial system in which each person *automatically* contributes to a cooperative *effect* that experts call "collective intelligence" – this effect itself increases individual capacities. Everything happens around the relationship and the individual, and is constructed around a major concept of behavioural science: cognitive bias. The intelligence of digital technology helps us avoid cognitive bias, trains us, and obtains cooperative effects.

Computer-assisted therapy, cognitive bias modification, intelligent personal assistants (Siri), diagnoses done by computers, continuous monitoring of fluctuations in a patient's state, etc. – we have a set of technology partners for the problem-solver.[64]

The Apple app Siri, an intelligent assistant, is a BFF to Gus, who is affected by autism. With robots and animals, he can use new support tools for autistics. "Gus had never noticed Siri before, but when he discovered there was someone who would not just find information on his various obsessions (trains, planes, buses, escalators and, of course, anything related to weather) but actually semi-discuss these subjects tirelessly, he was hooked. And I was grateful."[65] The assistant helps him develop certain skills, such as pronouncing words more clearly, so he can be better understood; it educates him on social cues or allows him to practise conversations that can be transposed to humans. SRI International, who created Siri, works on devices that can hold complex conversations. These machines have more patience than a human would and can be used as companions that encourage development in disabled children.

Avatars that are substituting for psychotherapists, like Sim Sensei, are another example, as described in "The Computer Will See You Now," in the *Economist*: "Ellie is a psychologist, and a damned good one at that. Smile in a certain way, and she knows precisely what your smile means. Develop a nervous tic or tension in an eye, and she instantly picks up on it. She listens to what you say, processes every word, works out the meaning of your pitch, your tone, your posture, everything. She is at the top of her game but, according to a new study, her greatest asset is that she is not human."[66] According to a study cited by this weekly magazine, those who thought a human was controlling the avatar were more reticent in giving out personal information. Individuals confide more easily in Ellie than in a human being. There is an advantage there for the treatment of certain populations, like military personnel who, since they have to put on a tough facade, avoid going to see a psychologist. "Just talking to it makes them feels better, just like if they were talking to their dog. And people open up a lot, and confide in the machine."[67]

It has become possible to create programs that are time-saving in the activity of psychotherapy, which can be very time-consuming. For example, with people who are addicted to drugs, teaching them alternative approaches in CBT is effective because it is repeated. These repetitive tasks drain the therapists' resources and the therapists themselves. Such tasks can be handed over to computer programs. One psychiatrist developed such a training exercise based on computer treatment that is applicable to CBT (CBT4CBT, Computer-Based Training for Cognitive Behavioural Therapy), which works like peer support. "The key characteristic is not the cognitive instruction,... it is the patient's ability to identify emotionally with characters in a brief vignette who experience the same challenges the patients face." It is a question of the patient being able to identify with people experiencing the same issues and hardships. In cases with patients suffering from addiction, proponents of these techniques think the traditional identification with a therapist is more difficult than with people having gone through the same experience. The idea is as follows. Actors awaken emotions that patients are susceptible to feel in a small psychodrama, often inspired by a TV series: "The computerized psychodrama supports not only repetition of problematic situations, but through the psychodrama, continues to involve the patient emotionally in these conflicted situations."[68] The limitation lies in the therapeutic tasks that cannot be digitized, like empathy from a therapist who helps patients discover the problematic aspects of their personality, or transference.

To treat the cognitive bias at the heart of anxiety and depression, in particular "an attentional bias toward threatening information," training procedures have been developed. A major portion of this research is centred on social anxiety, to reduce selective attention to threatening stimuli, using "a computerized attentional training task."[69] This task does not necessarily need a therapist and does not go through (actually on the contrary) an exploration of feelings and emotions. The basic idea is that anxious people have an unconscious tendency, in a crowd for example, to pay closer attention to faces that are hostile than to those that are welcoming or neutral, "as if they see only the bad apples in a bushel of mostly good ones." The goal is to train the subject to turn away from the hostile faces. The motive for the technique, according to the psychiatrist who developed it, consists in repeating the exercise to "train the eyes to automatically look away, or the frontal areas of the brain to exercise more top-down control."[70] It "does look extremely promising, if only because it offers a way out for those whose answer to the question, 'Do you want to talk about it?' is a resounding 'No.'"[71]

An entire movement around life skills has flourished and found a place online, organized around increasing connections, aided by the platform, the connected object, and the data. "Soon this technology will be all around us, helping us make more intelligent decisions or positively modifying our habits and routines. Simply put, it will help us help ourselves."[72] These new objects are designed to increase our ability to adopt adequate behaviours using small reminders or exercises to take on a multitude of everyday situations. Digitizing affective data – affective computing – helps accelerate how psychology is distributed as well as how it is used in various situations, even those that require working-out, notably for people with difficulty in social relations. "Therefore, we can succeed in using technology to forge new boundaries with ourselves, and is that not the biggest goal? After all, the clear effect of self-betterment is a world in which we can feel more empowered and able to work together towards a common good."[73] Expanding boundaries of the self – increasing one's value – all while cooperating with others, is influencing both individuals and their relationships. We understand the coherence of all these practices and ideas, but what is it that acts on the individual, and how? With this question, we have come to the moment in which we must question the understanding of humans by understanding their brain and organism.

BIOLOGICAL, PSYCHOLOGICAL, AND SOCIAL: ACTING ON NEURONAL CIRCUITS OR FINDING AN ACCEPTABLE WAY OF LIFE?

Cognitive neuroscience has followed to a *T* the movement of ideas and values by going, like in many other places, from standardized approaches to programs that are both flexible and individualized. But how do we distinguish and bring together the biological, psychological, and sociological aspects?

Biology: What the Bench Brings to the Bedside

Empirical evidence shows concomitant variations between brain circuits and thoughts or emotions. They can constitute a weak interpretation (correlations) or a strong interpretation (causes). In this case, acting on a human being is essentially acting on neuronal systems through the modification of synaptic connections. The concept of cerebral plasticity is the biological mechanism that ties these elements together. Practices that refer to neuroscience are therefore expressed using a language of mental physiology, which is to say these practices ultimately anchor behaviour to physiology. Still, it is important to remember that biological reasoning is not organicist, but functionalist: cerebral dynamics are at work, not lesions needing to be compensated for, which makes it possible not only to look at human complexity, but thanks to synaptic plasticity, to consider that the brain is able to modify itself internally, and we do not know its limits.

Let us look at a dossier on cognitive and social neuroscience applied to psychiatric pathologies published by the *American Journal of Psychiatry* in 2014. It attempted to systematically link psychology and physiology. The articles were presented by two editorials, one on the variety of psychosocial interventions from one of the principle proponents of recovery, John Strauss, and the other on the place taken up by cognitive neuroscience in explaining syndromes and treatments (where and how it acts). The first evokes the diversity of problems that individuals are treated for today, and it highlights that the most deficit-ridden patients are "capable of acting in a totally normal way."[74] It then applauds the diversity of psychological treatments that can be used. The second editorial presents, to use its title, a "cognitive neuroscience trifecta," that fulfills the new "translational" approach (in other words, from the biologist's bench in the lab to the patient's bedside in the hospital), since "what we do know is that these interventions exist and that we can now reliably identify and measure the brain functioning correlates of these processes."[75] Here we have manifestly entered into a veritable science of behaviour, taking into account individual singularity, a personalized science.

The file comprises three articles: a review of cognitive training, a meta-analysis comparing psychological interventions, and a study on cerebral activations in an observation/imitation task.

The review of cognitive training is "a sophisticated attempt to highlight the neurobiological benefits of cognitive training."[76] The goal of the training itself is the "improvement or restoration of physiological mechanisms in individuals at all levels of functioning."[77] It "aims to drive learning and adaptive neuroplastic changes in an individual's neuronal representation systems through specifically defined, neuroscience-based, and controlled learning events."[78] This type of training involves less the idea of compensating for a deficit than it does reviving a biological process. It concentrates on neuronal circuits more so than it does syndromes and "harness[es] neuroplasticity mechanisms for cognitive enhancement in impaired neural systems." It may one day be possible "to identify the key neural system impairments unique to individual patients and prescribe personalized cognitive training programs in order to enhance cognition, improve community functioning, and optimize well-being."[79] Cognitive training is "an intervention that uses specifically designed and behaviourally constrained cognitive or socio-affective learning events, delivered in a scalable and reproducible manner, to potentially improve neuronal system operations. The eventual goal of cognitive training is to target known neuronal mechanisms of behavioral impairment to affect clinical change."[80] These mechanisms could affect one's ability to imitate, resulting from mirror neurons activating differently in people with schizophrenia and leading to false perceptions of reality.[81] Such a result would support studies having shown that cognitive remediation therapies modify activity in the prefrontal cortex, which is essential to working memory in schizophrenic patients.

Now we can understand the assertion from a French university team that summarized the mindset in which cognitive neuroscience looks at mental disorders: "Cognitive remediation is part of a fundamental renewal in our way of looking at schizophrenic disorders, the biological substrate (cerebral dysfunction) of which is no longer viewed independently from a psychological approach renewed by cognitive neuroscientific contributions."[82] Experts continually repeat that psychology and biology are indissociable when it comes to bringing about change in patients. A French manual for therapists detailing the RECOS cognitive remediation program asserted that by "relying on cerebral plasticity and uncovering the often underestimated potential for rehabilitation, cognitive training encourages not only cognitive performance in patients, but also their social and professional reintegration thanks to a behaviour better adapted to their environment."[83] According to a state-of-the-art program established by the NIMH in 2012 on "cognitive training in mental disorders," methods that use "neuroplasticity mechanisms for cognitive enhancement in impaired neural systems show promise as evidence-based interventions in psychiatry."[84] "The eventual goal," the authors specify, "is to target known neural mechanisms of behavioral impairment to affect clinical change."[85] Paul Gilbert, a British psychologist who promotes a complex approach to cognitive behavioural therapy, summed up this mindset well: "Psychological interventions in the future are going to be much more sensitive to individual variation in physiology and genes, much more orientated to tailoring specific inputs, and brain-training exercises for particular people, and much more socially contextualised."[86] Behavioural science being organized according to individual variation, a personalized science of neurobiological dysfunction can then occupy a transversal spot, mobilizing clinical actors, like a social one.

Prestigious scientific journals, as well as manuals or practical guides depict problems and their solutions as mental physiology. If the explanations put forward all remain hypothetical, if there are debates within the social neuroscientific community, if we have no hard empirical evidence on the set of cerebral mechanisms correlating to factor X, the general philosophy of this entire venture is nevertheless to correlate cerebral mechanisms, behaviour, thoughts, and emotions. However, the strong explanatory function given in what we just read on the concept of cerebral plasticity goes happily beyond epistemological prudence. It rests on the idea that activating a region makes it possible to enhance a function. Therefore, according to Denis Forest, "Activating a region with a stimulus is not equivalent to determining a function. It is but an instrument of it, the observed effect remains subject to debate."[87] In other words, we must not confuse the correlation between stimulus and activation with that of causality. If, on an empirical level, it clearly appears that there are variations in these regions and in the brain–behaviour relationship, their *specific* effects on the individual are not assessable.

If we are interested in the effect of practising these exercises, it would not be possible to dissociate the neurobiological argument on plasticity from the moral/social argument. The epistemological/scientific issues and the moral/social issues are inseparable. It is seen on a therapeutic level, because on the level of a concrete individual three aspects (biological, psychological, and sociological) intertwine to such an extent that we confuse cerebral plasticity and plasticity in terms of an individual's educability or capacity to change.

Psychology: Holistic Indirect Effects of the Practical Subject's Exercises

We have already mentioned the model of the musician used to translate reasoning into an everyday language. Here are two other examples. An article written on the "social influences of neuroplasticity," in the "News in Focus" section of *Nature* from 2012, previously cited, refers to it: "Studies on intervention explicitly designed to promote positive emotional qualities, such as kindness and mindfulness, imply that such qualities might best be regarded as the product of skills that can be enhanced through training, just as practice will improve musical performance and produce correlated regionally specific anatomical changes."[88] Musicians' skill comes from corporal learning, and it becomes one with them. Such a reference can regularly be found the moment a non-reflexive self-understanding is mentioned. Philosopher Galen Strawson, in his influential article "Against Narrativity," uses this several times to take moral, and even therapeutic value away from the idea that a fulfilled life must necessarily be told: "People can develop and deepen in valuable ways without any sort of explicit specifically narrative reflection, just as musicians can improve by practice sessions without recalling those sessions."[89] If there is a tendency to favour self-examination and reflexive knowledge, there is no moral reason to consider an exercise in itself as producing inferior styles of life. It is a matter of self-knowledge by way of the body, a knowledge enabling one to be at ease and, consequently, facilitating the action to be performed. These exercises are for practical subjects who, in order to act, must adjust their means to an end, but in doing so, they have an indirect global effect on the individual.

Ellen Corrin, psychoanalyst and anthropologist, demonstrates that narratives from patients in recovery

> points to the importance of mastering everyday actions, to reinsert oneself into a project framework by setting, for example, short-term objectives and encouraging each other, and supporting each other in success and failure; the importance also to be able to decide for oneself the actions on which to center one's attention, to be able to feel proud of the accomplishments that, from the outside, may seem of little importance ... It could be said that, in this context, acquiring basic skills holds great importance, but the purpose is far from being essentially instrumental; such skills are often found as a sign or mediation value in reviving the being's activity, endowed with meaning that extends beyond instrument efficiency.[90]

Instrument or modular efficiency (relearning to run errands in town by being plunged into a virtual reality program, for example) goes beyond the practical mastery of adjusting one's means to an end. At the same time, it is likely to provide support for finding a place in the world, a personal place.

The benefits of training help individuals make new habits or reinforces a behaviour that enables them, through know-how achieved by a certain practical mastery, to acquire know-how-to-be.[91] Exercises influence the "restitution mechanisms" that are well-established in various traditions (German psychiatry, American psychoanalysis, indeed Lacanian psychoanalysis), the characteristics of which we have stated. Acquired skills facilitate positive subjective actions and motivate subjects to continue. The mechanics of practical exercises function, because they have indirect consequences on individuals when considered in their totality, in particular the increase of individuals' capacity to socialize. Although the mechanisms by which brain circuitry operates and acts on the entire being remain perfectly hypothetical, the psychological mechanism of indirect global effects is completely real.

By distinguishing between symptom and experience, and by placing emphasis on the assets best suited to reduce disabilities, recovery practices institutionally encourage these mechanisms. They are perfectly situated in the psychotherapeutic tradition of people suffering from psychoses, in which the therapist must not occupy any position of authority whatsoever. Therefore the action is not to interpret, but rather to instill a communication dynamic enabling people to come up with a solution on their own, including the most idiosyncratic one.[92] Before, having this kind of attitude was unconventional, but today, with coaching and peer support, and their computerized extension on the World Wide Brain, this attitude is very common. So this extension is the expression of a set of shared values gravitating around hidden potential. Today there is generalized social support, a system of beliefs and collective rituals for "restitution mechanisms."

This global attitude in individualist societies, regarding contingencies in which uncontrollable negative emotions are at work, is at the heart of psychotherapy and rehabilitation practices. Additionally, this set of psychodynamic practices act on suffering and call on the search for intelligibility, or cognitive behaviour, and refer to training practices. Our psychological mechanisms of restitution are *sociological* rituals for reconstructing one's moral being. If these rituals characterize all of human society – in anthropology they are called propitiatory rites – in individualist society it consists of making the illness affecting you a part of yourself by socializing it, by converting it into an asset.

Sociology: Individualist Rituals to Reconstruct One's Moral Being

A quick detour through anthropology will highlight the interest in considering these therapies as rituals to reconstruct one's moral being. We are not considering recovery or neuroscience and behavioural science as religious rituals, which would disregard science, but it is important to highlight the ritual dimension of any practice, including when it is steeped in science, and thus clarifying how collective representations become an active force moving through the individual.

A short, smart article by Edmond Ortigues on ritual healing helps to specify how the rite works. Lineage societies in sub-Saharan Africa are characterized by their identification with a common ancestor. Their conception of illness doesn't distinguish between fault and illness, and when someone is affected by misfortune or illness, the cause is always found to be external to the individual. The illness comes from without, such as an ancestral spirit the clan did not pay tribute to. As a consequence, the spirit errs and possesses a body to persecute. Therapy helps to appease the errant spirit by organizing a worship: the spirit is thus transferred from the individual's body to the alter. The persecution requires a projective response: the illness must be driven out from the individual's body. The interesting comparison point here is that "it is not only the rab [ancestral spirit], it is also the individual who is fastened at the alter and so becomes an officiant ... He is fastened to the ancestral powers presiding over his destiny. So now, he cannot live in good health without indefinitely repeating the rites." "The healing ritual displaces the symptoms."[93] It drives the illness out of the individual by attaching it to the alter. In this society, the individual's fate is in the hands of the ancestral spirits. There is no interest in the psychology of the subject, in the individual. Subjects cannot act on their own to get out of the situation. In fact, they are released from this task. The alter places the individual's health in the hands of the ancestor, who is involved both negatively as persecutor and positively through the worship and alter.

Modern individualist society structures misfortune and illness using an entirely different type of anthropology. Exercises in autonomy are organized so that individuals take their health into their own hands as much as possible, which involves being creative with solutions. "Restitution mechanisms" indicate this style of appeasing the ill: "Efforts to establish meaning," writes Leader in his essay on psychotherapy for psychoses, "to build bridges between ideas, or to invent new lifestyles can appear outrageous or idiosyncratic, but they are a testament to an authentic work of creation."[94] With recovery, such an idiosyncratic use has been considerably broadened in a social context. Therapeutic training is a ritual involving creativity, which makes it possible to care for oneself. Recovery of the individual is not so much the medical expectation of trying to get rid of any symptoms, but is more the *moral* expectation of taking (a little, a little more, etc.) responsibility for oneself. Individualist rites do not consist of driving out the illness, but making it part of the self. These rites of self-transformation teach people how to be agents of their own change. Instead of being fastened to the alter, an individualist healing ritual sets a course for personal transformation, which socializes the negative and integrates the illness as part of the self. These practices are, by the way, part of a long history of spiritual practices and exercises of interiority in Western society. Today they are emotional exercises for everyone to use.

So social life today offers an array of possibilities for converting uncontrollable emotions *by socializing negativity*. Indeed, the underlying idea of "restitution mechanisms" now has social support: the considerable broadening of our concept of capability through the ideal of hidden potential reconfigures them using a typical/atypical pairing embodied in the high-functioning autistic, as we saw in chapter 1. As they become increasingly common, and therefore legitimate to justify the action, they broaden the collective support that helps socialize the ill. Society as a whole, so to speak, participates in the healing ritual.

Here is an example. An individualist equivalent to the lineage alter makes it possible to socialize the ill, and it is the new mental health institution. Experts by experience can turn themselves to peer support, but they can also be professional therapists. An article by Larry Davidson and his team (one of the major references on recovery, from Yale University) published in 2006 in the *Schizophrenia Bulletin* found that in the United States "groups, programs, and organizations run by and for people with serious mental illness and their families now outnumber traditional, professionally run, mental health organizations." Furthermore, "as the idea of peer support has spread, in fact, it has become almost as common to encounter mental health professionals disclosing their own histories of mental illness as it has been to find people with histories of mental illness becoming providers of care."[95]

Patients and professionals are changing at the same time. Personal accounts published in the *Schizophrenia Bulletin* or *Psychiatric Services* often show that when people work, they exercise their activity specifically in mental health institutions. The increase in ambulatory institutions and diversity of professional skills intervening in these problems has built a social environment big enough to attain personal fulfillment: people who are in recovery can use their individual qualities that have social utility.

Peer supporters themselves have often found idiosyncratic solutions to re-establish life balance. Amy Johnson works at the Yale program. She was diagnosed with paranoid schizophrenia (because she does not trust reality, she says). In 2015, she described her struggle to achieve a consistent and reliable self. Her weapon is the language of cognitive neuroscience: "My understanding of neural plasticity is that the brain can both learn and unlearn unwanted ways of thinking in favor of new, better ways of coping. But this type of learning takes time. When I blame my brain cells, how brain cells function, rather than blame myself for repetitive mistakes, it creates a willingness in me to try new styles of coping. It allows me to sort of play around with or try on new ways of acting. Self-blame keeps me stuck. Realizing that it's my brain and not me that is keeping me stuck helps a lot." Neural plasticity guarantees her that the brain can "unlearn" the symptoms by separating them "into behavioral ones and cognitive ones," and that she can therefore change "those old neuronal relationships, those old neural pathways and connections, by *withstanding the uncertainty of the unknown*, i.e., by trying 'on' or trying out new responses, by engaging in new, unfamiliar behaviors." Yet, to do this, there needs to be reasoning that is as solid as a "math equation, where if I do A then I will get B, and if I do B then I will get C."[96] By setting goals in a ritual manner (rigid, repetitive) for this equation, support is created for experimenting and innovating – the complete opposite of lineage healing aims, on the contrary, to re-establish continuity of tradition, indeed a cyclic repetition of time. Individualist ritual healing enables people to exercise enough emotional self-control to live in society, including those affected by the most extreme ills.

Nancy Riffert is a consultant specialized in providing support systems for recovery. She also has a psychotic disorder. "Telling me that I have a brain disorder and that I should take medication does not solve my problems ... Whether it was a brain disease or not, I did not want to have a mental illness."[97] This account can be set against that of Lisa Halpern (who does community service work in Massachusetts), entitled "Brain Training: An Athletic Model for Brain Rehabilitation." She states that the process of reconstructing a brain ravaged by schizophrenia strikes her as analogous to reconstructing a badly injured body. Yet it is not the brain as such, but the athletic training that she describes – using her own athletic practice as a triathlete as a basis. Multiple uses of cerebral references could be described as showing all possible modalities for this use of metaphorical language.

If we turn to the voice hearers, Eleanor Longden published an article in 2013 in the *Guardian* "Learning from the Voices in My Head."[98] It sums up the book she had just published: "Over the years, these voices have changed, multiplied, terrorized, inspired, and encouraged. Today they are an intrinsic and valued part of my identity, but there was also a time when their presence drove me to delirious extremes of misery, desperation, and despair." They brought her to the brink of madness, but they also elevated her and helped her obtain a university degree and discover fundamental therapeutic truths about herself. By transforming the tormenting voices into ones that became an asset, she demonstrated a skill that allowed her to remain in the social arena. Today, Eleanor is a psychotherapist and participates as a researcher in programs on auditory hallucinations.[99] In the opening of *Living with Voices*, a call is made to allow "all experience and all forms of evidence to be used at all levels."[100] On British and North American websites and blogs, there is often this type of approach.[101] The expansion of our social skills in terms of different capabilities and adopting a recognized lifestyle paints the picture of a society that could be better organized on individual singularity than it has been.

These are some of the most spectacular examples of socializing an illness. The ritual dimension is a blatantly clear order to invent: the subject must set an idiosyncratic definition with the use of an aid: "This act," Leader writes, "may include speaking, but it also implies a material creation: writing, drawing, painting, sculpting or any human practice of forging or inscription."[102] It is not so much a question of setting an idiosyncratic definition using an aid that objectifies it, since it lacks stability and torments the subject. What is important here is to call it out by name. Therapists have often noted patients coming up with neologisms – "handicapable" is an excellent example. Naming and objectifying symptoms can be a big help for the subject. "That is why the cognitive therapies," states Leader (though a Lacanian psychoanalyst), "are sometimes useful in such cases: they give the subject a language, a way of naming and ordering their experience." Jacques Lacan considered that, in treating psychosis, the therapist must play the role of "'the secretary of the alienated subject.'"[103] Personal accounts published by American scientific journals show that people use a wide variety of language games. They represent a therapeutic ritual enabling creative activity, which is manifested in these practices of self-expression. The moment in which meaning is given to the experience beyond the symptoms, encouraging patients to write contributes to socializing disturbed perceptions and uncontrollable emotions. To establish meaning with the use of an aid is to socialize the negative.

But an advocate of neurobiological explanations could retort that it does not call into question our arguments, since the efficacy of a therapeutic action is independent from what patients think, and the patients can, in fact, use whatever language they deem fit. Regardless of what they think, infra-personal mechanisms are at work, and being completely impenetrable to the subjects' conscious mind, act without their knowing. Let us conclude this chapter by starting to examine this argument.

Limits of the Neurobiological Argument: An Oversight of Language?

I tried to understand how social normativity and therapeutic normativity were interwoven. Our ideas of the individual in society – the social mind – and our ideas of therapy – the caring mind – have evolved interdependently. "Restitution mechanisms," long observed in classic psychiatry and psychoanalysis through psychotherapy, occupied a rather marginal space in the clinic. The rise of a system of collective representations of the individual in society characterized by the ideals of autonomy provided the moral environment that allowed them to occupy an entirely new space. The ideal of hidden potential is fundamental, because it puts in play an idea essential to modernity: individuals who, creating value (by socializing), increase their own value. This ability to self-expand gravitates toward an idea of change. The ideal of hidden potential, the patient as moral partner, and the paradoxical definition of illness using the antonyms *handicap/asset*, all form a system of action that produces and points to several capacities to change. It creates as many mobilizing ideals as are needed to guide the action.

The limits of the neurobiological explanation are empirical, because they rely on partial and hypothetical results, which the neuroscientific community has voiced, but the explanations insist that they are centred on material causes conveyed in the omnipresent idea of all sorts of cerebral "mechanisms."[104] There are obviously solid epistemological reasons for those in neuroscience to proceed in this manner. However, these reasons are, in this regard, less a naturalism than they are a materialism thought of in terms of cerebral and mental cogs and counterbalances. They account for the biological benefits of rehabilitation practices by suggesting that such a technique or modality of training works on this or that function, governs this or that skill, or activates this or that domain, with an effect whose result is therapeutic. Yet sociology and anthropology disagree precisely on this point.

Those in favour of the neuroscientific program tackle the efficacy of these practices and exercises as empiricist philosophers of yore, by isolating the basic rites in a worship that a lineage society forfeits to the ancestral spirits of the tribe. Like them, they don't see the necessity of the moral dimension without which there can be no material benefit. In *The Elementary Forms of Religious Life*, Émile Durkheim rightly criticized this way of understanding the action of religious rites. First, he notes that believers do not just believe when practising religious rituals; they can do more, since "a god is not merely an authority upon whom we depend; it is a force upon which our strength lies."[105] "The moral efficacy of the rite, which is real," he specifies, "leads to the belief in its physical efficacy, which is imaginary; that of the whole, to the belief in that of each part by itself. The truly useful effects produced by the whole ceremony are like an experimental justification of the elementary practices out of which it is made, though in reality, all these practices are in no way indispensable to its success ... So if a price is attached to these various manoeuvres, it is not because of their intrinsic value, but because they are a part of a complex rite, whose utility as a whole is realized."[106] The elements of a rite do not act materially on this or that problem. It is the whole of the ceremony that acts, using its moral authority on individuals, reconstructing their moral being. The whole, which is to say the mind, is necessarily shared, in which different elementary rites of a ceremony are performed or different modes of therapy are carried out, and on which each element relies as parts that are indissociable from one another. How does this mind act concretely?

The limit of the neurobiological argument lies in the fact that it could never explain why in one case the illness is projected, and in the other, incorporated. Social life is a necessary angle to be used for explaining therapeutic efficacy, but on the condition to integrate an element missing in neurobiological explanations: language. Indeed, cognitive neuroscience uses language, but it is given a place and function that is too narrow, that of replicating the material world without needing concepts or categories. In other words, to use Olivier Favereau's remark, language is "isomorphic to the world": it has been reduced to "a collection of labels placed on objects from an external reality,"[107] which consequently means that language does nothing.

The only explanation lies in the different ways of living and acting. This means that in social life, which makes it possible to easily grasp why an illness is projected on some and incorporated in others, that is because is it normative. "Beliefs are active only when they are partaken by many,"[108] asserts Durkheim. Their shared character makes them active. It is not that we don't know how ideas and values make their way into one's head, nor is it a collective consciousness kicking down the door of individual consciousness, but because living in society (lineage-based, individualist, or other) is to participate in a common meaning – shared beliefs – on which individuals act spontaneously like others, and use the rules of social grammar, to which they pay no more attention than they do regular grammar when speaking. For example, when a child learns a noun, like *father*, it learns what a father is, and then, progressively, the system of parental relations in his society. To socialize oneself is to be introduced to categories of nouns that enable one to think, but more importantly to live.[109] Since language is co-extensive to society, it does not depend on human will; it is inherited and therefore natural. All individuals make their own place by appropriating it little by little, and to a greater or lesser extent.

The social is shown in the two major attitudes concerning contingency. Only the system of collective expectations of the second allows individuals to act by giving themselves authorization. Today, this attitude finds support in the public sphere to a degree that was unimaginable four or five decades ago. It is supported by these new collective representations, which are capacities defined through a typical/atypical lens and that mobilize multiple social actors, like with recovery, and are at the root of many different lifestyles. Now they make up a shared signification, a common language of autonomy-as-condition, which all actors use, even when they are in direct opposition. In other words, they show the mind in which the action takes place.

Given that "the brain is the most complex object in the universe" and that research "has only just begun," it has mainly opened paths of exploration, proof showing the efficacy of exercises is always situated at the individual level. It is the individual's functional evaluation that counts. Neurobiological reasoning is situated at the infra-personal level of neurophysiological mechanisms. The neurobiological – material – argument is therefore indissociable from the psychological one, which describes a real mechanism, used by the individual, therefore on a personal level, as well as from the moral/social argument, the ideal of hidden potential that imbues shared beliefs, structures the actions of social partners and their reasons for acting in the first place, and that, as for it, plays on a supra-personal level.

Exercises in autonomy, on the level of the practical subject, in the empiricist sense of the term, have indirect global consequences on the individual, and are the condition for which the mechanics of passions – learning through exercise – is effective. However, exercise is not all; we need to continue the search for meaning and comprehensibility so the patient has enough benchmarks.[110] Besides, we have seen that cognitive behavioural references and psychodynamic references are not necessarily contradictory. How can these two major ways of reconstructing one's moral being take the modern individual's path to personal transformation? That is what we will look at now.

6

Is It My Ideas or My Brain
That Is Making Me Sick?

Neuroscience and Self-Knowledge

Master the neural assemblage, and we might at long last master us.
Richard Powers, *The Echo Maker: A Novel*

Mindful of the scholastic adage that whenever you meet a contradiction you must make a distinction.
William James, *What Pragmatism Means*

Stories about the trials of illness make up a literary genre that has
largely developed over the last forty years. This phase began at the
same time an explosion of memoirs hit in the 1970s. As early as
1977, Milan Kundera spoke of acute "graphomania" in *The Book
of Laughter and Forgetting*.[1] Experts agree that what this explosion
"coincided with, indeed was incited by the rise of handicap memoirs
… [that] have recently [the book was published in 1997] generated
a vast collection of life stories in memoir form."[2] More generally
speaking, starting in the 1990s, there was a rollout of personal
accounts of one's own life: television went down the path paved
by radio with reality TV,[3] and the internet and YouTube eventually
inserted these practices into everyday life. As we saw, major scientific
journals regularly published accounts of psychiatric patients.

In 1940 literary critic Lionel Trilling saw psychoanalysis as the
"ultimate tragic courage in acquiescence to fate."[4] The new understanding of the individual proposed by cognitive neuroscience does
not prescribe tragedy, but facilitates action. Does it provide analogous knowledge to help someone to continue living with the illness,
misfortune, or evil? In the search for the self, while simultaneously

working to transform one's fate, where does the cerebral establish itself? Is it possible to be content with a concept composed of neuro-physiological accounts underpinned by materialist morality, which itself is based on an individual's neuronal networks? In real life, is this account not combined in more ways with the search for an intelligibility that strengthens psychodynamic therapy? Such are the questions we wish to explore.

The first neurocognitive memoirs written (or co-written) by high-functioning autistic people revealed how seeing the world through the brain could be the foundation for a way a life, and could be valuable to civilization. The brain appeared as the biological basis for a self-reliance sufficient enough to live a social life instead of being locked away in an institution (see chapter 1). These narratives have given us clues to understanding both the disabilities and assets of these people. They helped to better understand their world, but also to give it value beyond the pathology or disability. This method of valuation is based on a narrative that uses current motivations the reader can appropriate. While reading *Emergence* by Temple Grandin, for example, there is a palpable social purpose everyone can grasp: being misunderstood and how to cope with it. It was therefore possible to put words to and give an identifiable shape to a broader human experience.

This last chapter will look at three case studies in order to describe how cognitive behavioural or neuroscientific and psychodynamic references can be put to use in an individual's life, at the level of the total person, intertwining the biological, psychological, and socio-logical. This allows us to shift focus, with scientific, therapeutic, and philosophical debates becoming existential questions. In this context, we can describe the way in which the brain and cognitive neuroscience meld into all other elements of life. It is a question of exemplifying some of the ways in which we rebuild our moral being and the contingencies that accompany them. The three studies comprise two memoirs, one from author Siri Hustvedt, *The Shaking Woman or a History of My Nerves* (2010), the other from Allen Shawn, *Wish I Could Be There: Notes from a Phobic Life* (2007),[5] and the third is a novel by Richard Powers, *The Echo Maker*, published in 2006. These three cases show a marked tension between the psychodynamic, indeed psychoanalytical, viewpoint and the neuro-scientific viewpoint. In no way do they claim to be representative or typical neuro-psychoanalytical narratives, nor do they claim to be neurocognitive narratives in general. Rather, they represent a few modalities among many in the search for intelligibility.

The authors are sophisticated individuals whose narration, either autobiographical or literary, is very evolved. They make readers sensitive to the confusion that is most often obscure to them, but the types of tension they highlight apply to a substantial portion of people today.

Here is an example. A patient suffering from obsessive-compulsive disorder (OCD) is treated using an experimental protocol known as deep brain stimulation. This surgical technique, which places implants into certain cerebral zones, was first used to treat Parkinson's disease, a motor function disorder. The surgery was expanded to OCD at the end of the 1990s, when it was discovered that stimulation influenced obsessional rituals in Parkinson's patients who also had OCD. The surgical technique opened a concrete path for treating psychic disorders (rituals) expressed as motor actions, and raised hope for overcoming the long-standing division between neurology and psychiatry. Following the procedure, the patient, a bit confused by his symptoms after the surgery, asks the neurologist and the psychiatrist very bluntly, "Well, is it a neurological or psychiatric problem?"[6] Regarding the apparent issues of overcoming the differences between neurology and psychiatry, this patient suggests that while these perspectives can offer solutions, they can sometimes create new problems.

These three works make it possible to condense the steps organizing the whole of this book, which is to show that the brain provides the material for one of the great tales of individualism, and that tale is an echo chamber in which powerful ideals of action and personal change are invested, relying on the guarantee of the scientific method. The truth of the neurocognitive expression of these ideals and solutions that it is likely to bring cannot be understood without being tested on human reality in its entirety, from which it is inseparable. This is what cannot be demonstrated in a lab with controlled variables.

These three case studies are not representative of a statistical point of view, nor do they depict reality and the impact of life experiences, and therefore in no way claim to thoroughly explore the subject. They set out to simply elucidate a few methods.

It is not a matter of taking a position regarding the narrative (which can be as much a way to pull the wool over your eyes as it could to open them widely, with all the possible combinations in between), but to describe how individuals make use of the two main ways to reconstruct their moral being – exercising in order to adopt new habits and making relationships intelligible – and, more broadly, the ways in which collective representations act concretely on individuals as ideals for thinking and acting. These stories fall within a philosophical style that Stanley Cavell called moral perfectionism. Used largely in the world of autonomy-as-condition, moral perfectionism is, in my view, a philosophical conceptualization of the collective representation of hidden potential.

MORAL PERFECTIONISM:
A PHILOSOPHY OF PERSONAL TRANSFORMATION

At the heart of moral perfectionism is self-reliance, the ability to depend on oneself. Self-reliance evokes, and rightly so, the strength of personal affirmation, an ability to care for oneself and not depend on others, at least not to a very visible or unacceptable extent. Therein is a virtuosity that is admirable or enviable. Another aspect was brought to the fore by Stanley Cavell by way of Ralph Waldo Emerson, that of receptivity, listening to the self.[7]

Emerson's *Self-Reliance* (1841) is a famous American manifesto, which begins, "To believe your own thought, to believe that what is true for you in your private heart is true for all men, – that is genius. Speak your latent conviction, and it shall be the universal sense." Self-reliance is the attitude of the person who "has ventured to trust himself for a taskmaster." It is opposed to conformity, the greatest requirement from society, of which "self-reliance is its aversion."[8]

The expression for self-reliance in French, "*Confiance en soi,*" does not account for the essential aspects of the American expression, since the idea of reliance is not found in the French meaning, which is more an idea of *trust* or *confidence*. Reliance mixes the notion of independence and the ability to rely on oneself. To be self-reliant implies listening to the self.

There are situations in everyday life in which meanings are hidden, and they force us to listen to what is happening to us: crises, for example, when things are no longer going well with a partner, when we lose a job, when we have a mysterious malady, etc. Life's compass goes haywire, and we no longer know where we stand. We can no longer read ourselves. This type of moral crisis and confusion – "secret melancholy" (Emerson) – that it brings about are more pervasive than the two main types of moral dilemmas highlighted in traditional philosophy: Kant's categorical imperative of right action and the utilitarian motive of good action, the morality of "what I must" and "what I want." Cavell starts with Kant, for whom individuals see their own existence through two points of view: the sensible world of objects, which is causal knowledge, and the intelligible world, which is freedom and the moral law of reasoning that transcends sensible knowledge. He considers moral perfectionism, a philosophy according to which Kant's metaphysical division is transformed into an empirical division, to be existential, in which the ordinary person is engaged. This does not oppose the right action and the good action, but creates tension in the idea that there is a duty to the self. Moral perfectionism is an education of the self, which comes in the form of a conversation that is simultaneously a confrontation. Through it, the individual passes from the confusion of a split self to the (relative) clarity of an "unattained but attainable self."[9] Cavell describes the moral reasoning of this philosophy as "making ourselves intelligible" to others and to ourselves. For instance, it "recognizes difficulties in the moral life that arise not from an ignorance of your duties, or a conflict of duties, but from a confusion over your desires,"[10] over what you want. In a lifestyle that greatly values freedom of choice and individual initiative – our world of autonomy-as-condition – the moral canons that were elaborated in the eighteenth century come up a little short to be used as a guide to life.

They come up even shorter for mental pathology, in which the body (sensible)/mind (intelligible) debate and the recurring question of knowing if what happens is of a mechanical or intentional order are part of the nature of the illness. So for those affected, the Kantian idea of two worlds, sensible and intelligible, becomes exacerbated within their own empirical reality. This division is part of the solution. Moral perfectionism therefore represents an attitude toward adversity – which is neither Kantian duty nor empiricist and utilitarian good.

In the explosion of narratives on illness, a subgenre recently emerged, linked to the growing popularity of neuroscience, called a neuro-psychoanalytic narrative. A narrative enters this category when it refers to psychoanalysis (or to a psychodynamic approach) and neuroscience at the same time. First, such an account contains moral perfectionism for two reasons. Because subjects are affected by an illness that plunges them into confusion: they no longer recognize themselves, are no longer intelligible to themselves, and are looking for perspective on their lives. Second, because they wonder whether this illness results from neurological reasons, where the symptom is a sign, or whether the reason is psychological, in which the symptom is intentional. Is it an impersonal lesion or personal relationships? This is a typical moral debate on their involvement in their own illness: is the symptom merely due to mechanical issues and thus must be dealt with using "mental disinfection," or is it a confused response to problems that have a raison d'être? Unless it is both conflict and complementarity coming across in the language used by the individual.

Since the three cases are American, it is worth noting that they were first developed, during the 1980s, in a psychiatric context that was increasingly practising a non-narrative understanding of the self, like that of the schizophrenic who forgets the self, as the *Schizophrenia Bulletin* highlighted in 1989 (see chapter 5). This marginalized a decisive aspect of the illness regarding the patient's care, especially mental or neurological pathologies that tend to be chronic: suffering, confusion, despair. Arthur Kleinman, an American psychiatrist and anthropologist, published a famous defence in 1988 on illness narratives, in which he sharply criticizes reducing psychiatric practices to what is hardest in biomedicine, and which "disables the healer and disempowers the chronically ill." It is a practical and dramatic error to eliminate the patient's voice because the biomedical model is not capable of tackling "the problem of illness as suffering" and confusion. We go from illness as a nosographic entity, the signs of which are symptoms, in the medical sense of the term, to suffering as a "relationship," the narrative helping express the experience and the health professional helping "to assist the chronically ill and those around them to come to terms with – that is, accept, master, or change – those personal significances that can be shown to be operating in their lives and in their care. I take this to constitute the essence of what is now called empowering patients."[11]

These narratives continued their rise into the context of recovery. From that moment, health professionals encouraged patients to write. These practices in self-expression (personal accounts, blogs, books, narratives) tell about journeys through adversity and use a wide array of language games. Jeffrey Geller, who in 2000 reviewed the thirty-four first-person accounts, a section that Psychiatric Services had opened in 1994 and that he headed up, wrote in his conclusion, "The message ... here is clear: allow us to be partners in our own treatment and care ... [P]sychiatrists and other mental health professionals worked to empower patients, although the term 'empowerment' was not often used. Now individuals with chronic mental illness want to empower themselves."[12] That involves some duties that we will look at through two memoirs. They will help us to understand how "exercising" and making the self "intelligible" organizes the various aspects of life for a writer who shakes and a phobic musician.

CAUSES AND REASONS: A DILEMMA FOR ONE AND HARMONY FOR THE OTHER

Just to give a quick contrast of the two narratives: in one, the subject, writer Siri Hustvedt, the shaking woman, is lost between the mechanical and the intentional, perception and belief, and eventually identifies herself *as* the shaking woman, the being, yet without knowing why, without identifying *it*; in the other is composer Allen Shawn, who would have loved to have been there were it not for his being phobic, and who eventually finds himself and harmoniously articulates – like a musical composition – two ways to reconstruct his moral being.

The Ambiguous Shaking of Writer Siri Hustvedt

Siri Hustvedt gave a talk honouring her father two and a half years after his passing. As soon as she pronounced the first words, she started to shake violently from the back of her neck downward: "My arms flapped. My knees knocked. I shook as if I were having a seizure. Weirdly, my voice wasn't affected ... When the speech ended, the shaking stopped. I looked down at my legs. They had turned a deep red with a bluish cast" (3).

She wonders if her problem is psychiatric or neurological, psychopathological or neuropathological, and what *psychopathological* and *neuropathological* actually mean. The narrative flows into new situations, with increasing frequency, trying to redefine psychopathologies and neuropathologies, in which the individual does not know whether the illness is neurological or psychological: what role do I play in my symptoms? Are they telling me something about myself or are they devoid of meaning, mere tricks of cerebral mechanics? In that question resides a new moral debate that confronts an increasing number of patients.[13] This mystery calls for a conversation, in this case a conversation with oneself in the form of a narrative. Confusion/division of the self and mechanical/intentional make up the framework in the search for a perspective that can shed some light on this shaking that makes her unrecognizable to herself while echoing the absence of her father. Siri Hustvedt's book is an attempt to answer the questions asked by the patient being treated for OCD: Is this a neurological or psychiatric problem?

Siri Hustvedt invites us to travel with her through the hardships of the afflicted subject who is unable to distinguish if her brain or her ideas are making her sick, to the extent that she wonders if it is not just one and the same. The search for the causes of shaking range from possible hysteria to the hypothesis of a temporal lobe syndrome – "I confessed to Dr. L that I sometimes wondered if I had it – a temporal lobe personality" (162), as some temporal lobe lesions can lead to epileptic seizures, and it was seen that subjects demonstrated greater interest in religious and ethical questions, as well as excessive emotional sensitivity.

Her own "travels in the worlds of neurology, psychiatry and psychoanalysis" (5) started with migraines since early childhood. She was fascinated by psychoanalysis starting at the age of sixteen, read a lot of Freud, but was always scared by the idea of undertaking therapy. She also admits to being fascinated by neuroscience and attending conferences at the New York Psychoanalytic Society & Institute, and contributed to the narrative medicine program at Columbia University: "What began with curiosity about the mysteries of my own nervous system had developed into an overriding passion" (6) for the mystery she represents to herself. Since the surprise of the shaking itself, her sensory world plunged her into a drama of self-recognition, of her own intelligible world: "The shaking woman felt like me and not like me at the same time. From the chin up, I was my familiar self. From the neck down, I was a shuddering stranger. Whatever had happened to me, whatever name would be assigned to my affliction, my strange seizure must have had an emotional component that was somehow connected to my father. The problem was that I hadn't felt emotional. I had felt entirely calm and reasonable. Something seemed to have gone terribly wrong with me, but what exactly? I decided to go in search of the shaking woman" (7).

As early as 1982, she had felt "as if some superior power picked me up and tossed me about as if I were a doll. In an art gallery in Paris, I suddenly felt my left arm jerk upward and slam me backward into the wall. The whole event lasted no more than a few seconds. Not long after that, I felt euphoric, filled with supernatural joy, and then came the violent migraine that lasted for almost a year" (4). This incident was followed by a list of beta blockers and anti-depressants, "a sleeping-drug cocktail I took in the doctor's office in hopes that I would wake up headache-free ... Finally, that same neurologist sent me to the hospital and put me on the antipsychotic drug Thorazine (the first antipsychotic, discovered in Paris in 1952)" (4).

Her search for the shaking woman started with hysteria, given the context in which the shaking occurred and the symptoms' capacity to imitate neurological disorders. She noticed the similarity to epilepsy (which also produces migraines). She was treated by a psychologist who, over a period of months, taught her biofeedback techniques (relaxing, increasing blood circulation, warming the body's extremities, reducing pain). She continued to shake and took benzodiazepines, which did nothing to soothe her illness. For years she took beta blockers for her migraines, which she eventually gave up on – because she could feel the shaking from within: "It was like shaking without shaking" (40). The beta blocker stopped her from shaking physically, but not morally. Her drawn-out experience with migraines is a model demonstrating how an individual can go from an ailment that she *has* to becoming a characteristic of what she *is*: "Alas, my life is lived in the borderland of Headache. Most days I wake up with migraine, which subsides after coffee, but nearly every day includes some pain, some clouds in the head, heightened sensitivities to light, sounds, moisture in the air. Most afternoons I lie down to do my biofeedback exercises, which calm my nervous system. The headache is me, and understanding that has been my salvation. Perhaps the trick will now be to integrate the shaking woman as well, to acknowledge that she, too, is part of myself" (174).

Must she start working on herself concerning the shaking? "The strangeness of a duality in myself remains, a powerful sense of an 'I' and an uncontrollable other. The shaking woman is certainly not anyone with a name. She is a speechless alien who appears only during my speeches" (47). But what is this silence saying? Bringing up conferences given by Pierre Janet at Harvard (in 1906), regarding a case of hysterical anaesthesia, for which "it is the faculty that enables the subject to say clearly, 'It is I who feel, it is I who hear'" (83), she wonders, "But who owns the self? Is it the 'I'? What does it mean to be integrated and not in pieces? What is subjectivity?" (47). The enormity of the questions (or their banality), which are formulated in a perfectly rhetorical way, underscores the disarray, and the formulation is itself made to underscore it. The alien makes her doubt. She no longer recognizes herself.

Incidentally, the way she speaks of psychoanalysis is closer to the splits in consciousness from Janet's psychology and his idea of the shrinking of the sphere of consciousness in hysteria than it does Freudian conflict – sexuality, for example, is not present, and is actually absent, especially if we compare Hustvedt's memoir to Shawn's, as we will see a little bit later.

Is the shaking alien that splits her into two, not her double? Doubles proliferate in neurology, but also in literature. These individuals are doubles in that they are split-brain – their division, like that of Janet, is not conflictual, like that of the Freudian symptom. These are doubles who suffer from a disconnection syndrome between cerebral areas (Do I shake because I have a systematic disconnection?) (69). Disconnection, a very popular concept as we saw (chapter 3), is used in cognitive neuroscience today to explain several syndromes. Evoking anosognosic patients who are affected in the right hemisphere of the brain, who deny their affliction, she reintroduces splitting: "Neglect and denial of illness seem to redraw the boundaries of the body and liberate the conscious 'I' from having to worry about *the bad parts*" (85). Neuropathology and psychopathology seem to be presented under the same banner of symptoms that provide meaning for the affected subject. "Since childhood, I have experienced lifting sensations and euphorias, floods of deep feeling that arrive in my body as a lightness in my head and seem to pull me upward ... I attribute these flights and drops to my nerves, but that attribution doesn't mean the experiences have no meaning for me or haven't been important to who I am" (157–8).

Returning to the realm of psychoanalysis, she dreams of some inoperable cancer in which she is intensely conscious of tumours under her skin at her throat and around her neck, and the interpretation jumps right out at her: "The malignant tumor the doctors removed from my father's thigh, which left his leg stiff and useless" (the leg she clutched to when she was little) and the loss of his voice at the moment of his death (he could no longer speak to his daughter during their last phone conversations).

Treated by a psychiatrist and a neurologist ("but neither of them can tell me who the shaking woman is" [187]), she gets nowhere. She will have to get along with her shaking like she does her migraines, or like Prince Myshkin does with his epilepsy: "I cannot see where the illness ends and where I begin; or, rather, the headaches are me, and rejecting them would mean expelling myself from myself" (189). As the shaking occurred later in her life, it took her more time to integrate the shaking woman into her narrative: "But as she becomes familiar, she is moving out of the third person and into the first, no longer a detested double, but an admittedly handicapped part of my self" (190). She had to stop looking for the limits between brain and mind and stop dividing herself into categories to live her life as a whole by accepting her limitations, the migraines or shaking, the hysteria or temporal lobe syndrome, regardless of the words.

Narratives of this type can be considered practices through which the author examines her life as a whole, starting with her limitations. The difficulty in recognizing the self ("Who are we, anyway?" [69]) is the motivating factor for learning about oneself, the importance of which is "accepting responsibility for being the one you are."[14] Here we have an idea of duty toward the self. Accepting is to take the shaking woman from being alien to being familiar by situating the shaking in the long history of her own symptoms (neurotic, migrainous, etc.) and treatments (psychotherapy, pharmacotherapy, alternative medicine). The shaking woman goes from an external third person (she) to an internal first person (I) and personal pronoun (me): she is "no longer a detested double, but an admittedly handicapped part of my self" (190). Her grammar and the use of "me" is the way by which she can take hold of herself as a person: from "it is not part of me / it is not me" to "it is part of me / it is me." Siri Hustvedt sought "the route to coherence" (198) to escape the confusion into which ambiguity threw her – that of the body/mind rapport caused by the shaking. Nevertheless, she writes in the last paragraph, "Coherence cannot eliminate ambiguity, however ... [It] is inherently contradictory and insoluble, a bewildering truth of fogs and mists and the unrecognizable figure or phantom or memory or dream that cannot be contained or held in my hands because it is always flying away, and I can't tell what it is or if it is anything at all. I chase it with words even though it won't be captured and, every once in a while, I imagine I have come close to it." From there, the solution comes: "In May of 2006, I stood outside under a cloudless blue sky and started to speak about my father, who had been dead for over two years. As soon as I opened my mouth, I began to shake violently. I shook that day and then I shook again on other days. I am the shaking woman" (198–9).

Receptive, listening, can she be self-reliant? One thing is clear: it will not be easy, since the call to be self-reliant is not merely looking at life's struggles with a smile. It is not a state, but a journey, an activity that makes us cautious of "hope and despair,"[15] thus rebooting the ability to be self-reliant. The story of Siri Hustvedt's nerves narrates an experience of personal transformation. We get a first-hand look at it as she goes from being subjected by her shaking to finding her own individuality, and this personal evolution allowed her to create something that she owns, instead of it causing her to suffer.

Musician Allen Shawn's Missing Piece

Allen Shawn's journey is also organized around the question of knowing what is intentional and what is mechanical. Yet it is not a source of torment for him. As a musician, he is in harmony; his narrative is centred on what we will call asymmetrical complementarity between psychoanalysis and cognitive neuroscience.

Allen Shawn is a composer and pianist. Born in 1948, he is the son of an editor-in-chief of the *New Yorker*, William Shawn, who headed the magazine from 1951 to 1987 – he commissioned Hannah Arendt to write the famous articles on the Eichmann trial, which led to the *Banality of Evil*. His mother, who had received a first-class education, abandoned her career in literature and journalism to raise a family.

Wish I Could Be There, a memoir he published in 2007, refers to the fact that he would have been there were it not for his agoraphobia. The work is clearly neuro-psychoanalytical: "I have interwoven two distinctly different ways of approaching my subject. I have written about my own childhood as I remember it, from within, and about the subjects I investigated – the brain, the physiology of fear, the way we form habits of thought and behavior, what Freud was trying to describe in the inner life of the mind – as I understood them, as a layman trying to grasp the origins, both personal and universal, of his own predicament" (x).

His framework is different from that of the shaking woman: if Siri Hustvedt's narrative is structured with tensions between cause and reason (is it mechanical or intentional?), Shawn's unfolds in a complementarity between a psychoanalytic and cognitive neuroscientific perspective.

The narrative takes place on two levels, Oedipal and cerebral cognitive. In the Oedipal narrative, Shawn sheds light on the relational keys of *his* phobia within a psychoanalytical framework – this is the intelligible world. For the cerebral narrative, he presents various mechanisms as they can be seen essentially anywhere in scientific publications or works on personal development – this is the sensory world. The reader understands straightaway how utilitarian and symbolic are interdependent. "Ultimately it [the phobia] led me on a search that was not only fascinating, but actually life changing. The search was both internal, into my own personal past, and external, into regions of science and psychology which required every ounce of mental acuity I could muster ... To write about one's own difficulties and their possible origins is not a task that lends itself to clear conclusions ... This book is not about cure, and it offers no certainties" (ix–x). The book offers something else: both a reflexive recovery of the illness suffered and a transformation of bad into good, into a realizable self. It makes a spiritual journey intelligible. That is the real subject of the book.

The lesson is visible from the first scene of the first chapter: on Halloween night in the mid-1970s, three thieves attack him as he is entering his building and pin him to the floor; he feels his strength increase tenfold to get his adversaries off him, then a neighbour comes and helps him. "Then I realized that what had made me summon up all my strength in the vestibule was not the threat of being robbed or the threat of death or that of being hurt, but the fact that I was being *held down*. My lifelong claustrophobia had awakened in me an intensity of physical response that the realistic danger of being harmed might not have" (2).

The lesson is part of our shared baggage: weaknesses can be transformed into strengths, but only so long as they are worked on as a reflexive recovery in which the illness is transformed into a lifestyle that allows for the construction of a realizable self. If Siri Hustvedt is looking for the shaking woman, or how her shaking is a tense phenomenon between intentional and mechanic, Shawn wants to "reconstruct [his] hemming in" (15). He puts up defence mechanisms.

The narrative is centred on his internal constraints and is structured with coupled oppositions that override the "hemming in."

The book starts out with a short survey on phobias: "I now know just enough about phobias to see that they are immensely complicated. They involve both physical and mental symptoms, and these cannot be entirely separated from each other. They are two aspects of our experience that form a continuous loop, and both are registered in the same organ, the brain. It is this loop that has to be dealt with when psychological problems are discussed." All this obviously depends on what is meant by the word. Let us continue: "It is now known that what you feel, experience, and do changes your brain. What you learn becomes a part of you, making the history of your quirks and habits that are much more difficult to uncover" (24). The allusion to cerebral plasticity is inevitable since it ties the sensory world of the body to the intelligible world of the mind.

The story develops from a syncretic perspective in which neurology and psychoanalysis are complementary. It is a recurring theme in the memoir: "But the music of the mind, the way it sounds from its inner orchestra of its billions of neurons ... can be deduced only from what we humans report and by what we manifest in our bodies and behaviors" (171).

The second chapter, entitled "Father", is Oedipal, and in it the reader suspects that Allen's phobia could be a symptomatic expression of the system of familial relationships. That is the Freudian dimension of the "loop." This chapter is Oedipal because it identifies with the father, and therefore to an ideal: "Like me, he was agoraphobic and suffered from panic disorder. He also needed a high degree of predictability-order ... He was a creature of routine" (28). His brother and sister were also phobic. It is not the reproduction of the father's symptoms that is Oedipal, but the lesson Allen Shawn takes from what his father did with his symptoms that serves the ideal: instead of travelling – an impossible activity for him – when meeting intellectuals, artists, writers, or politicians, he received them in his office: "Through his work at the magazine he was able to filter the unruly and terrifying world ... without venturing very far" (44). "The paradox is that without his phobias he would not have achieved what he did. He might well have achieved other things, which might possibly have been more gratifying to him, but not what he proved masterful at ... His phobias and his accomplishments were inseparable" (42). Other elements of identification surface during the narration: "While unconsciously absorbing his anxieties, I consciously imitated my father's work habits" (85).

Between the first relational key, provided by the father, and the second, which we are about to discover, there are three neurological chapters in which evolution and Darwin, brain and the physiology of fear initiate the reader to the "neural thermostat" that regulates an individual's responses. "In order to understand my own limitations, which so often seem at odds with the very things I want to be doing, I have had to try to grasp something about the way the brain protects and facilitates our existence by coordinating our reactions and behaviour" (75).[16]

The model embodied by the father is a necessary condition. Yet a sufficient condition is missing: a second protagonist is introduced about a third of the way through the book ("Childhood"), without which it would be difficult to understand the "choice" of Shawn's symptom: Mary, his twin sister, his autistic sister,[17] was "another model of behavior who ... had accompanied me in my journey into the world" (93). She started to speak around the age of three, but her language was poorly structured and contained odd expressions – Allen was her interpreter. She loved to sing. Like most young girls, she played with dolls, but in a strange way; she had a special relationship with one of her arms that she chewed on and talked to as if it were her friend; she had fits of anger and screaming, and ritual behaviour, etc. Any attempt for her to have a normal education failed, despite an uncanny gift for mathematical problem solving. Her parents decided to place her in someone else's care in 1956, at the age of eight. It was a major caesura: Allen would understand afterwards that a part of him, his double, had been ripped away.

Not long after, he began having night terrors of death. Then, at the age of ten or eleven, he developed a fear of being alone or in social situations, just two to three years after his sister's "exile." After finishing high school, the number of anxiety-provoking situations increased, but he dealt with them and interpreted them as "inexplicable physical responses" (16). The toll taken on him from the absence of his twin sister was evident: the fear of voids reproduced symbolically the void created by his sister's departure. His phobias were, from a Freudian standpoint, "sexually suggestive" (198). And it was precisely when sexuality came into play that his symptoms developed. The chapter "Agoraphobia" recounts the moment in which things changed dramatically, and it may be the most Freudian chapter, since there is a lot on desire and sexuality: "I also know that I became increasingly agoraphobic at the very instant I began to emerge as an independent, sexually active man,... and learn to fly far from the nest. This was also the moment of true separation from my parents and from childhood, and although the memory of it was buried, separation anxiety had already marked me ... I had always feared banishment, and now that I was *choosing* to leave I wanted both to leave and *not to*" (199).

The traumatic separation from his sister, the separation from his childhood by entering into adult sexuality, in which the trauma replayed in the aftermath, the separation from his parents when he left home, which replayed the initial trauma, thus capping his definitive entrance into phobia, even if his agoraphobia started shortly after his first sexual encounter and one year before gaining financial independence.

Three opposing couples played into Allen Shaw's search for intelligibility. The first established a link between his twin sister's absence, twinship making her almost a part of Allen (like the shaking was almost a part of Siri Hustvedt, without being assimilable to her?), and the phobic anguish of voids. That was the missing piece of Allen Shawn.

A second couple opposed the keeping up of appearances. There were some skeletons in the closet, a long-kept family secret: William had lived a double life for decades with a journalist from the magazine, which became public after his death in 1992 (from the memoirs of the other son, whom William had adopted). Allen learned of his father's double life in the late 1970s, the moment at which he started cognitive therapy. There were long discussions on this point. He did not consider the double life as a betrayal, but as the expression of his father's solitude.[18] The family atmosphere was both warm and worrying. There was something dissonant: "Neither of us knew that our parents were struggling with each other; there was a much too evident harmony between them" (108). After the death of his father, he also learned that his parents had been seeing psychiatrists for decades, but that "my parents were very different in their ways of coping with life's tragedies ... Their relationship to reality was sometimes in itself 'agoraphobic'" (216).

The dissonance seems to have discreetly infiltrated nearly everything. The family life "was both unusually supportive and unusually restrictive" (16). So, "being Jewish was also a matter for some distant uneasiness ... Despite the fact that objectively, many of their character traits and habits could be seen as quintessentially Jewish, they belonged to a generation eager simply to be Americans. Their ambivalence made perfect sense, but it also shaded over into discomfort" (112). Continuously, Shawn looked to understand what happened and the reasons behind the behaviours: "Our parents merely participated in a process that they didn't understand any better than we do" (196). There was no victim, no guilty party, just an exploration of the relational territory of phobic suffering.

The third couple was the opposition between ritual and creativity, rigidity and spontaneity. Mary's internment brought out a dual tension, of banishment ("my sister's 'exile' must have made me reluctant to draw attention to anything that might signify some abnormality in me" [16]) and abnormality ("Furthermore, the worry that I *was* 'abnormal' lurked unconsciously behind my every move, as it does now" [16]). Will I myself be ousted from the familial cocoon because I am abnormal? In this tension, "music gave me an enormous outlet but also protected me to being understood. In music, I could be wild, aggressive, irreverent, and unpredictable; in life, I shunned behaviors that would remind me the chaos of Mary's mind. I tended to act like and feel like the soul of reasonableness – except when I was ambushed by my inner demons" (190–1).

He opposed the *creativity* of his music, for which he needed to lay himself bare, to *rituals*, which compensated for the bareness of the space and reassured him. He opposed them pragmatically, not as a contradiction, but as a distinction in which the opposed poles fed into each other and each found its own relative place.[19] Because it was "only when I feel some sense of danger and nakedness and newness in what I am writing is my work saying something individual enough to be of interest. I do see surprise in music" (194).

Here, it was a matter of desire: "Beneath the restrictions are things I would accomplish if I were less restricted" (214). Yet thanks to these restrictions he found actualization through his music. All that tortured him in real life and reduced his possibilities of living was simultaneously what made him create – the freedom to do one thing or another. The frightening immensity of the world – how to "filter the unruly and terrifying world" – was metabolized only through musical expression. The frightening immensity of the world corresponded to the reassuring immensity of music. The ritual/creativity duality was the logical result of a system of interdependent relationships between the protagonists in the play. Allen Shawn had a sense of relational interdependence, and his approach was structural.

What is the place, the role, and the meaning of cerebral and cognitive references in a story so Oedipal that we seem to understand everything about Shawn thanks to Freud? What do they do in the soma/psyche "loop"?

After "Childhood," in which the missing piece is introduced, Shawn describes his phobias and rituals so he can address them ("On the Road"). The rituals were cognitive and behavioural exercises. He evokes the "momentous discovery" of cognitive behavioural therapy (CBT) when therapists "found that people with agoraphobia and many specific phobias have a fear of the physical and psychological effects of fear which is stronger than their dread of the context in which they experience them ... After many years of being told so, I have finally begun to understand that the tangled thoughts accompanying my irrational fears are merely the sparks thrown off by the grinding machinery of panic when it has no external cause" (134). Science enables the discovery of general mechanisms by which the brain regulates and deregulates our moods and ideas (the sparks thrown off by the grinding machinery), but it appears less a cause of the illness than a natural potential whose deregulation is due to the relational system in which the main character had been brought up. Nevertheless, what was the thing that was personal in this cerebral understanding, that concerned *him* and allowed him to be in touch with *his* phobia? Not much, since "one also has to be prepared to dismantle all that has grown up around these fears and to face their personal significance and usefulness" (135). The objectivity of mechanisms is without consequence if the subject does not himself practise reflexive recovery, which makes it intelligible, subject, and personal.

In the final chapter, "Alone/Not Alone," he describes group cognitive therapy sessions that started at the end of the 1970s at the Center for Stress and Anxiety Disorders, and he describes how they helped him function with less anxiety, thanks to diversion techniques and placed him "in a community of fellow sufferers where shame could be forgotten" (228). The last cognitive activity he participated in, shortly before his book came out, was with a self-help group called Fly without Fear at La Guardia airport.

Shawn adopts a centrist position: "If Freud's account of the unraveling of phobias through the retracing of their origins may now seem overly optimistic, equally absurd, in many cases, is the idea that simply 'unlearning' them while ignoring their significance is efficacious" (168).

This position must be seen as pragmatic: the expressive, the search for intelligibility that tied the phobia to his father and his missing sister, and the instrumental or utilitarian exercises were not opposing entities, but relevant distinctions for directing his life. The psychoanalytic perspective brought to light the interdependence of the personal positions that drove the individual to these symptoms, into the vicious circle of neurosis. The idea behind CBT is learning to objectify – the phobia is triggered by the sparks in my brain, it is not me – and this objectifying helps to protect and lessen the illness, to confront it and live day-to-day with anxiety-provoking situations.

When, for example, during a short trip to the country with his new girlfriend, he could no longer move forward and froze at the halfway point, his first strategy for dealing with it was to remind himself that he was phobic, then to use the four aid accessories (a paper bag to calm his breathing down, since he pants like a dog in such situations, a bag with ginger ale – "a stand-in for sustenance, generally, and perhaps even maternal comfort" (118), a box of tranquilizers to relax the muscles, heart, and mind, and a cellphone to call for help). He was able to make the short trip, he says, because "it had been explained to me that the freezing response was part of the physical repertoire of fear and did not constitute true immobility. Once I had grasped that this sensation was not something peculiar to me but was merely one of the muscular results of the fight-or-flight response,... I mustered the trust in my own ability to continue walking to get to the end of the road ... Since then the walk has become easy, and I can do it without carrying anything" (118–19). The cognitive and behavioural part allowed him to dis-individualize the symptom. The cognitive and behavioural work occupies a specific place: objectify the illness as a biological or somatic entity in order to "learn to accept such sensations and not compound them with additional fear" (119). One must, depending on the situation, "subjectify" to understand and shed light on the interdependence of familial positions of which the phobia is the expression, or "objectify" in order to act, externalize entities and practise in such a way that it becomes possible to self-rely, despite everything.

On the road, he always had a travel log with him in which he jotted down thoughts that helped him focus, thoughts that showed "a preoccupation with the mystery of being in another context" (133). These were just notes on what he came across (a church, a sign), or sometimes a little phrase ("Feeling a member of society dwindles so easily" [133]). He realized very well that it was "magical thinking," but if the magic could be of use, there was no reason to forego it. His notes helped familiarize this "other context" and made the return trip more reassuring. This process is analogous to that of "a dog marking a tree with his urine" (128) – here we are in the sensory world of the body for which the difference with an animal is not of any import. It is important to form habits, and from those there is the necessity of ritual in order to familiarize.

For individual intelligence to be mobilized, the brain must guard permanent traces so they become embedded into the memory of the brain matter itself, which constitutes the physiological counterpart to these psychological processes. This is the most delicate problem, since it links cerebral mechanisms and behavioural responses, biology and psychology, in short, the infra-personal to the personal level.

The last pages of the book are dedicated to his attempts to see his sister and finishes with a paragraph of canonical tone: "I had made an important step toward reconnecting with her. I had also made a step toward reconnecting with the fundamental truths of my life" (244). The self at the beginning of the book was entirely accomplished musically but utterly divided in life. The self at the end reconciled with his life, despite the illness that persisted. If we ask ourselves to what extent this reconciliation is not rhetorical for Siri Hustvedt ("I am the shaking woman" is a sentence, but where is the thing?), for Shawn it came as an *act* of which he was *capable*.

Shawn's narrative supports one of the major contributions of psychoanalysis, that the symptom is a compromise. The fact that it is seen as a solution, albeit flawed, even if it is precisely what sews the seed for crises in everyday life – "the idea of free association still constitutes the only known way to get even a glimpse of the vast web of thought that may be entangled in a single perception, a single instant of mental activity" (174). Is this not what is essential? So, then, what is the purpose of neuroscience? Is it merely some trend? No, it is not.

Demonstrating that the individual changes when the brain really does, thanks to synaptic transmission and cerebral plasticity, cognitive neuroscience provided a biological theory highlighting that what matters in CBT practice is the concept of training, in the sporting sense, or comparable to the training of a musician, the idea of exercise. In other words, apart from psychoanalytical work, and more broadly, therapy referring to psychodynamism, which consists of talking things through with a professional, there is another type of work put forth, and it is closer to common sense because it connotes effort, hard work, perseverance, even courage. "Phobias are widespread, but they still bear the dual stigma of being both 'psychological' problems and not, statistically, 'normal.' In the minds of many, they demonstrate a failure of will and a flaw of character" (250).

The United States is the country of self-reliance, and the self-governed individual is considered to hold the highest value. In a neoliberal context, which began with Reagan at the beginning of the 1980s and continued to develop with welfare reform during the Clinton administration, psychological problems harboured suspicions about feeding into a culture of excuses. The drawback of "psychology" and "mental" is that they refer to intangible entities. Neither science nor morality can deal with such categories. It is lacking matter, if I may say so. With cognitive neuroscience, "the field we used to think of as somehow pertaining to 'the mind' now, finally, describes the intersection of mental life, experience, behavior, genetics, neurology, physiology, and evolution" (250).

The brain and mind have been brought together again, thanks to cognitive neuroscience. The brain itself, continually modifiable, is presented with an idea of endless labour and practice, and the American ideal that it is always possible to get by and succeed with hard work. "Even the adult brain can build new connections. The old ones can become undone – if a person is ready to undo them – and eventually, with hard work, replaced" (194). Allen Shawn's memoir recounts the harmonious marriage between practice of training and the perfectionist narrative of personal transformation by referring to the ultimate ideal of autonomy, the ability to (finally) be self-reliant.

By definition, neuroscientific research is oriented toward discovering mechanisms that cause illness. But in real life, individuals are rarely "reductionist": if they take an interest in causes (therefore mechanical), they are also searching for reason and meaning, and most often, that has to do with circumstances. They are searching for global intelligibility. In real life, causes and reasons do not form separate entities, but practical distinctions. It is also possible that they make up a torturous division, as is the case for Siri Hustvedt, herself a divided cerebral and talking subject.

THE BRAIN'S ENCLOSURE:
WHAT IT FEELS LIKE TO BE ANYBODY[20]

Faces and the information they relay is central to psychiatry, particularly in cases of psychosis, like schizophrenia. A special issue of *L'Évolution psychiatrique* published in 2009, stated,

> The face is at the centre of every interaction. We can understand what the other wants or is feeling only by a relevant reading of the facial, and more specifically emotional, information that is conveyed. Psychiatric disorders are very often characterized by deeply disturbed social interactions, and underpinned by difficulties in understanding what others want, think, or feel. These difficulties are normally interpreted with clinical help; however, another level of interpretation (which does not compete with the first, but in fact completes it) is now available and deserves consideration. Indeed, how can we not take into account the progress made in understanding how the brain works and, more specifically, the way in which the brain manages facial information?[21]

To what extent can we push the neurophysiological explanation? Is it possible to include the moral element, which consists of making individuals intelligible to themselves? How would this explanation complete the clinical reading? What else does it bring?

The Echo Maker helps us delve deeper into these questions. It has to do with the difference between not recognizing any face and not recognizing a close friend or family member, between neurophysiological and personal, which is always relational and historical. The novel is about how the first can only be the echo of the second.

The "echo maker" is the name Algonquians gave to cranes because of the particular sound of their call, which is similar to an echo. But it also refers to the brain. The novel has two different levels. One is ecological, the environment, which has to do with the cranes. The other is human nature, the brain plot. Cognitive neuroscience is the narrative's main thread, where recognition, empathy, consciousness, but also pretence, confusion, and crisis are patterns that unfold in each character's life. At work is the neuroscience of subjective and social experience, which both solves the problem of consciousness and uncovers the secret of human sociality. Neuroscience abandoned archaic localization for modern networks of tangled neuronal sub-systems and distributed knowledge, and went beyond the mechanics of the mind in favour of a cerebral dynamic capable of explaining the individual completely. At the heart of the novel, like neuroscience, is the relationship between cognition and emotion. It is the book of "the reason of emotions," from "Descartes' error" (without emotion, there is no reason). It is also a book about today's psychopathologies, which took the neuropsychiatric turn and aim to surmount "the great divide" between neurology and psychiatry. The story puts this division to the test through an individual case in its full context and enables us to understand that this new insight raises as many questions as it does answers.

The protagonists in the novel are linked by Capgras syndrome,[22] a rare psychiatric disorder in which the subject is affected by a delusional misidentification of a close friend or relative who, he thinks, is a double, or an impostor. In the early 1990s, the syndrome was passed on from psychiatry, which defined it as a delusional certitude, to neurology, or cognitive neuroscience rather, where it was thought of as a false perception resulting from a rupture between emotional and cognitive circuitry.

Let us quickly specify this before going into the story.

From Delusional Certitude to Disconnection Syndrome

The illusion of doubles is part of the delirium family. The first case, described by psychiatrist Joseph Capgras in the 1920s, was a woman plagued by the certainty that someone else had replaced her daughter several times a day for years. She can no longer identify her daughter's face, which has lost its meaning. Her daughter is a double, an empty echo of the real person. "The illusion of doubles," writes Capgras, "has ... a greatly varied reach and genesis. It can spread and create a sort of metabolic delirium. Yet it can also be limited to a small category of people or even one single individual ... These are likely phenomena ... that are essentially affective, despite their sensory and mnemonic appearance." They were grouped under the label of "systematic misidentification."[23] "Everywhere the patient sees a resemblance and everywhere she misidentifies"[24] and projects this loss onto others. This can be limited to one person, or even an animal or a place. For Capgras, it is "agnosia of identification." Agnosia is a recognition disorder. It could easily have a neurological origin, and, in this case, be a matter of sensory, and not affective, causality. Thus, anosognosia, which is the result of lesions in the somatosensory region of the brain's right hemisphere, is characterized by the fact that such patients are unaware of their illness; prosopagnosia is a disorder of recognizing faces, a psychological blindness caused by a cerebral disturbance.

We saw (chapter 1) that syndromes expressed by excess and affecting higher brain functions, those which bring will and perception into play, made up the basis for a neurology of identity, dedicated to cerebral disorders affecting the self. Their role is strategic for those who question the separation between neurology and psychiatry.[25] Agnosias are a category of choice.

Oliver Sacks describes in detail a case of anosognosia, that of Greg, "the last hippie," who was unaware of his blindness, caused by a lesion in the frontal lobe (from an untreated benign tumour): "His singular blindness to his blindness, his no longer knowing what 'seeing' or 'looking' meant ... seemed to point to something stranger, and more complex, than a mere 'deficit,' to point, rather, to some radical alteration within him in the very structure of knowledge, in consciousness, in identity itself."[26] American neurologist V.S. Ramachandran described a patient whose left arm was paralyzed, but behaved as if it were normal: "Talking to denial patients can be an uncanny experience. They bring us face to face with some of the most fundamental questions one can ask ourselves as a conscious human being: What is the self? What brings about the unity of my conscious experience? What does it mean to will an action?"[27] These experiences convince him of the existence of repressed memories. He pays tribute to Freud (despite, he thinks, his many obscurities and absence of experimental work) since anosognosic patients "engaging in the same types of Freudian defense mechanisms – denial, rationalization, confabulation, repression, reaction formation and so forth – that all of us use every day of our lives."[28] He is also a participant in the New York group of neuro-psychoanalysis.

During the 1980s, much progress was made in understanding how the brain treats facial information. In fact, it was demonstrated that there are two cerebral pathways for recognition. One is covered recognition, or ventral, which joins the visual cortex and the temporal lobe and limbic structures, and the other is dorsal, which passes through the parietal lobe and transports affective information or, perhaps, what concerns familiarity. Prosopagnosia is caused by damage to the ventral pathway (tests measuring skin conductance indicate that there is implicit recognition of familiar faces) and Capgras in the dorsal pathway. It was concluded that facial recognition necessitates a visual and an emotional circuit. In 1990, two British neurologists, Hayden Ellis and Andrew Young, drew the conclusion that the syndrome was a mirror image of pro-sopagnosia.[29] So it is directly in the brain that we can establish, depending on which pathway is affected, the diagnostic differ-ence between Capgras and prosopagnosia. This "outlandish brain disorder," writes Ramachandran, "that most people regard as a psychiatric problem can be explained in terms of known brain circuitry. And once again, these ideas can be tested in the labora-tory."[30] Arthur, the patient, was both capable of feeling emotions and recognizing faces, but it was the linking of the two, and thus having to use two types of circuits, that was cut – he recognized his father when he spoke with him on the phone, but not when he saw him. "This implied that Arthur did not have amnesia with regard to his parents and that he was not simply 'crazy.' For, if that were true, why would he be normal when listening to them on the tele-phone and delusional regarding his parents' identities only when he looked at them?"[31] This explains that the problem was focused on the parents and not just someone he knew and did not care much about (like the mail carrier), and that there was no "emo-tional arousal": his delusion of misidentification (impostors) was therefore a response to this absence of emotion toward his parents. But what causes the absence of emotion?

In the case of prosopagnosia, we have a general disorder in the per-ception of faces (we can mistake our wife for a hat). With Capgras, the object of non-recognition is elective; it is someone close, who has *affective* value for the person and holds a symbolic position. Unlike prosopagnosia, Capgras is directed. In the first case, it has to do with an error of perception, a cognitive-cerebral mechanism, and in the second, an interpretive delusion. Whereas Capgras only individual-izes close relations (someone with whom the patient shares a world), prosopagnosics continue to individualize others through details that allows them to recognize indirectly. Unlike prosopagnosia, there needs to be a shared world between the patients and the person they no longer identify, and that is an affective relationship.

A Tragedy of Recognition in Delusion of Identification

The Echo Maker, which received the National Book Award for fiction, takes place in Nebraska, around the small town of Kearney, which sits along the Platte River, a place where cranes stop during their seasonal migration. The book is very complex. In our study, we will examine three of the protagonists:[32] Mark, his sister Karin, and the neurologist who looks after Mark, Dr Gerald Weber, as well as other characters who intervene in key moments. Mark (twenty-seven years old) is driving a delivery truck down a straight road one night and has a strange accident during which he sustains a head injury and develops Capgras: upon waking from his coma, he believes that his beloved sister, Karin (thirty-two years old), has been replaced by a double.[33]

We are going to concentrate on Gerald Weber for two reasons. He is the only one to examine Mark's life as a whole and, through this examination, he tests the tension between cognitive neuroscience and psychodynamic approaches. He becomes the site of tension between the cerebral subject and the talking subject, in which the question of self-intelligibility is played out.

The entire book is organized around doubles and itself has a double meaning: the double who echoes and the double who contrasts, like impostor and sincerity. This novel is thus a push and pull of betrayals, lies, empathy, and lack of empathy: who can be trusted and how? "The root of all his accidents: too caring by half," his sister thought (14). "It seems to me," declares Powers, "that evil – the word of the hour, again – might be the willful destruction of empathy. Evil is the refusal to see oneself in others."[34]

The book describes a division, seen through the syndrome that reveals the inconsistencies of three lives (and a few others) and their mending.[35] The characters no longer know who they are or where they are, with themselves and with others. The common theme is a narrative of misidentification, impostors, and lies, all that sounds hollow like an echo. The narrative is not very "Damasian" in that it recounts how the head injury modifies the system of social relations of the afflicted character. The syndrome reveals relational truths and difficulties between Karin and her brother, and Gerald Weber, who falls into an existential crisis (should I go back to real science or do I keep publishing case stories?). It also covers the contrast between Nebraska, a rural state in which Hayes, a very "mechanic" local neurologist, looks after Mark, and the globalized city of New York, where Gerald Weber, himself an internationally renowned neurologist, resides. Here, there are three relational pairings: Mark and Karin, Mark and Gerald, and Gerald and Hayes. Is it Mark's brain or is it Mark who is grappling with this new situation? His brain is what ties the characters' relationships together.

Neuroscience comes into play when Karin requests that Weber treat her brother; it is the lifeline. When Karin introduces Gerald to her brother, she says, "'He's a neuropsychologist. And a famous writer.' 'Cognitive neurologist,' Weber corrected" (112).

Gerald (fifty-five years old) is the author of two bestsellers and comes into the fold right when his new book is going to be published, and it, like the other two, is a series of cases – *The Country of Surprise*. During a conversation with his editor, he says that he will no longer publish using this style and wants to write a serious book on memory, which will not be a series of case studies. Gerald is at a turning point in his career and his life. He is heading into a dilemma of recognition and confidence, his self-intelligibility and that of his patients becomes muddled, and his certitudes are shaken. That is when he receives Karin's letter.

Upon receiving it, he is tempted by a case that was "unbelievably rare, and immensely resonant. A species he'd never seen. But he was finished with that kind of ethnography" (102) – this is reminiscent of how Sacks presents his stories through the lens of a neurologist who must act as an anthropologist. "True Capgras resulting from closed-head trauma: the odds against it were unimaginable. A case so definitive challenged any psychological account of the condition and undermined basic assumptions about cognition and recognition" (102). We are cast into the great philosophical debate on the brain. There is nevertheless a Freudian tinge to the syndrome that "makes it so fantastic. It's the kind of neither-both case that could help arbitrate between two very different paradigms of mind" (105). Yet there is no arbitration between the two theories of consciousness, but a third solution, that all the characters more or less blindly devises things in order to free themselves from the quagmire of their own lives.

Weber is a mix of Damasio (a leader in the world of cognitive neuroscience) and Sacks[36] (a subtle neurologist and keen expert of the human soul who popularized stories of neurological cases). Like Damasio, he views human relations through the brain, and like Sacks, he makes these odd human beings more relatable (yet, it would seem, with much less subtlety). Gerald started his career as an advocate for the cerebral subject at a time in which the strong program was being developed in labs during the 1980s. He "chanced to be working at the precise moment when the race was making its first real headway into the basic riddle of conscious existence: How does the brain erect a mind, and how does the mind erect everything else?... Questions that had been embarrassingly speculative since the beginnings of awareness were now on the verge of empirical answer ... Some days it seemed that every problem facing the species was awaiting the insight that neuroscience might bring. Politics, technology, sociology, art: all originated in the brain. Master the neural assemblage, and we might at long last master us" (134).

Mark's case, teetering between neurology and psychiatry, and Weber falling into existential crisis destabilizes these nice patterns. Becoming aware that the social or historical individual exists would hinge on the incapacity of science and personal crisis.

To understand how neurology and psychiatry are confronted, we should start with a discussion between the neurologist from Nebraska, Dr Hayes, who treated Mark after the accident, and Weber during his first visit. We will then look into Weber's personal crisis and his search for self-intelligibility tied to that of Mark.

In their discussion, the interest of *this* Capgras with regards to neurological etiology is that they cannot use the "current dominant hypothesis" used by Dr Hayes: "Both the amygdala and the inferotemporal cortex [are] intact, but [there is] a possible interruption of connection between them" (131) because, responds Weber, "Mark doesn't double every person he cared for before the accident" (132). For the former, it is a disconnection syndrome, and for the latter, the interrupted connection reflects something more. Since "there's a higher-order component to all this, too ... Capgras may not be caused so much by the lesion per se as by large-scale psychological reasons to the disorientation" (132). Weber follows the course of the cerebral subject and is ready to delve into psychoanalysis. The Capgras was not so much caused by the lesion itself (as was just discussed by the two neurologists) than by the psychological reactions to his disorientation. "I have always found it worthwhile to consider a delusion as both an attempt to make sense – as well as the result – of a deeply upsetting development" (132). In this case, Weber is manifestly in full regression, since it is the classic psychiatric concept of delusion that appears to him to be the best interpretation. Mark

Schluter's Capgras is not primarily psychiatric because he retains (more or less) his rationality over everything that is not linked to his sister. It is a borderline case. But his brain, Weber thinks, is struggling with complex interactions, and "We owe him more than a simple, one-way, functionalist, causal model" (133).

Weber looks back over the change in the epistemological status of Capgras: "Wilder reversals were on their way, should Weber live to witness them. The day would come when the last clean cause and effect would disappear into the thickets of tangled networks" (157). The effect of Capgras on Gerald, which came into his life right at a time when people started to turn against him – he gets accused of exploiting his patients' suffering and lacking empathy toward them – is the collapsing of this utopia. Worried about how his book will be received, he says to himself, "Each of his twelve subjects had been changed so profoundly by illness or accident that each called into question the solidity of the self. We were not one, continuous, indivisible whole, but instead, hundreds of separate subsystems, with changes in any one sufficient to dispense the provisional confedera- tion into unrecognizable new countries. Who could take issue with that?" (170–1). Therein lies the problem. We cannot disagree with the reasoning in terms of complex systems being deployed depending on multiple modalities in order to account for human fragility, but what can we do about it, at least at an individual level? Weber, convinced of the immorality of his books, becomes progressively overwhelmed by the feeling of being an impostor. He lost his true self and is no more than the echo of himself. He feels guilty about what he is accused of, namely that he lacks empathy toward his patients, whom he instru- mentalized for his own benefit. The solution? Write an entire book on Mark and maybe solve the problem of the "great divide." But he is quickly assailed by Mark's illness, not knowing which approach to take between neuroscience and psychoanalysis, prosopagnosia and Capgras: "But his own mirror neurons failed to fire. Mark Schluter had gradually dismantled his most basic sense of acquaintance, and nothing would ever seem familiar or linked again" (355).

Out promoting his book, which is going worse than expected, he becomes disoriented, no longer recognizing the world in which he used to feel so comfortable. But this personal disorientation appears "cere- brally" – upon waking in his hotel room, he can no longer decipher if his arm is on top of or underneath him. This brings him to reflect at length about humankind, which gives a slight metaphysical nod to works on cognitive neuroscience: "Our sense of physical embodiment did not come from the body itself. Several layers of brain stood in between, cobbling up from raw signals the reassuring illusion of solidity" (258). His world, that of "Famous Gerald," is crumbling – and yet his fame is from the neurology of yore, of case studies. He is but a "neurological opportunist" (273). From that moment, "even if Capgras were entirely understandable in modular terms, as a matter of lesions and severed connections between regions in a distributed network, it still manifested in psycho-dynamic processes – individual response, personal history, repression, sublimation, and wish fulfillment that could not be reduced entirely to low-level phenomena" (191). So how do you treat this borderline case?

Weber recommends the "conventional method": "intensive, persistent cognitive behavioral therapy" because it "has a track record in delusions" (185). Yet, with this trauma-induced Capgras, CBT has no effect. So it is back to "emotional adjustment. Training patients to explore their belief systems. Helping them work on their sense of self. Giving them exercises to change," to "make it easier to live with" (208). Yet again, the therapy does nothing to lessen the emotional impact of Mark's delusional cognition, to change his relationship to the belief, or to make it less emotionally charged.

Mark has Weber at wit's end, and all the more so since he puts him in an awkward position regarding the dominant scientific opinion: "Surely the phenomenon had to be something more than a dissociation between ventral and dorsal recognition pathways. But what did *psychological* mean anymore, except a process that did not yet have a known neurobiological substrate?" How is it psychological since it takes no interest in relationships? "What did it feel like to be Mark Schluter?... He needed his delusions to close that gap. The self's whole end was self-continuation" (301). Here we have hit precisely on the concept that classic psychiatry had developed: delusions are autotherapeutic. They allow Mark to remain himself, whereas Weber does not know where he is or who he is. "Mark, at least, was still himself – more than Gerald Weber could claim ... He could no longer even imagine what it felt like to be Gerald Weber, that confident researcher from last spring" (301). After that, there was a reversal of roles. Gerald hopes to cure his own illness through his patient, Mark. He recharges his battery, discovers a truth, a hallucinatory one, like ones that can be found in old case studies.

So he makes his way back to Nebraska to treat Mark using something other than CBT. "Neuroscience might finally be powerless to settle this desperately improvising mind. But he might help Mark improvise" (299). Mechanics are of little use in relationships, because what do people do, if not improvise? Or else find restoration mechanisms, with possible assistance from a therapist? Weber seems to find out that, in order to help the patient, he must take an interest in the person and not just the syndrome, not only his sensory world, but his intelligible world as well, and that is exactly what it means to be empathetic.

Mark found a delusional solution to a real question: he has good reason to believe that he is being lied to, that there is an impostor in his accident, a conspiracy, this impostor having taken Karin's place. He also understands eventually that his two closest friends lied about events on that night. The lie is not a conspiracy, but an understandable reaction to those present at Mark's accident. Once he understands the truth and takes an antipsychotic prescribed by Weber, Mark is able to put himself back together, and these two elements, chemical and narrative, allow him to get back to a stable world. "What more can I do but hand him some chemical shotgun – 'Here, take this, and let's cross our fingers and hope for the best'?" (324). The last part of the book is short and has to do with recognition. Mark recognizes his sister (and also discovers the truth about his accident), and Gerald recognizes his truth; he lets go of a knowledge that leads only to large generalizations and deception, and is at home with himself.

Looking for the answer to the great divide, Weber stumbles into great confusion. He forces himself to understand Mark through the multimodal complexity of the brain, but brings to light only elements that no one can disagree with. His knowledge rings hollow, like the echo of real knowledge that could be useful to Mark. He has to dig deeper, into history, because the secret of the encounter between neurological trauma and psychiatric delusion is found in the epigraph of Alexander Luria's book: "To find the soul, it is necessary to lose it." The book is a well-told story about how the fates of Mark and Weber come together. But the previous sentence from the novel states, "To discover the sources of free action it is necessary to go outside the limits of the organism, not into the intimate sphere of the mind, but into the objective forms of social life; it is necessary to seek the sources of human consciousness and freedom in the social history of humanity."[37] The only reference to cerebral mechanics shuts the subject in the enclosure of the subject's brain and fails to deepen the relationships between the protagonists, relationships situated in the profundity of their history.

The Solution: Distinguish Two Main Ways to Reconstruct Our Moral Being

If mechanics hold no sway over this case of Capgras, if they leave the shaking woman uncertain about her life, they represent a physical support when all else fails for the phobic person. It is evident that we can think that exploring "the biological mechanisms underlying social interactions" is "one of the major programs for neuroscience in the 21st century," to again cite Frith and Wolpert,[38] but, when illness necessitates an understanding of the self and others, the mechanics of passions quickly reaches its limits. Intelligence destined for human relations gets lost in the maze of neuronal networks.

If we wait for cognitive neuroscience to deliver a more certain model of morality, we are deluding ourselves, because its limits are on the level of the reality it treats: the practical subject, in the empirical sense, centred on finding a means to an end, for which the question of purpose of what the individual desires is not a question, and does not require self-comprehension. Physical knowledge enabled by cognitive behavioural exercises clearly has its raison d'être, yet their efficacy is better explained by indirect global effects than by cerebral mechanisms alone. Being comfortable also helps provide support for finding a place in the world, as was shown by the cognitive behavioural techniques used by Allen Shawn. It does not suffice to invoke the unique complexity of the brain and the nascent state of research to hope that future empirical results will provide a complete neurobiological explanation.

CBT and its training exercises, heir of empirical tradition, convert passions by adjusting the sensorial to obtain regularity. If the concept of cerebral plasticity is in a position to account for these therapies and forms of support (repeated exercise increases synaptic plasticity, like in the musician's model), it is hard to see how it could explain therapies advocating the search for intelligibility. Exercise and forming habits are not always the most important part of therapy, and, more generally, rituals used in individualist societies to reconstruct one's moral being. It all depends on context, people, and opportunity.

Moreover, as we just saw with our three case studies, there are several modalities of articulation, but also tensions between vocabularies used to refer to exercises and the search for intelligibility. We could multiply the number of case studies to enrich the description of these modalities. For example, patients with OCD treated with deep brain stimulation, for the most part, unite in different "naturalist and psychodynamic styles": they "are alternatively mobilized without constantly being disputed … 'Biological,' 'psychological,' and 'sociological' styles of causality are never exclusive and continue to coexist and intermingle in order to respond to our need to clarify the part of these different dimensions in a way that is consistent with our actions and our understanding of who we are."[39] The intermingling of styles, instead of compartmentalizing, corresponds to a situation of the practical subject in real life. Different styles used by different patients and individuals offer a variety of ways to act on their suffering by using several types of causality that are also ideal for their issues. What lacks in the compartmental approach of cognitive neuroscience is the understanding of the active power of ideals. The different styles used by patients, users, and individuals are ways of acting on what they are suffering from, by relying on several types of causality, which are ideals for acting on the illness.

The main distinction between the two ways of reconstructing our moral being is that neuroscience and cognitive behavioural neuroscience are part of practices that convert passions into action through exercise with self-regulation in mind, whereas psychoanalysis transforms passions (symptoms from which one suffers) into questions (symptoms are likely to speak because they conceal intention of which the subject is unaware, an unconscious intention) and questions into actions, the cure being, to use Freud's 1923 definition, "freedom to decide one way or another."[40] The mechanism Freud brings to light, what he calls the unconscious, is repression. This separates affect from the threatening representation and dismisses it, which reappears disguised in the symptom. Therapy aims to bring to subjects' attention what they do not want to see, thus raising the question of their desires. The neuroscientific mechanism is ultimately biological; it works through synaptic communication and cerebral plasticity. Yet, given the extensive use of this concept, mechanism remains to this day hypothetical. Even though empirical evidence would move forward by leaps and bounds, we cannot see how this mechanism could integrate the moral element other than through language, as we saw in the previous chapter's conclusion. Furthermore, using one way over another is, in any case, reflexive, since, according to Hume, we cannot keep ourselves from thinking and breathing.

Acquiring the ability to act by converting symptoms, or acquiring intelligibility by interpreting them to understand what one desires constitutes henceforth not oppositions of nature, but practical distinctions that are combined according to multiple modalities, within societies imbued with strong collective expectations regarding individual autonomy.

Making something intelligible to have a more clearly acting conscious, or practising to acquire automatisms, this alternative underlies disputes between advocates of neuroscience for which the goal is a cerebral subject, and supporters of psychoanalysis who think in terms of speaking subjects. This head-on opposition must be sociologically relativized.

Tensions and complementarities between the sensory world and the intelligible world is not a matter of philosophical position (Hume against Kant), nor is it that of a therapeutic concept, but a practical necessity that expresses Cavell's moral perfectionism, since these tensions and complementarities are central to contemporary individualism, in which autonomy has become normative and the individual is expected to make choices and self-actualize throughout life. For that, there needs to be a morality that does not condemn the individual to choose between duty (Kant) and want (Hume), a morality that enables possessing self-comprehension and social relations, and a sufficient ability to act in the thick of these relations for which the neuroscientific community holds the highest of hopes to one day discover the mechanisms within our organism.

Henceforth, the attitude shown in our narratives underlines the importance of certain traits of our form of life. In the world of autonomy-as-condition, in a kind of society highly oriented toward a proactive concept of action and in which the relationship to the future is much more characterized by infinite contingencies of change than by an assurance of undefined progress, practices referring to moral perfectionism constitute a way to reconstruct one's moral being in such a manner that life can continue despite there being illness, and asserting oneself as an individual. Of course, Siri Hustvedt is a writer, Allen Shawn a musician, and Gerald Weber a character in a novel, but this attitude in the face of adversity, this new individualism, now concerns masses of individuals who, capitalizing on the "creative potential" of illness, search arduously "to rely on themselves as such."

The Brain's Place

From the Neuronal Being to the Total Being

> Thus sociology encounters the biological totality. What sociology always and everywhere observes is not the human divided into psychological or even into sociological compartments, but the entire human being.
>
> Marcel Mauss, *The Nature of Sociology*

By following the common thread of the brain–behaviour link, my intention here was to reveal the success cognitive neuroscience had in exploring the connections between the social ideals and scientific concepts that had gone unnoticed. By describing these connections from an ethnological point of view, the idea was to highlight the coherence of their production regarding the goal of explaining human beings cerebrally. The main players, who had to build their authority on scientific hypotheses and experimental protocols in which collecting evidence and deeming something true or false, improbable or plausible, are at the centre of the debate.

From there, my approach was to treat these sciences on two levels: first, as a phenomenon of social authority so as to grasp the effectiveness of their successes, and second, as a practical knowledge by examining some of the ways in which these sciences were applied in real life, and weighing the value that could be accorded to purely neurobiological explanations in these non-experimental or "total" situations. On the first level, I attempted to show how neuroscience and cognitive behavioural science drew their moral authority of transfiguration, in their concepts, their presentation methods, and their language, on a major aspect of individualist modernity upon which lies a good portion of how we act and live. Their success is attached to the meshing of a system of social ideas and scientific theory, the latter of which provides a solid basis to our most common social concepts and therefore possesses the greatest value. On the second level, following the same descriptive path, I wanted to understand just how far I could take this understanding of thinking, feeling, and acting individuals from understanding their brain with the aim to make allowances between the coherence of these sciences and their pertinence, what they really show.

This approach involved avoiding two common pitfalls in sociology and anthropology. The first consists of opposing "our" anti-reductionism to "their" reductionism, which leads to not taking seriously their advances using a (oversimplified) strategy highlighting the distance between their partial character and their unabashed, grandiose claims. Inversely, the second pitfall that can be found in those advocating for methodological individualism seeks to use these same advances to improve our own disciplines.

THE NARRATIVE OF INDIVIDUALISM: AN ECHO CHAMBER OF OUR IDEALS OF CAPABILITY

The narrative of individualism developed under the auspices of a "physiology of autonomy," a "mental physiology" combining neuroscience and cognitive behavioural psychology. A staunch supporter of this combination, psychologist Olivier Houdé, writes that we must develop "a pedagogy of the prefrontal cortex."[1] Psychology lent its language to neuroscience, and as we saw, this language is filled with collective representations of humankind in society and evolves with them. That is why Durkheim had solid reasons to assert that "the value which we attribute to science depends upon the idea which we collectively form of its nature and role in life; that is as much as to say that it expresses a state of public opinion."[2] The science this examination tried to portray was able to gain sufficient value for the masses to refer to it with the hope of finding a guide by which to lead their lives, notably because it is linked to our collective representations of autonomy.

Since the early 1980s, brain science and cognitive behavioural science have been associated with a changing system of action that has been marked by broadening the ideas and values of autonomy. These were related, on the one hand, to the expansion of value creation to lifestyle, thus opening the door to possible choices for everyone, encouraging diversity and creativity, or innovation as an aesthetic of existence and, on the other hand, to ways of acting that promote individual initiative, competition, and cooperation. The value attributed to links and chosen ways of living, with an emphasis on relationships and individuals, especially concerning work and couples, represents a shift from vertical relations toward horizontal ones and an increased reference to trust at the (relative) expense of obedience. Within this framework, new forms of regulating behaviour, which reinforce the capacity for individuals to both self-guide and self-control were developed. The system of action for the autonomous condition is structured by this dual supposition, an excess of self-control paralyzing action, its insufficiency deregulating it.

Globalization, the transformation of employment, work, and consumption (the goods and services we purchase from the industrial society to the services society), the evolution of technology, and the new sharing economy with its multiple platforms have greatly increased the value of change and innovation (to the point of "disruption"), and lead to a sociable commerce and global trade that has reinforced the authority of how we regulate individual behaviour that is measured by social skills.[3] This dynamic plunged societies into a freedom of sociability and exchange on a level that has not been witnessed since it began in eighteenth-century United Kingdom, at a time when the modern question of contingency emerged. By raising this question, the Scottish developed a morality of humankind reliable enough to maintain a sufficient sociability to live confidently among strangers. At the turn of the twentieth century, with the industrial society (the big factory and the big city), the question of contingency was played out in new circumstances to which psychoanalysis and behaviourism offered sociologically complementary answers.[4] Today, we have entered into a world of infinite contingencies (with innovation taking the place of standardization and globalization, that of internationalization) within which trust has become a central issue in social relations. From that comes the dual concern for cooperation and emotional self-regulation of social competency, which cognitive neuroscience seized upon.

In a form of life in which diversity and choice are among the shared ideas and values, hidden potential brings into play a notion essential to modernity: individuals who, creating value (by socializing it), increase their own value by transforming a deficit into an asset. Broadening considerably the concept of capability through the

typical/atypical polarity sets this idea in motion in a very concrete
way. The ability to come up with the solution is in *your* hands, so
that *you* may be the agent of your own change. This is a powerful
force in a society of individuals.

Cognitive neuroscience, which emerged and rose to prominence in
this moral and social context, was an echo chamber for our ways of
socialization. It made the broad narrative of the individual resonate,
a narrative that appeared in Scotland during the Enlightenment as a
conversion on passions. Everyone is engaged in social commerce, and,
consequently, is an agent who has to confront relational contingency.
The materialistic reference to a biological basis, to neuronal assembly,
and the infra-personal contributes to our ideals of self-control and stable social relationships, not because we currently know enough about
neurobiological mechanisms, but because it feeds our shared ideal of
personal transformation through the recycling of highly valued social
concepts like regularity, predictability, and consistency using scientific
language. The naturalism of a biological foundation always speaks to
us at the same time as a naturalism of regularity.

The extensive use of the biological concept of cerebral plasticity,
this "synaptic selection" that Edelman called "experiential" (see
chapter 3), transformed it into a social concept: the capacity of the
brain to modify itself throughout an entire life solidifies the opinion
that the possibilities for humans to progress, increase their value,
or metamorphose are themselves limitless.[5] This guarantee is built
on the authority of the methods and values of coherence, on the
simplicity and plausibility of cognitive neuroscience, which feeds the
optimism of action by demonstrating that human beings can always
stretch their boundaries and that no one is condemned by any determinism whatsoever, be it biological or social.

The ambition of this program is embodied by the new model of
identification, which is the high-functioning autistic. This individual
exemplifies the possibility to transform a deficit into an asset. This
can happen because, on the one hand, he or she is situated at the
intersection of new moral boundaries where individuals are able to
assert themselves and take responsibility for their life regardless of
what is affecting them. Furthermore, they must be able to show they
are capable, despite it all, to live autonomously by finding a personal
solution. On the other hand, cognitive neuroscience offers scientific
methods for exploring these boundaries. If every brain is different,
then nature has given us all we need to be able to enrich ourselves

with all our differences and use the diversity of our abilities in a society where encouragement to innovate and create in forms of life is rooted in our mores. The plastic brain transfigures these collective representations, and thus contributes to making socially acceptable what was once considered a pathology to treat, a deficit to compensate for, or a deviance to remedy. It also contributes to the widening access to individuality. The brain appears as a biological system that guarantees some development is definitely possible, or that guarantees that each of us is endowed with the resources in our own cerebral mechanisms to transform a deficit into an asset. Assisted by the brain, individuals cannot only dare to explore their plethora of possibilities, but *must* do so.[6] This morality instructs that you must do what you can do. Doing what you are capable of doing is undoubtedly one of the great expectations in a society where autonomy is the condition of everyone.

With a bodily understanding that allows one to be more at ease in thought and action, as well as appealing to everyday virtues of choice, courage, and creativity, these disciplines provide a heroic psychobiological narrative that individuals can exploit with the certainty of being able to ingrain their virtues on a brain that can change itself all while providing stability to the human being confronted with the unknown. Individuals, whatever their issues, have a base – the brain – allowing them to explore any capacity, be it innovative or just crazy, because intelligence has become multiple.[7]

In short, by asserting a biologically based naturalism, the mechanisms, which cause mental pathologies and social behaviours, have remained up to now a scientific hypothesis that is more or less plausible. If not philosophical speculation, they most certainly transfigure another naturalism central to our shared, fundamental ideals of individualist modernity. They are fundamental because they provide the conditions under which men and women conduct themselves as sociable individuals (regularity, exercise, habit, trust, cooperation, empathy, etc.) and, at the same time, can be developed into forms of regulated self-expansion. Cognitive neuroscience has become one of the main narratives of contemporary individualism by associating the ideals of regularity with those of infinite possibility to change and innovate. Therefore, cognitive neuroscience is at the centre of moral and social expectations, which spread widely in societies during the last third of the twentieth century, and were met with a series of practices organized around the idea of exercise.

The new brain does not possess the disciplined model of obedience created during Taylorized industrialization, in which one central supervisor gave out orders. The new brain triggers itself proactively, is able to make hypotheses, simulate action, and foresee consequences. It is equipped with all the concepts that characterize a type of person capable of self-activation and self-control in the face of any contingency. The authority acquired by cognitive neuroscience results as much from their insertion into our ideals as from their discoveries. So the issue is to differentiate between the ways of expressing the metaphysics of our morals using biological language and what is actually being referenced.

ORDINARY USES AND PRACTICAL KNOWLEDGE: REFORMING THE NEURONAL BEING BY THE TOTAL BEING

To put it differently, the explicative pretences from those espousing the strong program of cognitive neuroscience lead us to wonder about the extent to which they have no other choice but to use, without realizing it, our social concepts in order to put forward partial biological hypotheses, which come down to *idealizing* biological mechanisms. If this is the case, Hilary Putnam's evaluation on utilitarianism could be applied to it: "an attempt to make simple and non arbitrary a series of ideas which have deep and complex roots in our culture, – values of equality, liberal values of choice, and values of fraternity and happiness."[8]

Cognitive neuroscience amply demonstrated cerebral functioning to be systematic: motor activity is a component of feeling, and therefore experience. The brain is ever-evolving and develops throughout a person's life, providing each of us the necessary capacities to self-actualize. This discipline, therefore, is exactly right when it asserts that the "social" is within the individual.

Some overstepping occurs with the tendency to reify concepts, such as cerebral plasticity, as if such a concept possessed the same qualities as an independent entity, and to therefore think that variations in regions of the brain make it possible to draw conclusions concerning effects on the individual. So, through reification, we are dealing with nothing other than ordinary ways of speaking in accordance with our social ideals, and moreover, an idealization of biological concepts. Indeed, what more is there to learn if we already know that "to learn is to modify one's neuronal connec-tions"?[9] Therefore, the actual epistemological interest in science can consist only of progressing in what *we already* know.[10] However, the sociological appeal this science has through their strong program, the one that is generally covered by media (something along the lines of "Cognitive neuroscience proves that..." or "Cognitive neurosci-ence demonstrates that..."), must satisfy individualist aspirations and capabilities that today possess the highest value.

The last two chapters showed that the sensory motor and intelligi-ble intentions cannot be described *independently* from one another. Therefore it is futile to criticize cognitive neuroscience, since it would be a power-knowledge much like reducing the mind to the brain, to change human practices on a biological basis, or to make the "social" disappear thanks to "neural" advancements. It is, how-ever, just as futile to call on social sciences to reform in response to "results" in neuroscience and cognitive science. The logical and inevitable conclusion we must draw is that they demonstrate that the human brain has natural potential activated through the learn-ing process. It is therefore entirely possible to extract cognitive neuroscience from their solipsistic leanings (an exterior and interior connected by "neuronal representations") without it affecting their achievements. Cognitive neuroscience found a problematic solution to the brain–mind dualism in the materialistic monism of the neuro-nal individual. We remember that Dewey saw the empirical subject of behaviourism as a first step toward the pragmatic program for controlling forces that make up society.

In his subtle *Histoire des aphasies*, Denis Forest, who claims to be a naturalist philosopher, writes, regarding studies going from the discovery of Broca's area in the 1860s to that of mirror neurons in the 1990s, that the neurophysiological research was neither nec-essarily individualist nor solipsistic, that it does not look only to understand how mental states mysteriously enter into contact with other mental states. "Broca's area does not control words any more than the motor cortex ... controls hand movement; it does, however, enable us to program intentional gestures to articulate such a phrase and it also contributes to detecting that which is executed in front of me – to grasp its intention. The material substrate of the function is only in preparation of fulfilling it in the world of exchange"[11] – in the world of exchange, meaning that of customs, mores, learn-ing, in short, of human second nature. Sociologist Norbert Elias clearly laid out the idea for brain potential: "We have not yet sufficiently recorded the natural process of human maturing and the social process of learning self-regulation in terms of a civilizing code suitable for society, far from being opposed, one presupposes the other and are intertwined."[12] In other words, we are dealing with an untangleable web in all aspects of biology, psychology, and social: "Processes of natural and unlearned growth combine with processes of learned development linked to experience in such a manner that it is futile to look to distinguish results from each other."[13] Biology (cerebral circuitry, putative at least), psychology ("restitution mechanisms" to which behavioural and cognitive exercises apply and in which power to do fuels power to be), sociology (social expectations in the specific form by which these populations befall individual existence, hidden potential, different capabilities, asset/deficit) join together inextricably in the individual's body.

No observable behaviour can be understood without the mediation of shared customs that provide us with a code of conduct, and therefore those of misconduct as well, codes that are formulated using language established by society, without which it would be impossible to even access the meaning of behaviour. It is not the brain that stipulates, in one society, to cast the illness out while remaining atop a pedestal and, in another, make the illness become part of the self and get on with life despite it all. The reason for this opposition, highlighted in the conclusion to chapter 5, must absolutely involve a description of the collective beliefs and customs that imbue the grammar of social relations and regulate the expert's game.

If dividing biological, psychological, and social factors is an incontestable necessity when in the service of methodological reductionism that is indispensable to experimental research, in the case of epidemiology or the evaluation of public policy, an epistemological problem arises when members of the community forget that reductionism, like any method, obviously has its limits. To go beyond them proscribes authors to general formulas that describe nothing and only exacerbates our ordinary manners of speaking in a scientific language.

Since the true fate of the "neuronal human being," at least if looked at as a social phenomenon, is a shift toward the "total human being" of Marcel Mauss. This fate is social in that the authority begotten by cognitive neuroscience is the fulcrum for *ordinary* uses of new references and objects. This authority is the result of both a change in our scientific approach to the brain (which, between 1950 and 1980, went from a mechanical system that reacts against illness to a dynamic system that acts by creating categories) and our ways of acting and enduring, which are imbued with collective expectations regarding individual autonomy. The paradox is that, if the most ambitious program in cognitive neuroscience is to demonstrate the causal power of the brain, it is nevertheless social life that makes possible what it is able to do – like knowing if it can be (and under which conditions) a support for new forms of life worthy of being lived.

We can thus describe the place cognitive neuroscience occupies, the meanings it has procured for us, the uses we have taken from it, but also the concrete effects that therapeutic methods, to which it makes reference, have on the individual without having to *also* examine the different modalities by which it mixes with the rest of existence. Where the psychologist, neuroscientist, or sociologist look to compartmentalize the human being, they discover that everything is woven together.

Acknowledgments

My sincerest thanks to Jacques Donzelot, Corinne Ehrenberg, and Éliane Rothier-Bautzer for reading and discussing the text. A special thanks to Pierre-Henri Castel and Nicolas Marquis for their close reading of the manuscript and their help in clarifying my thoughts. I also owe a big thanks to my editor, Laurence Devillairs, for her attentive reading and her support, as well as to the unshakable Odile Jacob. And a final thanks to Irène Théry for helping unlock the introduction of this book.

Notes

INTRODUCTION

1 Anonymous, "Focus on Social Neuroscience," 645.

2 Berthoz, *Le Sens du Mouvement*, and *La Décision*.

3 Edelman, *La Biologie de la conscience*.

4 Forrester, *Dispatches from the Freud Wars*. "If often he was wrong and, at times, absurd, / to us his is no more a person / now but a whole climate of opinion / Under whom we conduct our different lives: / Like weather he can only hinder or help," Auden, "In Memoriam Sigmund Freud," a poem from 1940.

5 This is the case of Bronner and Géhin, *Le danger sociologique*. See chapter 3 in particular: "La crainte des science cognitives: une peur injustifiée." This sociology is closely linked to behavioural economics, which will be examined in chapter 4.

6 Rabinow, "Artificiality and Enlightenment."

7 Rose and Abi-Rached, *Neuro*, 227.

8 Choudury and Slaby, *Critical Neuroscience*, 33. "Critical neuroscience aims to analyse the ways in which, and conditions through which, behaviours and categories of people are 'neuro-naturalized.'" For an overview on the connections between social and life sciences, which circumvents both critical and apologetic approaches and shows that these connections are highly variable and that reciprocal borrowing is constant, see Guillo, *Sciences sociales et sciences de la vie*.

9 Durkheim, *Elementary Forms of the Religious Life*, 438.

10 Dumont, *Homo aequalis*, 128.

11 For a precise and thorough ethnographic enquiry on therapeutic practices based on neuroscience applied to psychiatry, see Moutaud, *"C'est un problem neurologique ou psychiatrique?*

12 Baudelaire, *Mirror of Art*, 37.

13 Seigel, *Paris Bohême*.
14 Goffman, *Asylums*.
15 Germany had a strong tradition of scientific psychology known as Gestalt psychology. It came about at the same time as American behaviourism, at the beginning of the twentieth century, but is situated in another perspective: American scientific psychology infers according to a logic of parts whereas the German version directly perceives a whole. It involves animal models in experimental psychology that are totally different. Gestalt comes from philosophy and aesthetics, behaviourism from biology. See Ash, *Gestalt Psychology in German Culture*. Gestalt is proposed as an alternative to Kantian idealism and empiricism, like Durkheim's sociology in France and John Dewey's pragmatism in the United States.
16 In the same sense, Nicolas Marquis did a good job showing that publications on personal development had a moral axiom saying no situation was totally negative: the trained eye could always find a means to feel better, to go further, to get back on one's feet despite it all. If all we see is the bad in a given situation, it means that we have not yet discovered what good it has to offer. See Marquis, *Du bien-être au marché du malaise*.
17 I will continue the analysis of two stories, including Ehrenberg, "Suis-je malade."

CHAPTER ONE

1 Damasio, *Descartes' Error*, 7.
2 Harlow, cited by Damasio, *Descartes' Error*, 8.
3 See, for example, Adolphs, "Social Cognition and the Human Brain"; or Kennedy and Adolphs, "The Social Brain in Psychiatric and Neurological Disorders."
4 Damasio, *Descartes' Error*, 10.
5 As noted by Damasio, *Descartes' Error*, 10.
6 Damasio, *Descartes' Error*, 13.
7 Henri Hécaen talks about "the enigma of the frontal lobe and its pathology in humans," "H.-L. Teuber et la fondation de la neuropsychologie expérimentale," 122.
8 Damasio, *Descartes' Error*, 32.
9 Damasio, *Descartes' Error*, 19.
10 Damasio, *Descartes' Error*, 19.
11 Damasio, *Descartes' Error*, 19.
12 Signoret, "Entre cerveau et cognition," 157.
13 See Ehrenberg, *La Société du malaise*, chap. 3.

14 Damasio, *Descartes' Error*, 40.
15 Damasio, *Descartes' Error*, 36.
16 Damasio, *Descartes' Error*, 44.
17 Damasio, *Descartes' Error*, 45.
18 Anderson et al., "Impairment for Social and Moral Behaviour," 1032.
19 Anderson et al., "Impairment for Social and Moral Behaviour," 1033.
20 Anderson et al., "Impairment for Social and Moral Behaviour," 1035.
21 Anderson et al., "Impairment for Social and Moral Behaviour," 1035.
22 Anderson et al., "Impairment for Social and Moral Behaviour," 1036.
23 Damasio, *Descartes' Error*, 70.
24 Damasio, *Descartes' Error*, 174; my emphasis.
25 "I see the essence of emotion as the collection of changes in body state that are induced in myriad organs by nerve cell terminals, under the control of a dedicated brain system, which is responding to the content of thoughts relative to a particular entity or event." Damasio, *Descartes' Error*, 139.
26 Damasio, *Descartes' Error*, 174.
27 Damasio, *Descartes' Error*, 90.
28 Damasio, *Descartes' Error*, 94.
29 Damasio, *Descartes' Error*, 99–100.
30 Damasio, *Descartes' Error*, 103.
31 Damasio, *Descartes' Error*, 106.
32 Damasio makes a distinction between primary, innate, genetically programmed emotions, and secondary emotions, learned and mobilized using other cerebral areas – Gage and Elliot suffer from a lack of secondary emotions. The neural systems, on which emotions depend, were studied starting from cerebral lesions having affected determined structures. They are all located in the right hemisphere. For primary and secondary emotions, see Damasio, *Descartes' Error*, 130–9, and for the right hemisphere, 151.
33 Sacks, *Man Who Mistook His Wife for a Hat*, 87.
34 "Sacks, reluctantly at first, would soon become the most well-known and influential translator of the patient experience to a wide lay audience." Kushner, "The Cursing Patient," 153.
35 Jacyna and Casper, *Neurological Patient in History*, 11.
36 Sacks, *Anthropologist on Mars*, xiii.
37 Sacks, *Man Who Mistook His Wife for a Hat*, viii.
38 They all appear to be pathologies of recognition, be it the ignorance of one's own pathology in agnosia or of social normativity in frontal lobe syndromes and personality disorders.

39 I am referencing Foley's study, "Encephalitis Lethargica Patient as a Window on the Soul."

40 Foley, "Encephalitis Lethargica Patient as a Window on the Soul," 191.

41 Foley, "Encephalitis Lethargica Patient as a Window on the Soul," 204.

42 See Moutaud, "C'est un problème neurologique ou psychiatrique?"

43 Sacks, *Man Who Mistook His Wife for a Hat*, 89.

44 Sacks, *Man Who Mistook His Wife for a Hat*, 89 and 91.

45 Sacks, *Man Who Mistook His Wife for a Hat*, 6.

46 Sacks, *Anthropologist on Mars*, xvi.

47 Sacks, *Anthropologist on Mars*, xii.

48 Sacks, *Man Who Mistook His Wife for a Hat*, "neurological excess or deficit," 87 and 130.

49 Sacks, *Man Who Mistook His Wife for a Hat*, 146.

50 Sacks makes a distinction between left hemisphere and right hemisphere, the right being able to control the ability to recognize reality. For Luria, "These still completely unstudied defects lead us to one of the most fundamental problems – to the role of the right hemisphere in direct consciousness." Sacks, *Man Who Mistook His Wife for a Hat*, 5.

51 Sacks, *Man Who Mistook His Wife for a Hat*, 96.

52 Sacks, *Anthropologist on Mars*, 77.

53 Sacks, *Man Who Mistook His Wife for a Hat*, 98.

54 Sacks, *Man Who Mistook His Wife for a Hat*, 99.

55 Freud, "Ego and the Id."

56 Sacks, *Man Who Mistook His Wife for a Hat*, 95.

57 Sacks, *Man Who Mistook His Wife for a Hat*, 124.

58 Sacks, *Man Who Mistook His Wife for a Hat*, 95.

59 Sacks, *Man Who Mistook His Wife for a Hat*, 124.

60 Wolfe, "The 'Me' Decade and the Third Great Awakening." The first awakening took place in the first half of the eighteenth century; the second, which saw the birth of Mormonism, took place at the beginning of the nineteenth century.

61 The book came out at about the same time as *Rain Man*, a 1988 film depicting a high-functioning autistic, meaning someone who is characterized as being socially inept and, at the same time, having hypertrophy of a particular skill.

62 Cited by Hacking, "Autistic Autobiography," 1469.

63 Sacks, *Anthropologist on Mars*.

64 "Sensory-perceptual idiosyncrasies and difficulties in processing information were portrayed as contributing to high levels of distress, fear and

anxiety, but also as a source of pleasure." Chamak et al., "What Can We Learn about Autism from Autistic Persons?," 275.

65 Evans-Pritchard, *Nuer*.

66 Grandin and Panek, *Autistic Brain*, vii.

67 Grandin and Panek, *Autistic Brain*, 27.

68 Grandin and Panek, *Autistic Brain*, 38.

69 Evans-Pritchard, *Nuer*, 37.

70 Grandin and Panek, *Autistic Brain*, 174–5.

71 "Many of those who are born with these differences and are able to advocate for themselves are wary of research into eliminating their conditions, on the basis that it would eliminate much of what makes them *them*." Rothstein, "Mental Disorder or Neurodiversity," 112.

72 Evans, "How Autism Became Autism," 3–31.

73 Evans, "How Autism Became Autism," 17.

74 Wing and Gould, "Severe Impairments of Social Interaction and Associated Abnormalities in Children," 26, cited by Evans, "How Autism Became Autism," 23.

75 Happé, "Autism: Cognitive Deficit or Cognitive Style?," 221.

76 Happé, "Autism: Cognitive Deficit or Cognitive Style?," 220.

77 Sacks, *Anthropologist on Mars*, 215.

78 Mottron, "Power of Autism," 33.

79 Mottron, "Power of Autism," 35.

80 Dawson, *Misbehaviour of Behaviourists*.

81 Mottron, "Power of Autism," 34.

82 Treffert, "The Savant Syndrome," 1356.

83 Grandin and Panek, *Autistic Brain*, 204.

84 Benjamin, *Walter Benjamin: Selected Writings*, 44.

85 Pachet, *Le premier venu*.

86 Benjamin, *Charles Baudelaire*, 110. This is how Baudelaire defined suicide, which is to say not as a renunciation, but as a "nihilist" act. Benjamin refers to Nietzsche. I am taking the idea of democratic heroism that was attributed to sport (Ehrenberg, *Le Culte de la performance*), but am looking to highlight another aspect. Competiveness is an institution of sport, and it depicts the democratic contradiction of equality in principle and inequality in practice, resolving the contradiction in the idea of just inequality, just competition – in sport, first is best, whereas in everyday life… Sport tells the story of how the layperson can rise out of the obscure mass of facelessness and become self-made through competition regulated by justice. Another version of the

layperson, the *"frêle athlète de la vie"* (frail athlete of life), as Baudelaire writes in "L'Âme du vin," puts on display correlations of equality other than those of justice.

87 Auerbach, "De la *Passio* aux passions."

88 Sacks, *Anthropologist on Mars*, 276 (my emphasis).

89 "Reflecting on this paradox, Dekker proposes an 'autistic utopia' in which society would be 'organised around [the] individual.'" Van Goidsenhoven and Masschelein, "Posting Autism." The majority of self-help groups are in Great Britain and the United States. Anne Idoux-Thivet, "Écouter l'autisme." See also Davidson, "Autistic Culture Online," 791–806.

90 Emerson, *Essays*.

91 For elements on the history of cognitive science and neuroscience, see Chamak, "The Emergence of Cognitive Science in France: A Comparison with the USA," 463–504; Chamak, "Dynamique d'un mouvement académique et intellectuel aux contours flous," 13–34; and Plas, "La psychologie cognitive française dans ses relations avec les neurosciences," 125–42.

CHAPTER TWO

1 For example, see Danziger, *Naming the Mind*, 37–8.

2 Damrosch, *Fictions of Reality in the Age of Hume and Johnson*, 22–3.

3 "It is remarkable," notes Mauss, "that the issue of civil freedom, of metaphysical freedom, and the founding of social sciences were all raised at the same time. The development of societies, and possibly even of modern nations, was needed so the notion of civil, political, religious, and economic freedom could apply the notion of pure freedom to individual consciousness. Neither one nor any other of these forms of the notion freedom expresses the considerable increase in the number of possible actions offered to the choice of the individual, the citizen in our nations. That is the reality and the number of contingencies that delivered a sense of contingency." Mauss, "Catégories collectives de pensée et liberté," 124.

4 See the very enlightening work of Bruno Bernardi, *Le Principe d'obligation* in particular.

5 Gautier, *L'Invention de la société civile*, 42.

6 "What is a given? An experience, one of a collection or a succession of distinct and independent perceptions. Since all is there, this given is no longer given to a subject, on the contrary: the subject … is formed in the given and the experience is to be understood only as a simple abstraction of passivity." Gautier, *L'Invention de la société civile*, 42.

7 Hirschman, *Les Passions et les intérêts*.

8 Hume, *An Enquiry Concerning the Principles of Morals*, cited by Benoist, "Le naturalisme, avec ou sans le scepticisme?" 130. I draw heavily on this article.

9 Hume, *Treatise of Human Nature,* 179.

10 "The *natural,* for Hume, is not what is determined primitively: the *naturel* is fundamentally ... what is regular, what obeys laws and what can be uttered." Cléro, introduction to *Dissertation sur les passions* and *Des passions,* 36.

11 Hume, *Treatise of Human Nature,* 183.

12 "Thinking is like seeing, in the exact sense in which, at a certain level, one activity or the other appears to be absolutely involuntary, automatic, naturalized." Benoist, "Le naturalisme, avec ou sans le scepticism?" 133.

13 Hume, *Treatise of Human Nature,* 422–3.

14 Hume, *Treatise of Human Nature,* 405.

15 Hume, *Treatise of Human Nature,* 403.

16 Gautier, *L'invention de la société civile,* 233 (emphasis in original).

17 Le Jallé, "Hayeck lecteur des philosophes de l'ordre spontané," 1, http://asterion.revue.org/17.

18 Cited by Gautier, *L'invention de la société civile,* 231.

19 Biziou, Gautier, and Pradeau, "Structure et argument de la *Théorie des sentiments moraux,*" 6.

20 Hume, *Treatise of Human Nature,* 592.

21 The theories of action put forward by empiricists are "founded upon a principle of movement or a *concatenation of passions,*" writes Gautier, *L'Invention de la société civile,* 35 (emphasis in original).

22 The work used to understand Scottish ideas is Pocock's *Virtue, Commerce and History,* 69.

23 Pocock, *Virtue, Commerce and History,* 99.

24 Pocock, *Virtue, Commerce and History,* 98.

25 "If there is meaning to be given to the Scottish school of individualism ... it is this: contingency became an integral part in the elaboration of the model for *individual* action." Gautier, *L'Invention de la société civile,* 181.

26 Deleuze, *Empirisme et subjectivité,* 124.

27 Pocock, *Virtue, Commerce, and History,* 115.

28 Pocock, *Virtue, Commerce, and History,* 114 and 121.

29 Mizuta, "Moral Philosophy and Civil Society," 114–31, cited by Silver, "Friendship in Commercial Society," 1483.

30 Granovetter, "The Strength of Weak Ties," 1360–80.

31 Silver, "Friendship in Commercial Society," 1482.

32 Smith, *Theory of Moral Sentiments,* 101. Kant praised Mandeville for having discovered the governing principles of society: "The more civilized

human beings are, the more they are actors" (*Anthropology from a Pragmatic Point of View*, 42). From the theatre to mentoring in the digital age, the idea of reputation is everywhere today.

33 Phillipson's biography, *Adam Smith: An Enlightened Life*, paints a pretty good picture.

34 Hundert, "Sociability and Self-Love in the Theatre of Moral Sentiments," 41.

35 Dumont, *Homo aequalis*, 108.

36 Dumont, *Homo aequalis*, 92.

37 Dumont, *Homo aequalis*, 101.

38 Hirschman, *Les Passions et les intérêts*, 17.

39 Halévy, *La Formation du radicalisme philosophique*, tome III, 221.

40 Cited by Halévy, *La Formation du radicalisme philosophique*, tome III, 198.

41 For the following, I use Collini's *Public Moralists*, in particular "The Culture of Altruism: Selfishness and the Decay of Motive" and "The Idea of Character: Private Habits and Public Virtues."

42 Collini, *Public Moralists*, 98.

43 Collini, *Public Moralists*, 85 and 113.

44 Collini, *Public Moralists*, 114.

45 For psychoanalysis, see the first section of my book, *La Société du malaise*. With scientific psychology, I use a similar approach and present a history complementary to that of psychoanalysis. I will refer to this work repeatedly, being as it covers the same time period.

46 Mandler, "Origins of the Cognitive (R)evolution," 339–53.

47 Dewey, *Individualism*, 16.

48 Dewey, *Individualism*, 17 and 18.

49 Dewey, *Individualism*, 27.

50 Danziger, *Naming the Mind*, 54.

51 Danziger, *Naming the Mind*, 98.

52 Danziger, *Naming the Mind*, 101.

53 Watson, "Psychology as the Behaviorist Views It," 158.

54 Buckley, *Mechanical Man*, 179.

55 Regarding this, see Bakan, "Behaviorism and American Urbanization," 5–27; and Buckley, *Mechanical Man*. Every work on the birth of social science in the United States draws the same conclusions regarding the changes to American society.

56 These issues are not exclusive to the American experience. Georg Simmel, for example, makes the stranger a central part of his analysis and, for him, the city is a key theme.

57 Bakan, "Behaviorism and American Urbanization," 11.

58 Bakan, "Behaviorism and American Urbanization," 12.

59 For more on the crisis of character being the first crisis of American individualism, see Ehrenberg, *La Société du malaise*, chap. 1.

60 Bakan, "Behaviorism and American Urbanization," 12. See also, among others, Lemov, *World as Laboratory*; Buckley, *Mechanical Man*; Plas, "Aux origines des thérapies comportementales et cognitives," 143–66.

61 Bakan, "Behaviorism and American Urbanization," 21.

62 Buckley, *Mechanical Man*, 175.

63 "Mazes won out because in a sense they were the most general, the most representative, and the most perfect models available of the original problem situation, life itself," Lemov, *World as Laboratory*, 21.

64 For Neal Miller and John Dollard, who tried to behaviourize psychoanalysis, "Culture, as conceived by social scientists, is a statement of the design of the human maze." *Social Learning and Imitation*, cited by Lemov, *World as Laboratory*, 265. On the beginnings of behavioural therapy and the attempt to behaviourize psychoanalysis, see Castel, *La Fin des coupables*, 2:269–302.

65 Dewey, "Need for Social Psychology," 277 and 266.

66 Dewey, "Need for Social Psychology," 267.

67 Buckley, *Mechanical Man*, 175.

68 Famous expression from Alfred Chandler, *The Visible Hand*.

69 Buckley, *Mechanical Man*, 148.

70 Buckley, *Mechanical Man*, 175–6. Burnham, "Psychiatry, Psychology, and the Progressive Movement," 457–65, had already highlighted the "radical environmentalism" from that period.

71 Dewey, "Need for Social Psychology," 273.

72 Burnham and Bakan had already brought this to our attention more than a half century ago. See also Sears, "Psychoanalysis and Behavior Theory," 208–20.

73 Watson, "Behavior and the Concept of Mental Disease," 590, cited by Buckley, *Mechanical Man*, 93.

74 Danziger, *Naming the Mind*, chap. 9.

75 See part 2 of Lemov, *World as Laboratory*: "Rooms: Freud and Behaviorism Come Together," 71–146, and chap. 7 in particular.

76 Danziger, *Naming the Mind*, 131.

77 Riesman, Glazer, and Denney, *Lonely Crowd*, 22. For more on Riesman and the post-war era, see Ehrenberg, *La société du malaise*, 76–81.

78 Ehrenberg, *La société du malaise*, 76.
79 Cohen-Cole, "Reflexivity of Cognitive Science"; Cohen-Cole, *Open Mind*; Crowther-Heyck, *Herbert A. Simon*; Crowther-Heyck, "Patrons of the Revolution"; Crowther-Heyck, "Herbert Simon and the GSIA," 311–34; Heukelom, "Measurement and Decision Making," 189–207.
80 Clyde Coombs, cited by Heukelom, "Measurement and Decision Making," 199.
81 As is pointed out in Amadae, *Rationalizing Capitalist Democracy*.
82 Amadae, *Rationalizing Capitalist Democracy*, 107.
83 "Arrow's philosophical system rests on objective scientific knowledge, universal law, rationality defined as a well-ordered set of transitive preferences as opposed to deliberation, and individual freedom to determine ends and values." Amadae, *Rationalizing Capitalist Democracy*, 131.
84 Gigerenzer, "From Tools to Theories," 254–67.
85 Heukelom, "Kahneman and Tversky and the Making of Behavioral Economics," 31.
86 Skinner, *Beyond Freedom and Dignity*, 206.
87 Miller, "Cognitive Revolution," 142 and 144.
88 Crowther-Heyck, "Herbert Simon and the GSIA," 312.
89 Crowther-Heyck, *Herbert A. Simon*, 167.
90 Crowther-Heyck, *Herbert A. Simon*, 200 and 201.
91 Andler, "Calcul et représentation," 42–3. This collective work is the result of a conference that took place in 1987, at the same time a report was submitted to the European Commission under the direction of one its participants with a mission to stimulate European reseach (Imbert et al., *Cognitive Science in Europe*). The CNRS started to come up with strategies to favour the development of a French scientific environment. As Étienne Balibar noted, "Descartes, basing himself on classic Latin etymology (*conscientia = cum + scientia*, which suggests a 'private' knowledge that we 'share' with no one but ourselves), introduced a meaning that today we would call 'cognitive': direct knowledge that is sufficient in itself, and in that respect, benefits from a particular evidence." "L'invention européenne de la conscience"; Lechevalier, Eustache, and Viader, *La conscience et ses troubles*, 169.
92 Cohen-Cole, "Reflexivity of Cognitive Science, 122.
93 Newell, Shaw, and Simon, "Report on a General Problem-Solving Program," 1–3. "The theory of problem solving is concerned with understanding systems of heuristics," 2.
94 Crowther-Heyck, *Herbert A. Simon*, 15.

95 Cohen-Cole, "Reflexivity of Cognitive Science," 121.

96 Miller, Galanter, Pribram, *Plans and the Structure of Behavior*, 2.

97 Cited by Cohen-Cole, "Reflexivity of Cognitive Science," 108.

98 Hebb, "American Revolution," 740.

99 Hebb, "American Revolution," 736.

100 Hebb, "American Revolution," 737–8.

101 Buchanan, "Legislative Warriors," 225–49; Capshew, *Psychologists on the March*, chap. 10, "Toward a Reflexive Science."

102 For more on Rieff, see Ehrenberg, *La Société du malaise*, 133–6.

103 Buchanan, "On Not 'Giving Psychology Away.'"

104 "Amid a searching self-examination, disciplinary leaders sought to realign their science with an ethos of personal autonomy and life optimization." Buchanan, "On Not 'Giving Psychology Away,'" 297.

105 See Capshew, *Psychologists on the March*, chap. 11, "Beyond the Laboratory," for the 1969 APA convention, 255 and after.

106 Miller, "Psychology as a Means of Promoting Human Welfare," 1067.

107 Miller, "Psychology as a Means of Promoting Human Welfare," 1069.

108 Miller, "Psychology as a Means of Promoting Human Welfare," 1073.

109 Castel, "La Fin des coupables," 273.

110 McGregor, *Human Side of Enterprise*, 47–8.

111 Miller, "Psychology as a Means of Promoting Human Welfare," 1070–1.

112 Bandura, "Behavior Theory and the Models of Man," 862–3.

113 Bandura, "Self-Efficacy," 193. It is not enough to practise. So that the experience leaves a lasting effect, they must be "coded and retained in symbols for memory representation," 192.

114 Bandura, "Behavior Theory and the Models of Man," 866. Baistow analyzed these changes in "Problems of Powerlessness." Bandura is the principal psychologist of this dynamic in the article.

115 Rieff, *Triumph of the Therapeutic*, 41.

116 Bandura, *Social Learning Theory*, 203. "While the therapeutic jungle was awash with options by the early 1970s, cognitive therapies began to supplant behavioral and humanistic approaches. Psychologists increasingly saw themselves as helping people help themselves, treating those who were not 'ill' but simply not performing optimally." Buchanan, "Legislative Warriors," 244.

117 Pocock, *Virtue, Commerce, and History*, 115.

118 Baistow, "Liberation and Regulation?" The paradox exists only if we limit the analysis to politics. Albee, "Competency Model Must Replace the Defect Model."

CHAPTER THREE

1 Hebb, *Organization of Behavior*, chaps 11 and 18.
2 Blanc, "Conscience et inconscient dans la pensée neurobiologique actuelle," 181.
3 Blanc, "Conscience et inconscient dans la pensée neurobiologique actuelle," 213.
4 Blanc, "Conscience et inconscient dans la pensée neurobiologique actuelle," 221.
5 It should be noted that there is a French tradition regarding psychophysiological questions and, as Denis Forest highlights, "an important part of French thought is defined in connection with neuropsychological explanations in general." *Histoires des aphasies*, 1. For more on how neuroscience made its way into French philosophy, see Feuerhahn, "Un tournant cognitivist en phénoménologie?"
6 Gazzaniga, *Social Brain*, ix.
7 Edelman, *Bright Air, Brilliant Fire*, 209.
8 Kandel, "Biology and the Future of Psychoanalysis," 509.
9 Korn, "Neurosciences et maladies du système nerveux."
10 Albright et al., "Neural Science," S1.
11 Edelman, "Building a Picture of the Brain," 37.
12 Andreasen, *Brave New Brain*, chaps 9–10.
13 Changeux, *L'Homme neuronal*, xvii.
14 Jeannerod, *La Fabrique des idées*, 60.
15 Jeannerod, *La Fabrique des idées*, 22.
16 Marcus Raichle, one of the pioneers of the positron emission tomography (PET) scan, writes, "This result was a new scientific discipline known as cognitive neuroscience, and, more recently, social neuroscience, with a combined agenda ... that now emcompasses virtually all aspects of human behavior in health and disease." Raichle and Mintum, "Brain Work and Brain Imaging," 450.
17 Hécaen, *Introduction à la neuropsychologie*, chap. 11.
18 Hécaen, *Introduction à la neuropsychologie*, chap. 11.
19 Gazzaniga, *Handbook of Cognitive Neuroscience*, vii.
20 Lanteri-Laura, *Histoire de la phrénologie*, 235. The defining moment of the nineteenth century was the "passage of the organ of the soul to that of the brain." Hagner, *Des cerveaux de genie*, 6.
21 Lantéri-Laura, *Histoire de la phrénologie*, 202. Neurologists referring to Gall "are those who researched cybernetics as possible models for how the central nervous system functions and are part of a group of anatomists

and physiologists who wonder about the possibility to renew the applications of neurophysiology to human behaviour through such applications."

22 Lantéri-Laura, *Histoire de la phrénologie*, 230.

23 Henri Hécaen wrote in the editorial of the first instalment of *Neuropsychologia* in 1963, 1:1–6 (in English, German, and French): "Under the term 'neuropsychology,' we have in mind a particular area of neurology of common interest to neurologists, psychophysiologists, and neurophysiologists. This interest is focused mainly, though not of course exclusively, on the cerebral cortex. Among topics of particular concern to us are disorders of language, perception and action."

24 Jeannerod, *Le Cerveau volontaire*, back cover.

25 Jeannerod, *Le Cerveau volontaire*, 11.

26 Cited in Jeannerod, *Le Cerveau volontaire*, 29.

27 Jeannerod, *Le Cerveau volontaire*, 30.

28 Jeannerod, *Le Cerveau volontaire*, 23.

29 Hécaen, *Introduction à la neuropsychologie*, 299.

30 Hécaen and Lantéri-Laura, *Évolution des connaissances et des doctrines sur les localisations cérébrales*, 253.

31 "It represents a specifically human trait, no experiment having ever shown in animals differences in symmetrical cortical areas nor an alteration in performances when one of the areas is respected." Hécaen, *Introduction à la neuropsychologie*, 303.

32 Signoret, "Entre cerveau et cognition," 154.

33 Catani and Ffytche, "The Rises and Falls of Disconnection Syndromes," 2225.

34 Geschwind, "Disconnexion Syndromes in Animals and Man, Part 1," 279.

35 Geschwind, "Disconnexion Syndromes in Animals and Man, Part 2," 637.

36 Geschwind, "Disconnexion Syndromes in Animals and Man, Part 2," 637.

37 Heilman, Boller, and Damasio, "Founding of the Behavioral Neurology Society"; Farah and Feinberg, *Behavioral Neurology and Neuropsychology*.

38 Jeannerod, *Le Cerveau volontaire*, 41.

39 Jeannerod, *Le Cerveau volontaire*, 43.

40 "'Executive' functions, which is to say strategy, planning, organization, resolution of problems, inhibition of irrelevant strategies, are one of the frontal lobes' roles. They are deficient in schizophrenic patients … Such a deficit [lowering of metabolism in the dorsolateral prefrontal cortex] is no longer interpreted using a localizationist perspective. It is analyzed in terms of functional disconnection between the frontal regions and hippocampal circuits," Montreuil and North, "Apports de la neuropsychologie à la recherche en psychopathologies."

41 Catani and Ffytche, "The Rises and Falls of Disconnection Syndromes," 2224.
42 Varela, *Connaître les sciences cognitives*.
43 Jeannerod, *Le Cerveau volontaire*, 80–1.
44 Jeannerod, *Le Cerveau volontaire*, 40.
45 Teuber, "Brain and Human Behavior," 900.
46 Jeannerod, *Le Cerveau volontaire*, 127.
47 Philosopher William Bechtel was one of the main proponents of this idea. "If the conception of the brain as endogenously active is taken seriously, it profoundly challenges the reactive perspective that has dominated much of cognitive science as well as neuroscience: stimuli or tasks must be regarded not as initiating activity in an inactive system, but rather as perturbing endogenous dynamic behaviour." Bechtel and Abrahamsen, "Understanding the Brain as an Endogenously Active Mechanism."
48 Jeannerod, *Le Cerveau volontaire*, 86.
49 Jeannerod, *Le Cerveau volontaire*, 91–2. "A living organism is in a state of permanent disequilibrium, and it is more accurate to speak of a central fluctuating state than of a consistent internal environment." Vincent, *Biologie des passions*, 168.
50 Cited by Jeannerod, *Le Cerveau volontaire*, 84–5.
51 Jeannerod, *Le Cerveau volontaire*, 141–4.
52 Jeannerod, *La Frabrique des idées*, 138.
53 Varela, *Connaître les sciences cognitives*, 56.
54 Varela, *Connaître les sciences cognitives*, 76–7.
55 Varela, *Connaître les sciences cognitives*, 112–13.
56 Varela, *Connaître les sciences cognitives*, 61. For more on this trend, see Feuerhahn, "Un tournant neurocognitivisite en phénoménologie?" 59–79. For Varela, "information must appear not as an intrinsic order, but as an order that emerges from cognitive activities themselves." *Connaître les sciences cognitives*, 65.
57 Mountcastle, "Brain Science at the Century's Ebb," 17. This text is the introduction to an instalment dedicated to the brain, of which Mountcastle is the editor.
58 Varela, *Connaître les sciences cognitives*, 113.
59 For an analysis on the meaning and uses of the concept in biology and psychology, see Forest, *Neuroscepticisme*, 106–16.
60 Mountcastle, "Brain Science at the Century's Ebb," 5 and 7.
61 Markram, Gerstner, and Sjöström, "A History of Spike-Timing-Dependent Plasticity," 1.
62 Cooper, "Donald O. Hebb's Synapse and Learning Style," 861.

63 Hebb, *The Organization of Behavior*, 70.

64 Markram, Gerstner, and Sjöström, "A History of Spike-Timing-Dependent Plasticity," 7 and 19.

65 Markram, Gerstner, and Sjöström, "A History of Spike-Timing-Dependent Plasticity," 19.

66 According to philosopher Catherine Malabou, cerebral plasticity is the precondition for "neuronal liberation." Malabou, *Que faire de notre Cerveau?* For anthropologist Tobia Rees, who did work in the laboratory directed by Alain Prochaintz, cerebral plasticity is not a liberation, but a "way of life": "The coevolution of adult cerebral plasticity and the political and economic figure of flexibility is a striking … phenomenon." Rees, "Being Neurologically Human Today," 158–9. These philosophies, to some extent activist, do not consider the notion's extensions and plural uses. On this important epistemological point, see Forest, *Neuroscepticisme*, 106–15.

67 Dupont, Éléments d'histoire de la neurotransmission.

68 Jeannerod, *La Frabrique des idées*, 47.

69 Edelman, "Building a Picture of the Brain," 38.

70 Edelman, *Bright Air, Brilliant Fire*, 30.

71 Edelman, *Bright Air, Brilliant Fire*, 28. Edelman's theory, elaborated in collaboration with Vernon Mountcastle, was perfected in the 1970s. See Edelman and Mountcastle, *Mindful Brain*.

72 Edelman, "Building a Picture of the Brain," 42.

73 Mountcastle, "Brain Science at the Century's Ebb," 7 (emphasis in original).

74 Signoret, "Entre cerveau et cognition," 154.

75 Edelman, "Building a Picture of the Brain," 42.

76 Varela, *Connaître les sciences cognitives*, 111.

77 Edelman, "Building a Picture of the Brain," 43.

78 Andler, *Introduction aux sciences cognitives*, 517.

79 Gaillard, "Ce que le développement des outils d'exploration fonctionnelle du cerveau doit à la psychologie."

80 Raichle, "Behind the Scenes of Functional Brain Imaging," 766.

81 Brodie, "Imaging for the Clinical Psychiatrist," 145.

82 Cited by Pine and Freedman, "Imaging a Brighter Future," 885.

83 Pine and Freedman, "Imaging a Brighter Future," 885. But this was to specify that a new perspective had come about: reduce the distance between animal and human models.

84 "It is the authors' belief that from and beyond this confrontation, a new discipline is emerging, which couples brain and thought as its object of

study, and anatomical and functional cerebral imaging as its experimental method." Houdé, Mazoyer, and Tzourio-Mazoyer, *Cerveau et psychologie*, 2–3.

85 Beaulieu, "Space for Measuring Mind and Brain." Anne Beaulieu's work is essential for understanding all of these transformations. In these paragraphs, I rely heavily on her work.

86 Raichle, "Behind the Scenes of Functional Brain Imaging," 766.

87 Frakowiak, "Functional Architecture of the Brain," 110.

88 Beaulieu, "Space for Measuring Mind and Brain," 16.

89 With the PET, the regional distribuation of radioactivity is measured, which provides information on the biological function in which the tracer participates. The fMRI provides images without radiation from the PET and can therefore be more easily used in a repetitive manner on normal subjects, including children. See Forest, *Neuroscepticisme*, chap. 1.

90 Beaulieu, "From Brainbank to Database."

91 Dumit, *Picturing Personhood*, 77–8.

92 Beaulieu, "Voxels in the Brain," 657.

93 Project on the Decade of the Brain. "Presidential Proclamation 6158."

94 Beaulieu, "Voxels in the Brain," 646.

95 Beaulieu, "From Brainbank to Database," 383.

96 Beaulieu, "From Brainbank to Database," 383.

97 Beaulieu, "Voxels in the Brain," 650. "Traditional distinctions between atlas, model and database collapse. This collapse is related to the structures of these resources, which become more fluid because their digital format allows different types of data to be abstracted easily from gathered scans." 644.

98 "The study of human cognition with PET was aided greatly by the involvement of cognitive psychologists in the 1980s whose experimental designs for dissecting human behaviors by using information-processing theory fit extremely well with the emerging functional brain imaging strategies." Raichle, "Behind the Scenes of Functional Brain Imaging," 766.

99 Jeannerod, *La Fabrique des idées*, 159.

100 Mountcastle, "Brain Science at the Century's Ebb," 16.

101 Mountcastle, "Brain Science at the Century's Ebb," 24.

102 Mountcastle, "Brain Science at the Century's Ebb."

103 Edelman, "Building a Picture of the Brain," 41.

104 Mountcastle, "Brain Science at the Century's Ebb," 17.

105 Here we have the ambiguity of expressions like that of Stanislas Dehaene in his inaugural lesson at the Collège de France in which he followed Jean-Pierre Changeux: "Imaging's goal is, first and foremost, breaking down the

functional architecture of mental representations and it offers more direct access to thought mechanisms than does behavioural analysis alone." Dehaene, *Vers une science de la vie mentale*, 25. Functional architecture does not give access to such mechanisms. The geographical character is well laid out in a manual for psychologists: "For the trip to the center of the cognitive brain, the reader will thus be equipped with his geography map – a 'geography of the mind.'" Houdé, Mazoyer, and Tzourio-Mazoyer, *Cerveau et psychologie*, 26.

106 Price, Adams, and Coyle, "Neurology and Psychiatry," 11.

107 Insel at al., "Neuroscience Networks," 1. Emphasis in original.

108 To clarify the issues of the DSM, see Demazeux, *Qu'est-ce que le DSM?*

109 For the following, I am referring to the NIMH document detailing their strategic plan. You can find the most recent plan at National Institute of Mental Health, "National Institute of National Health Strategic Plan."

110 Insel et al., "Research Domain Criteria (RDOC)," 749.

111 Insel et al., "Research Domain Criteria (RDOC)," 749.

112 Insel et al., "Research Domain Criteria (RDOC)," 749.

113 Gorman, "Brain in Exquisite Detail."

114 Hyman, "Grouping Diagnoses of Mental Disorders by Their Common Risk Factors," 2.

115 Insel et al., "Research Domain Criteria (RDOC)," 749.

116 Insel et al., 750.

117 Sacks, *Anthropologist on Mars*, xiii.

118 According to the anthropologist Nicolas Langlitz, the reconceptualization of the brain via its "plasticity" requires "neuroscientific explanations of the social and social explanations of the neurosciences – to critically engage with one another. Langlitz, "Book Forum Introduction," 262. *BioSocieties* is the main publication medium for critical neuroscience brought up in the introduction of this book. The founding of this critical dialogue hinges on the belief that the nature–culture relationship has been renewed by neuroscientific discoveries and, more broadly, contemporary biology.

CHAPTER FOUR

1 Feuerhahn, "Instituer les neurosciences sociales."

2 Decety and Keenan, "Social Neuroscience," 1.

3 See, for example, Camerer, "Wanting, Liking, and Learning."

4 Thaler, "Public Policies, Made to Fit People."

5 Institute for Government and Cabinet Office, MINDSPACE, 14. It is an official government report from when David Cameron was prime minister.

6 Kahn et al., *L'An 2000*, 343.

7 Crozier, "La crise des régulations traditionnelles," 377 and 378.

8 Elias, "Le concept freudien de société et au-delà," 160.

9 Elias, "Civilizing of Parents," in *The Norbert Elias Reader*, 199.

10 Lutz and White, "Anthropology of Emotions," 405.

11 Hochschild, *Managed Heart*.

12 "We cannot describe the state of an 'obligated' individual, which is to say morally held by his obligations, for example a point of honour, that if we knew the physiological effect and not only the psychological, of this obligation's meaning." Mauss, "Rapports réels et pratiques de la psychologie et de la sociologie," 305.

13 Davidson and McEwan, "Social Influences on Neuroplasticity," 691.

14 Damasio, *Descartes' Error*, 254 and 246.

15 Cacioppo et al., "Social Neuroscience," 109.

16 Lieberman, "Social Cognitive Neuroscience," 21.

17 Adolphs, "Social Cognition and the Human Brain," 469.

18 Cacioppo et al., "Social Neuroscience," 111.

19 Brothers, "The Social Brain," 27–51.

20 Buckholtz and Marois, "Roots of Modern Justice," 655.

21 Zaki and Ochner, "Neuroscience of Empathy," 675.

22 Davidson and McEwan, "Social Influences on Neuroplasticity," 689.

23 Buckholtz and Marois, "Roots of Modern Justice," 655.

24 Frith and Wolpert, *Neuroscience of Social Interaction*, xiv.

25 Decety and Keenan, "Social Neuroscience," 1. Also Lieberman thinks that "social cognitive neuroscience can both draw on and contribute to social psychological theory." Lieberman, "Social Cognitive Neuroscience," 1.

26 Decety and Keenan, "Social Neuroscience," 2.

27 Adolphs, "Cognitive Neuroscience of Human Social Behaviour," 165. "*Descartes' Error* is the 'Theory and evidence that the orbitofrontal cortex implements the triggering of somatic markers that guide decision making.'" 177.

28 Adolphs, "Cognitive Neuroscience of Human Social Behaviour," 165.

29 Hume, *Treatise of Human Nature*, 244.

30 Pocock, *Virtue, Commerce, and History*, 115.

31 Adolphs, "Social Cognition and the Human Brain," 470.

32 Silbersweig et al., "Failure of Frontolimbic Inhibitory Function," 1833. The article was signed by fifteen authors, among which was psychoanalyst Otto Kernberg and one of the inventors of the PET, Michael Posner.

33 Cited by Kay, "Toward a Clinically More Useful Model," 1381.
34 New and Stanley, "Opioid Deficit in Borderline Personality Disorder," 882–5; Stanley and Siever, "Interpersonal Dimension of Borderline Personality Disorder"; Berlin, Rolls, and Iversen, "Borderline Personality Disorder."
35 Siegle, "Brain Mechanisms of Borderline Personality Disorder," 1777.
36 Decety, "L'empathie est-elle une simulation mentale de la subjectivité d'autrui?" 141.
37 Cacioppo et al., "Social Neuroscience," 107.
38 Kennett, "Autism, Empathy, and Moral Agency," 355.
39 Premack and Woodruff, "Does the Chimpanzee Have a Theory of the Mind?"
40 Baron-Cohen et al., "Does the Autistic Child Have a 'Theory of the Mind'?"
41 See the review dedicated to this subject, by Klin et al., "Defining and Quantifying the Social Phenotype in Austism."
42 Brothers, "Social Brain," 367–85.
43 Frith and Wolpert, *Neuroscience of Social Interaction*, chaps 13 and 14.
44 Singer and Lamm, "Social Neuroscience of Empathy," 83.
45 Decety, "L'empathie est-elle une simulation mentale de la subjectivité d'autrui?" 70.
46 Jeannerod, *Le Cerveau volontaire*, 34.
47 The extensive use of mirror neurons gave rise to controversies among researchers. For more on this, see Ogien, "Normativité sociale et normativité neuronale."
48 Trust is identified with cooperation, which is a bit of a stretch, since building it takes time. Trust is a phenomenon for which heterogeneity must first be recognized before venturing further into its rudiments. See Ogien and Quéré, "Introduction," 1–5; and Ogien, "Éléments pour une grammaire de la confiance."
49 Quervain et al., "Neural Basis of Altruistic Punishment."
50 Quervain et al., "Neural Basis of Altruistic Punishment," 1256.
51 Quervain et al., "Neural Basis of Altruistic Punishment," 1257 and 1258.
52 For a general overview, see Buckholtz and Marois, "Roots of Modern Justice."
53 Buckholtz and Marois, "Roots of Modern Justice," 656.
54 Tabibnia, Satpute, and Lieberman, "Sunny Side of Fairness," 345.
55 Tabibnia, Satpute, and Lieberman, "Sunny Side of Fairness," 346.
56 Quervain et al., "Neural Basis of Altruistic Punishment," 1258.
57 Buckholtz and Marois, "Roots of Modern Justice," 660. This article covers both methods.

58 Freud, *Psychopathology of Everyday Life*, 277. http://www.reasoned.org/dir/lit/PEL_freud.pdf.

59 Tierney, "Do You Suffer from Decision Fatigue?"; Baumeister and Tierney, *Willpower: Rediscovering the Greatest Human Strength*.

60 Dyson, "How to Dispel Your Illusions," 43 and 41.

61 Brooks, "Who You Are."

62 On the back cover of Kahneman's *Thinking, Fast and Slow*.

63 Kahneman, *Thinking, Fast and Slow*, 8, 10, 11.

64 Kahneman, *Thinking, Fast and Slow*, 4 and 11.

65 Kahneman, *Thinking, Fast and Slow*, 13.

66 Thaler and Sunstein, *Nudge*, 3.

67 Thaler and Sunstein, *Nudge*, 5.

68 Thaler and Sunstein, *Nudge*, 23.

69 Department of Work and Pensions, *Automatic Enrolment Evaluation Report*, #45, December 2016.

70 Institute for Government and Cabinet Office, MINDSPACE, 73. MINDSPACE is an acronym. The *D*, which stands for "default," is at the heart of it, while the other letters refer more to minimizing decisions.

71 Thaler and Sunstein, *Nudge*, 249.

72 Institute for Government and Cabinet Office, MINDSPACE, 73.

73 Institute for Government and Cabinet Office, MINDSPACE, 77.

CHAPTER FIVE

1 Pillet, "Thérapie de remediation cognitive et psychothérapie," 3.

2 Massé, "Pour une réhabilitation psychosociale à la française," 292.

3 Tondora et al., "Getting in the Driver's Seat of Your Treatment." Yale is one of the places where the reconceptualization of schizophrenia as a pathology from which one can recover was developed, with John Strauss, Larry Davidson, etc.

4 Wolfe, "'Me' Decade and the Third Great Awakening."

5 From Charles Webster's manifesto in 1976 and Roy Porter's 1985 article, "The Patient's View." Cooter, "Neuropatients in Historyland," 215.

6 Fraser explains, "A blanket 'dependent-incapable-status' approach is gradually being replaced by a functional approach which focuses on the person's relative abilities." Fraser, "Three Decades after Penrose," 10.

7 Leader, *What Is Madness?* The author gives a precise and synthetic perspective on this mechanism. I will put his ideas to use in this chapter.

8 Leader, *What Is Madness?*, chap. 8: "Stabilization and Creation."

9 Will, "Preface," *Schizophrenia as a Lifestyle*, x.

10 Burton, Lopez Ibor, and Mendel, "Avant Propos."

11 Wood, who dedicated a study to these Personal Accounts, rightly estimates that they establish a credibility of insight in people with mental illness. Wood, "Rethinking 'Patient Testimony' in the Medical Humanities," 43.

12 Jääskeläinen et al., "A Systematic Review and Meta-Analysis of Recovery."

13 Keshavan et al., "Cognitive Training in Mental Disorders," 511.

14 Romme and Escher, "Hearing Voices." A second article came out shortly after in the *British Journal of Psychiatry*: Romme et al., "Coping with Voices: An Emancipatory Approach," 99–103.

15 Estroff and Strauss, "Epilogue," 177–8.

16 Johnstone, "Voice Hearers Are People with Problems, Not Patients with Illnesses," 27–36.

17 Leguay et al., "La piste cognitive," 310.

18 We can draw a parallel to people with autism: "I was taught socialization in therapy," declares Stéphany Bonnot Briey, founder of SAtedI (Spectre Autistique troubles envahissants du développement International). Briey and Constant, "On ne peut pas parler de nous sans nous."

19 Simonet, "La piste cognitive," 312.

20 Lamb, "A Century and a Half of Psychiatric Rehabilitation in the United States," 1015.

21 Lieberman and Kopelowicz, "Rehab Rounds," 1377.

22 Lieberman and Kopelowicz, "Rehab Rounds," 1379.

23 Olivier et al., "Une priorité pour la réhabilitation des patients psychotiques."

24 For a prensentation on this reasoning, see Ehrenberg, *La Société du malaise*, chap. 8, "Rendre l'individu capable d'être l'agent de son propre changemement ou le nouvel esprit institutionnel," 325–7.

25 Hogarty and Flescher, "Developmental Theory for a Cognitive Enhancement Therapy of Schizophrenia." See also Amado and Tod, "Cognitive Remediation Therapy (CRT)."

26 Barch and Yarkoni, "Introduction to the Special Issue," 486. Barch is a codirector of the BRAIN initiative announced by Barack Obama, see above, chapter 3.

27 Insel and Fernald, "How the Brain Processes Social Information," Introduction.

28 Eack, Schooler, and Ganguli, "Gerard E. Hogarty," 1060.

29 Bazin, Passerieux, and Hardy-Baylé, "Un atelier de remédiation cognitive basé sur l'attribution d'intention."

30 McGurk et al., "A Meta-Analysis of Cognitive Remediation in Schizophrenia," 1799.

31 The one led by Marie-Christine Hardy-Baylé. For a presentation on the approach, see Hardy-Baylé, "Sciences cognitive et psychiatrie"; Sarfati et al. "Attibution of Mental States to Others by Schizophrenic Patients."

32 Hardy-Baylé, "Sciences cognitive et psychiatrie," 91.

33 Hardy-Baylé, "Sciences cognitive et psychiatrie," 91

34 Oker et al., "How and Why Affective and Reactive Virtual Agents Will Bring New Insights," 133.

35 Bazin, Passerieux, and Hardy-Baylé, "Un atelier de remédiation cognitive basé sur l'attribution d'intention."

36 Amado and Todd, "Cognitive Remediation Therapy (CRT)."

37 Amado and Todd, "Cognitive Remediation Therapy (CRT)," 4.

38 EEGInfo, "What Is Neurofeedback?"

39 Fovet et al., "Translating Neurocognitive Models of Auditory-Verbal Associations into Therapy," 103. See also the article in *L'Information psychiatrique* introduced by Jardri and Thomas, "Hallucinations et neurosciences de la subjectivité."

40 Micoulau-Franchi, Fond, and Dumas, "Cyborg Psychiatry to Ensure Agency and Autonomy in Mental Disorders," 463.

41 Turner et al., "Psychological Interventions for Psychosis," 523.

42 Turkington, Kingdon, and Weiden, "Cognitive Behavior Therapy for Schizophrenia," 367 and 369.

43 See Marks, "Cognitive Behaviour Therapies in Britain."

44 Gilbert, "Moving Beyond Cognitive Behaviour Therapy," 400.

45 Gilbert, "Moving Beyond Cognitive Behaviour Therapy," 401.

46 Rhodes and Jakes, *Narrative CBT for Psychosis*.

47 For a review of virtual reality applications in psychopathology, see Baus and Bouchard, "Moving from Virtual Reality Exposure-Based Therapy."

48 Peyroux, Franck, "RC2S," 112.

49 Which stands for "Theory of Mind."

50 Peyroux, Franck, "RC2S."

51 "The therapist's role in CRT can also be to 'digest,' or to work out the clinical material brought up by patients during sessions, allowing them to reapproapriate it and give meaning to those places in which division and dislocation of the self create risk. This could only ameliorate the effects of cognitive remediation." Pillet, "Thérapie de remédiation cognitive et psychothérapie." See also Tisseron and Gutton, *Avatars et mondes virtuels*.

52 "Resorting to virtual reality can be likened to a psychodrama, with the psychologist controlling the virtual stimuli." Bouchard, "Qu'est-ce que la cyberpsychologie?"

53 CERNA, *Éthique de la recherche en robotique*, 36.

54 ALIZ.E, http://www.aliz-e.org.

55 Scassellati, Admoni, Matarić, "Robots for Use in Autism Research," 276.

56 Dumouchel and Damiano, *Vivre avec des robots*, 177.

57 Simut et al., "Children with Autism Spectrum Disorders Make a Fruit Salad with Probo."

58 Dumouchel and Damiano, *Vivre avec des robots*, 179–80.

59 Insel, "Look Who Is Getting into Mental Health Research."

60 Carey, "Head of Mental Health Institute Leaving for Google Life Sciences"; and Insel, "Dr. Tom Insel to Step Down as NIMH Director."

61 Regalado, "Why America's Top Mental Health Researcher Joined Alphabet."

62 One example: Bedi et al., "Automated Analysis of Free Speech Predicts Psychosis Onset in High-Risk Youths," 43–52.

63 Regalado, "Why America's Top Mental Health Researcher Joined Alphabet."

64 Rosenberg, "Depressed? Try Therapy without the Therapist." MoodGYM programs also help modify negative thoughts to change a subject's feelings and behaviour. Kaltenthaler and Cavanagh, "Computerized Cognitive Behavioral Therapy and Its Uses."

65 Newman, "To Siri, with Love."

66 *Economist*, "The Computer Will See You Now," 59.

67 Senk, "Les psy virtuels sont arrivés."

68 Freedman, "Computerization of the Therapeutic Task of Working Through," 389. See also Kiluk et al., "Methodological Analysis of Randomized Clinical Trials."

69 MacLeod and Holmes, "Cognitive Bias Modification." The article evokes the idea of a "cognitive vaccine."

70 Carey, "Therapist May See You Anytime, Anywhere."

71 *Economist*, "Therapist-Free Therapy," 78–9. See other specialized scientific journals, such as Maples-Keller et al., "Use of Virtual Reality Technology in the Treatment of Anxiety"; Smith et al., "Job Offers to Individuals with Severe Mental Illness; Smith et al., "Brief Report."

72 PFSKLab, "Will Your Next Gadget Be Your New Guru."

73 PFSKLab, "Will Your Next Gadget Be Your New Guru." There are several reflections on this topic found on http://www.internetactu.net.

74 Strauss, "'Psychological Interventions for Psychosis,'" 479–81.

75 Harvey, "Cognitive Neuroscience Trifecta," 482 and 483.

76 Harvey, "Cognitive Neuroscience Trifecta," 483.

77 Keshavan et al., "Cognitive Training in Mental Disorders," 511.

78 Keshavan et al., "Cognitive Training in Mental Disorders," 510.

79 Keshavan et al., "Cognitive Training in Mental Disorders."

80 Keshavan et al., "Cognitive Training in Mental Disorders."

81 Thakkar, Peterman, and Park, "Altered Brain Activation," 545.

82 Passerieux and Bazin, "La rééducation cognitive," 166–7.

83 Vianin, *Programme de remédiation cognitive*, 62.

84 Keshavan et al., "Cognitive Training in Mental Disorders," 510.

85 Keshavan et al., "Cognitive Training in Mental Disorders."

86 Gilbert, "Moving beyond Cognitive Behaviour Therapy," 403.

87 Forest, *Neuroscepticisme*, 189.

88 Davidson and McEwen, "Social Influences on Neuroplasticity," 694.

89 Strawson, "Against Narrativity," 448. Also 432.

90 Rodriguez, Corrin, and Guay, "La thérapie alternative."

91 D. Vuillaume demonstrates the openings that training rituals make possible with Alcoholics Anonymous. See "Ouvrir les débats actuels."

92 Leader, *What Is Madness?*, 294.

93 Ortigues, "Qu'est-ce qu'une guérison rituelle?" 97–103.

94 Leader, *What Is Madness?*, 321.

95 Davidson et al., "Peer Support among Adults with Serious Mental Illness," 444. In France, there is Le Cardinal, "Les pair-aidants ou médiateurs de Santé-Paris: enjeux d'un nouveau métier dans le champ de la santé mentale," 85–6. Girard et al., "La relation thérapeutique sans le savoir," 75–85.

96 Johnson, "How Understanding Neuroscience Helps Me Get Unstuck."

97 Riffert, "It's a Brain Disease," 773.

98 Longden, "Learning from the Voices in My Head."

99 Cortens et al., "Emerging Perspective for the Hearing Voices Movement."

100 Romme et al., *Living with Voices*. This book is the third in a series and comes after *Accepting Voices* published in 1993 and *Making Sense of Voices* published in 2000, both of which were edited by Romme and Escher.

101 One movement started to develop in France; see the Réseau français sur l'entente de voix, www.revfrance.org.

102 Leader, *What Is Madness?*, 322.

103 Cited by Leader, *What Is Madness?*, 305.

104 See Forest, *Neuroscepticisme*, 13–14.

105 Durkheim, *Elementary Forms of Religious Life*, 209.

106 Durkheim, *Elementary Forms of Religious Life*, 359–60.

107 Favereau, "La pièce manquante de la sociologie de l'acteur rationnel," 278.

108 Durkheim, *Elementary Forms of Religious Life*, 429.

109 I refer to this argument that is further developed in Ehrenberg, "L'institution, la règle sociale et la personne: autorité morale et dressage logique," *La Société du malaise*, 295–304. For more on "learning a noun," see Cavell, *The Claim of Reason. Wittgenstein, Skepticism, Morality, and Tragedy*, 271.

110 For an example of exceeding the limits in cognitive training, which leaves the subjects as bystanders using a more realistic approach, see Winter and Franck, "Remédiation cognitive et informations faciales."

CHAPTER SIX

1 Lejeune, *Je est un autre*, 315.

2 Couser, *Recovering Bodies*.

3 On the emergence of telling one's life story in the new cultural context of psychic suffering, see Ehrenberg, *L'Invididu incertain*.

4 Cited by Dorothy Ross, "Freud and the Vicissitudes of Modernism in the United States," 169.

5 Shawn, *Wish I Could Be There*.

6 Moutaud, "Un 'Alien' dans le cerveau," 177. On the patient's use of naturalist references, see Moutaud, "C'est un problème neurologique ou psychiatrique?"

7 For a distinction between virtuosity and receptivity, see Cavell, *Cities of Words*.

8 Emerson, *Essays*, 147, 233, 164.

9 Cavell, *Cities of Words*, 31.

10 Cavell, *Cities of Words*, 41. "This is the aim of moral reasoning in perfectionism, not to assess pluses or minuses of advantage, nor to assess whether the act is recommendable universally, but yet to see to what those two standard theories wish to accomplish, namely that the one in question make himself intelligible, to others and himself." Cavell, *Cities of Words*, 41.

11 Kleinman, *The Illness Narratives*, 29 and 42–3.

12 Geller, "First-Person Accounts in the Journal's Second 25 Years," 716.

13 On cases concerning patients with OCD, see Moutaud, "C'est un problem neurologique ou psychiatrique?"

14 Cavell, *Cities of Words*, 197.

15 Cavell, *Cities of Words*, 198.

16 Janet Malcolm notes in her review that the book circles back on itself rather than move forward. The book's subtitle, *Notes from a Phobic Life*, "may be more than a disclaimer, the double meaning of the word 'notes'

(fittingly enough) may point to a musical model for the book's organization." Malcolm, "The Not Returning Part of It," 6.

17 In *Twin: A Memoir*, the second of his memoirs, Allen Shawn writes that "even more surprising was that Mary became its central character, as if as the center of my ungovernable anxiety when I am at a height or in open or closed spaces, or far from what I deem to be 'safe' territory, were Mary's own furies and my reactions to them" (19). "My singular experience," he adds, "was a contrapuntal one, and that only when I confronted the sense of loss and the duality at the heart of my life would I begin to achieve some semblance of wholeness" (10).

18 Janet Malcolm pins it down: "Allen Shawn writes of his father not as the callous agent of his sufferings, but as a fellow sufferer, to be no less tenderly treated by the attending narrator-physician than he treats himself. He writes of his father's adultery not as a transgression, but as an attempt to cure a loneliness so extreme that no one woman could fill it." Malcolm, "The Not Returning Part of It," 4.

19 Relations are essential in pragmatism. See Lapoujade's elucidating *Fictions du pragmatisme*.

20 "Powerless to know what anyone else might do. To know what it feels like to be anybody." Powers, *Echo* Maker, 450.

21 Franck, "Éditorial," 1.

22 Capgras and Reboul-Lechaux, "L'illusion des 'sosies' dans un délire sys-tématisé chronique," 6–16.

23 Capgras and Carrette, "Illusion des sosies et complexe d'Oedipe, 1924," 146–7.

24 Cited by Thibierge, *Pathologies de l'image du corps, 14*.

25 Denis Forest argues for the idea that this type of pathology "disputes the validity of the distinction between disorders of the brain and mental disorders." Forest, "La frontière entre psychiatrie et neurosciences," 159.

26 Sacks, *Anthropologist on Mars*, 45. "Though his frontal lobe damage had taken away his identity in a way, it had also given him a sort of identity or personality, albeit an odd and perhaps a primitive sort." 54.

27 Ramachandran, with Blakeslee, *Le Fantôme intérieur*, 98.

28 Ramachandran, with Blakeslee, *Phantoms in the Brain*, 111.

29 Draaisma, "Echos, Doubles, and Delusions"; Ellis, "Role of the Right Hemisphere in the Capgras Delusion."

30 Ramachandran, with Blakeslee, *Phantoms in the Brain*, 119.

31 Ramachandran, with Blakeslee, *Phantoms in the Brain*, 114.

32 For a deep yet subtle analysis, see Atwood, "In the Heart of Heartland." I also recommend Draaisma, "Echos, Doubles, and Delusions," which contrasts the two ages of the syndrome in the novel.

33 The delusion also appears with his dog, but obviously the relationship is not very complex, and eventually he adopts the "fake Blackie," which he calls "Blackie Two." The same goes for his favourite restaurant, but unlike his dog and Karine, he does not care too much about the restaurant, and he never goes back.

34 Michod, "An Interview with Richard Powers."

35 "When I stumbled upon a description of Capgras syndrome ... I started to think more broadly about recognizing and not recognizing, about familiarity and foreignness. Can we see ourselves in others? Can we see something human in other creatures?" Richard Powers [?], "A Power-Full Presence," presentation at the College of Liberal Arts and Science (University of Illinois), taken from the college's website 20 December 2006.

36 At the end of the book, on the plane back to New York, a passenger mistakes him for Sacks ("You're the brain guy," 449). Gerald thus becomes the object of misidentification on two levels: he is not Sacks, but he is no longer "Famous Gerald" either.

37 Luria, *Language and Cognition*, 23, cited by Draaisma, "Echos, Doubles, and Delusions," 439.

38 Frith and Wolpert, *Neuroscience of Social Interaction*, iv.

39 Moutaud, "Un 'Alien' dans le cerveau," 177. See also a study done by Pickersgill, Cunningham-Burley, and Martin, "Constituting Neurologic Subjects." An overview on the anchoring of neuroscientific ideas aiming to "[cast] light on either the extent to which brain-related ideas are spontaneously recruited in naturalistic thought and conversation, or the meanings that these ideas carry for people" concludes that "neuroscience will dramatically alter people's relations with their selves, other and the world are overstated. In many cases, neuroscientific ideas have assimilated in ways that perpetuate rather than challenge existing modes of understanding." O'Connor and Joffe, "How Has Neuroscience Affected Lay Understandings of Personhood?" 262. The discovery of cerebral plasticity is interpreted against the theory of cerebral determinism. It also reinforces the idea that we can train our brains.

40 Freud, *Ego and the Id*, 28.

CONCLUSION

1 Houdé, "Apprendre à résister aux automatismes," 20.
2 Durkheim, *Elementary Forms of the Religious Life*, 438.
3 "Globally, our analysis suggests that automatization has created an increased need for 'social competence,' so much so that there truly exists a complementarity between man and machine." Le Ru, "L'effet de l'automatisation sur l'emploi." The report from the Conseil d'orientation pour l'emploi, entitled *Automatisation, numérisation et emploi*, published in 2017, estimates that "technology will also cause a general increase in demand for social and situational skills," tome II, "L'impact sur les compétences," 6.
4 And a good part of sociology emerging at the turn of the twentieth century, particularly in Germany and the United States, where the figure of the stranger and topic of the city were very present. Think of Georg Simmel in Germany and Robert Park in the United States.
5 See, for example, the metabolization of imagination of plasticity in teachers and pedagogues who put on a dazzling display in the report on "Neurosciences et pédagogie" in the *Cahiers pédagogiques*. In the introduction, it states, "Today, it is difficult for us to ignore the myriad studies that can shed light on how we practice our profession, beginning with those that pertain to cerebral plasticity, for which we have not finished exploring the pedagogical implications." Bouin and Zakhartchouk, "Place au débat," 20.
6 These topics are found in all of the literature on personal development, as Nicolas Marquis showed us in *Du bien-être au marché du malaise*.
7 In the same issue of *Cahier pédagogiques*, an English professor discusses Howard Gardner's concept of multiple intelligences: "I can also talk about autism ... and the movie *Rain Man*, which shows the incredible calculations done by the main character who is played by Dustin Hoffman. This makes intelligence an object of discovery rather than a quantitative, discriminatory assessment. The eight kinds of intelligence proposed by Gardner are useful when expressing our differences." Abdelgaber, "Intelligence(s): du quantitatif au qualitatif," 31.
8 Putnam, *Many Faces of Realism*, 60.
9 A director of a Canadian research lab in neuroeducation thinks that "in the most fundamental way, this mechanism [cerebral plasticity] leads us to redefine the very concept of learning. On a cerebral level, learning is not just modifying one's behaviour to answer a question or carry out a task.

To learn is to modify one's neuronal connections." Masson, "Pour que s'activent les neurones," 18.

10 Unlike other practices we call sciences," Cavell writes, "one sometimes feels that academic psychology tells us less than we already know. As though what stops it from being physics, or even economics, say, is not that it isn't as precise and predictive, but that it doesn't know how to use what we already know about its subjects." Cavell, *Claim of Reason*, 98.

11 Forest, *Histoire des aphasies*, 78.

12 Elias, "Le concept freudien de société et au-delà," 183.

13 Elias, "Le concept freudien de société et au-delà," 170. "The capacity, itself not learned, to use learned models to curb and channel relatively elementary and spontaneous impulses of the organism is a trait found only in humans," 170–1.

Bibliography

Abdelgaber, Sylvie. "Intelligence(s): du quantitatif au qualitatif." *Cahiers pedagogiques* 71, no. 527 (2016): 31.

Adlolphs, R. "Cognitive Neuroscience of Human Social Behaviour." *Nature Reviews Neuroscience* 4, no. 3 (2003): 165–78.

– "Social Cognition and the Human Brain." *Trends in Cognitive Sciences* 3, no. 12 (1999): 469–79.

Albee, George W. "A Competency Model to Replace the Defect Model." In *Community Psychology: Theoretical and Empirical Approaches*, edited by Margaret S. Gibbs, Juliana Rasic Lachenmeyer, and Janet Sigal, 213–38, New York: Gardner, 1980.

Albright, Thomas D., Thomas M. Jessell, Eric R. Kandel, and Michael I. Posner. "Neural Science: A Century of Progress and the Mysteries that Remain." *Neuron* 25, no. 1 (2000): S1–S55.

Amadae, Sonja Michelle. *Rationalizing Capitalist Democracy: The Cold War Origins of Rational Choice Liberalism*. Chicago: University of Chicago Press, 2003.

Amado, I., and A. Todd. "Cognitive Remediation Therapy (CRT): Un programme de remédiation cognitive pour la schizophrénie et les troubles des fonctions exécutives en pathologie mentale." *EMC Psychiatrie* 9, no. 2 (2012): 1–8.

Anderson, Steven W., Antoine Bechara, Hanna Damasio, Daniel Tranel, and Antonio R. Damasio. "Impairment of Social and Moral Behavior Related to Early Damage in Human Prefrontal Cortex." *Nature Neuroscience* 2, no. 11 (1999): 1032–7.

Andler, Daniel. "Calcul et représentation: Les sources." In *Introduction aux Sciences Cognitives*, 9–46, Paris: Gallimard, 1992.

– *Introduction aux sciences cognitives*. Paris: Gallimard, 1992.

Andreasen, Nancy C. *Brave New Brain: Conquering Mental Illness in the Era of the Genome*. Oxford: Oxford University Press, 2001.

Anonymous. "Focus on Social Neuroscience." *Nature Neuroscience* 15, no. 5 (2012): 645.

Ash, Mitchell G. *Gestalt Psychology in German Culture, 1890–1967: Holism and the Quest for Objectivity*. Cambridge: Cambridge University Press, 1997.

Atwood, Margaret. "In the Heart of the Heartland." *New York Review of Books* 21 (2006).

Auden, W.H. *Another Time*. London: Faber & Faber, 1940.

Auerbach, Erich. "De la Passio aux Passions." In *Le culte des passions: Essais sur le XVIIe siècle français*, 51–79. Translated by Diane Meur. Paris: Macula, 1998.

Baistow, Karen. "Liberation and Regulation? Some Paradoxes of Empowerment." *Critical Social Policy* 14, no. 42 (1994): 34–46.

– "Problems of Powerlessness: Psychological Explanations of Social Inequality and Civil Unrest in Post-War America." *History of the Human Sciences* 13, no. 3 (2000): 95–116.

Bakan, David. "Behaviorism and American Urbanization." *Journal of the History of the Behavioral Sciences* 2, no. 1 (1966): 5–28.

Balibar, E. "L'invention européenne de la conscience." In *La conscience et ses troubles: Séminar Jean-Louis Signoret*, 169–92. Bruxelles: De Boeck, 1998.

Bandura, Albert. "Behavior Theory and the Models of Man." *American Psychologist* 29, no. 12 (1974): 859–69.

– "Self-Efficacy: Toward a Unifying Theory of Behavioral Change." *Psychological review* 84, no. 2 (1977): 191–215.

Bandura, Albert, and Richard H. Walters. *Social Learning Theory*. Englewood Cliffs, NJ: Prentice-hall, 1977.

Barch, Deanna M., and Tal Yarkoni. "Introduction to the Special Issue on Reliability and Replication in Cognitive and Affective Neuroscience Research." *Cognitive, Affective, & Behavioral Neurscience* 13, no. 4 (December 2013): 687–9.

Baron-Cohen, Simon, Alan M. Leslie, and Uta Frith. "Does the Autistic Child Have a 'Theory of Mind'?" *Cognition* 21, no. 1 (1985): 37–46.

Baumeister, Roy F., and John Tierney. *Willpower: Rediscovering the Greatest Human Strength*. New York: Penguin, 2011.

Baus, Oliver, and Stéphane Bouchard. "Moving from Virtual Reality Exposure-Based Therapy to Augmented Reality Exposure-Based Therapy: A Review." *Frontiers in Human Neuroscience* 8, no. 112 (2014): 112.

Bazin, N., Ch. Passerieux, and M.-C. Hardy-Baylé. "Un atelier de remédiation cognitive basé sur l'attribution d'intention." *L'Information psychiatrique* 82, no. 4 (2006): 317–19.

Baudelaire, Charles. "L'Âme du Vin." In *Les Fleurs du Mal*. Paris: Auguste
Poulet-Malassis, 1857.

Baudelaire, Charles. *The Mirror of Art*. Garden City, NY: Doubleday
Anchor Books, 1956.

Baumeister, Roy F., and John Tierney. *Willpower: Rediscovering the
Greatest Human Strength*. New York: Penguin, 2012.

Beaulieu, Anne. "From Brainbank to Database: The Informational Turn in
the Study of the Brain." *Studies in History and Philosophy of Science
Part C: Studies in History and Philosophy of Biological and Biomedical
Sciences* 35, no. 2 (2004): 367–90.

– "A Space for Measuring Mind and Brain: Interdisciplinarity and Digital
Tools in the Development of Brain Mapping and Functional Imaging,
1980–1990." *Brain and Cognition* 49, no. 1 (2002): 13–33.

– "Voxels in the Brain: Neuroscience, Informatics and Changing Notions
of Objectivity." *Social Studies of Science* 31, no. 5 (2001): 635–80.

Bechtel, William, and Adele Abrahamsen. "Understanding the Brain as an
Endogenously Active Mechanism." In *Proceedings of the 32nd Annual
Meeting of the Cognitive Science Society*, 31–6. Red Hook, NJ: Curran
Associates, 2010.

Bedi, Gillinder, Facundo Carrillo, Guillermo A. Cecchi, Diego Fernández
Slezak, Mariano Sigman, Natália B. Mota, Sidarta Ribeiro, Daniel C.
Javitt, Mauro Copelli, and Cheryl M. Corcoran. "Automated Analysis
of Free Speech Predicts Psychosis Onset in High-Risk Youths." *npj
Schizophrenia* 1 (2015): art. 15030.

Benjamin, Walter. *Charles Baudelaire. Un poète lyrique à l'apogée du
capitalism*. Paris: Payot, 1982.

– *Walter Benjamin: Selected Writings 4, 1938–1940*. Cambridge, MA:
Harvard University Press, 2003.

Benoist, Jocelyn. "Le naturalisme, avec ou sans le scepticisme?" *Revue de
métaphysique et de morale* 2 (April–June 2003): 127–44.

Berlin, Heather A., Edmund T. Rolls, and Susan D. Iversen. "Borderline
Personality Disorder, Impulsivity, and the Orbitofrontal Cortex."
American Journal of Psychiatry 162, no. 12 (2005): 2360–73.

Bernardi, Bruno. *Le principe d'obligation: sur une aporie de la modernité
politique*. Paris: Vrin, 2007.

Berthoz, Alain. *La Décision*. Paris: Odile Jacob, 2003.

– *Le sens du mouvement*. Paris: Odile Jacob, 1997.

Biziou, M., C. Gautier, and J.F. Pradeau. "Introduction: Structure et Argument de la Théorie des Sentiments Moraux." In *La Théorie des Sentiments Moraux*, by Adam Smith, 1–13. Paris: Presses universitaires de France, 1999.

Blanc, Claude. "Conscience et inconscient dans la pensée neurobiologique actuelle. Quelques réflexions sur les faits et les méthodes." In *l'Inconscient (VIᵉ Colloque de Bonneval)*, edited by Henri Ey and A. Green. Paris: Desclée de Brouwer, 1966.

Briey, Stéfany Bonnot, and Jacques Constant. "On ne peut pas parler de nous sans nous..." *L'information psychiatrique* 85, no. 9 (2009): 813–20.

Bouchard, Stéphane. "Qu'est-ce que la cyberpsychologie?" *Rhizome* 3 (2016): 17–18.

Bouin, N., and J.M. Zakhartchouk. "Avant Propos: Place au débat." *Cahiers Pédagogiques* 71, no. 527 (2016): 10.

Brodie, Jonathan D. "Imaging for the Clinical Psychiatrist: Facts, Fantasies, and Other Musings." *American Journal of Psychiatry* 153, no. 2 (1996): 145–9.

Bronner, Gérald, and Étienne Géhin. *Le danger sociologique*. Paris: Presses universitaires de France, 2017.

Brothers, Leslie. "The Social Brain: A Project for Integrating Primate Behaviour and Neurophysiology in a New Domain." *Concepts in Neuroscience* 1 (1990): 367–85.

Brooks, David. "Who You Are." *New York Times*, 21 October 2011.

Buchanan, Roderick D. "Legislative Warriors: American Psychiatrists, Psychologists, and Competing Claims over Psychotherapy in the 1950s." *Journal of the History of the Behavioral Sciences* 39, no. 3 (2003): 225–49.

– "On Not 'Giving Psychology Away': The Minnesota Multiphasic Inventory and Public Controversy over Testing in the 1960s." *History of Psychology* 5, no. 3 (2002): 284–309.

Buckholtz, Joshua W., and René Marois. "The Roots of Modern Justice: Cognitive and Neural Foundations of Social Norms and Their Enforcement." *Nature Neuroscience* 15, no. 5 (2012): 655–61.

Buckley, Kerry W. *Mechanical Man: John Broadus Watson and the Beginnings of Behaviorism*. London: Guilford, 1989.

Burnham, John Chynoweth. "Psychiatry, Psychology and the Progressive Movement." *American Quarterly* 12, no. 4 (1960): 457–65.

Cacioppo, John T., David G. Amaral, Jack J. Blanchard, Judy L. Cameron, C. Sue Carter, David Crews, Susan Fiske et al. "Social Neuroscience:

Progress and Implications for Mental Health." *Perspectives on Psychological Science* 2, no. 2 (2007): 99–123.

Camerer, Colin F. "Wanting, Liking, and Learning: Neuroscience and Paternalism." *University of Chicago Law Review* 73, no. 1 (2006): 87–110.

Capgras, Joseph, and P. Carrette, "Illusion des sosies et complexe d'Oedipe (1924)." Reprint, *La Revue Lacanienne* 4 (2016): 145–58.

Capgras, Joseph, and J. Reboul-Lachaux. "L'Illusion des 'sosies' dans un délire systématisé chronique." *Bulletin de la société clinique de médecine mentale* 11 (1923): 6–16.

Capshew, James H. *Psychologists on the March: Science, Practice, and Professional Identity in America, 1929–1969.* Cambridge, MA: Cambridge University Press, 1999.

Carey, Benedict. "Head of Mental Health Institute Leaving for Google Life Sciences." *New York Times*, 15 September 2015.

– "The Therapist May See You Anytime, Anywhere." *New York Times*, 13 February 2012.

Castel, Pierre-Henri. "La fin des coupables." *Obsessions et contrainte intérieure de la psychanalyse aux neurosciences II*. Paris: Ithaque, 2012.

Catani, Marco, and Dominic H. Ffytche. "The Rises and Falls of Disconnection Syndromes." *Brain* 128, no. 10 (2005): 2224–39.

Cavell, Stanley. *Cities of Words*. Vol. 34. New Haven, CT: Harvard University Press, 2005.

– *The Claim of Reason: Wittgenstein, Skepticism, Morality, and Tragedy*. Oxford: Oxford University Press, 1999.

– *Philosophie des salles obscures. Lettres pédagogiques sur un registre de la vie morale*. Paris: Flammarion, 2011.

CERNA. Éthique de la recherche en robotique. Rennes: Allistene, 2014.

Chamak, Brigitte. "Dynamique d'un mouvement scientifique et intellectuel aux contours flous: Les sciences cognitives (États-Unis, France)." *Revue d'histoire des sciences humaines* 2 (2011): 13–33.

– "The Emergence of Cognitive Science in France: A Comparison with the USA." *Social Studies of Science* 29, no. 5 (1999): 643–84.

Chamak, Brigitte, Beatrice Bonniau, Emmanuel Jaunay, and David Cohen. "What Can We Learn about Autism from Autistic Persons?" *Psychotherapy and Psychosomatics* 77, no. 5 (2008): 271–9.

Chamak, Brigitte, and Baptiste Moutaud, eds. *Neurosciences et société: Enjeux des savoirs et pratiques sur le cerveau*. Paris: Armand Colin, 2014.

Chandler, Alfred. *The Visible Hand: The Managerial Revolution in American Business*. Cambridge, MA: Harvard University Press, 1977.

Changeux, Jean-Pierre. *L'homme neuronal*. Paris: Fayard, 1983.

Choudhury, Suparna, and Jan Slaby, eds. *Critical Neuroscience: A Handbook of the Social and Cultural Contexts of Neuroscience*. Oxford: John Wiley & Sons, 2016.

Cohen-Cole, Jamie. *The Open Mind: Cold War Politics and the Sciences of Human Nature*. Chicago: University of Chicago Press, 2014.

– "The Reflexivity of Cognitive Science: The Scientist as Model of Human Nature." *History of the Human Sciences* 18, no. 4 (2005): 107–39.

Collini, Stefan. *Public Moralists: Political Thought and Intellectual Life in Britain, 1850–1930*. Oxford: Oxford University Press, 1998.

Conseil d'orientation pour l'emploi. *Automatisation, numérisation et employ. Tome 2: L'impact sur les competences*. Paris, 2017. https://www.vie-publique.fr/sites/default/files/rapport/pdf/174000708.pdf.

Cooper, Steven J. "Donald O. Hebb's Synapse and Learning Style: A History and Commentary." *Neuroscience & Biobehavioral Reviews* 28, no. 8 (2005): 851–74.

Cooter, Roger. "Neuropatients in Historyland." *Neurological Patient in History* 20 (2012): 215–22.

Cortens, Dirk, Eleanor Longden, Simon McCarthy-Jones, Rachel Waddingham, and Neil Thomas. "Emerging Perspectives from the Hearing Voices Movement: Implications for Research and Practice." *Schizophrenia Bulletin* 40, no. S4 (2014): S285–S294.

Couser, G. Thomas. *Recovering Bodies: Illness, Disability, and Life Writing*. Madison: University of Wisconsin Press, 1997.

Crowther-Heyck, Hunter. *Herbert A. Simon: The Bounds of Reason in Modern America*. Baltimore, MD: Johns Hopkins University Press, 2005.

– "Herbert Simon and the GSIA: Building an Interdisciplinary Community." *Journal of the History of the Behavioral Sciences* 42, no. 4 (2006): 311–34.

– "Patrons of the Revolution: Ideals and Institutions in Postwar Behavioral Science." *Isis* 97, no. 3 (2006): 420–46.

Crozier, Michel. "La crise des régulations traditionnelles." *La sagesse et le désordre* (1980): 371–87.

Damasio, Antonio R. *Descartes' Error: Emotion, Reason, and the Human Brain*. New York: G.P. Putnam, 1994.

Damrosch, Leopold. *Fictions of Reality in the Age of Hume and Johnson*. Madison: University of Wisconsin Press, 1989.

Danziger, Kurt. *Naming the Mind: How Psychology Found Its Language*. London: Sage, 1997.

Davidson, Joyce. "Autistic Culture Online: Virtual Communication and Cultural Expression on the Spectrum." *Social & Cultural Geography* 9, no. 7 (2008): 791–806.

Davidson, Larry, Matthew Chinman, David Sells, and Michael Rowe. "Peer Support among Adults with Serious Mental Illness: A Report from the Field." *Schizophrenia Bulletin* 32, no. 3 (2006): 443–50.

Davidson, Richard J., and Bruce S. McEwen. "Social Influences on Neuroplasticity: Stress and Interventions to Promote Well-Being." *Nature Neuroscience* 15, no. 5 (2012): 689–95.

Dawson, Michelle. "The Misbehaviour of Behaviourists." 2004. https://www.sentex.ca/~nexus23/naa_aba.html.

Decety, Jean. "L'empathie est-elle une simulation mentale de la subjectivité d'autrui." *L'empathie* (2004): 53–88.

Decety, Jean, and Julian Paul Keenan. "Social Neuroscience: A New Journal." *Social Neuroscience* 1, no. 1 (2006): 1–4.

Dehaene, Stanislas. *Vers une science de la vie mentale: Leçon inaugurale prononcée le jeudi 6 avril 2006*. Paris: Collège de France, 2013.

Deleuze, Gilles. *Empirisme et subjectivité*. Paris: Presses universitaires de France, 1953.

Demazeux, Steeves. *Qu'est-ce que le DSM? Genèse et transformations de la bible américaine de la psychiatrie*. Paris: Ithaque, 2013.

Department for Work and Pensions. *Making Automatic Enrolment Work: A Review for the Department for Work and Pensions*. Vol. 7954. London: The Stationery Office, 2010.

Dewey, John. *La quête de certitude. Une étude de la relation entre connaissance et action*. Paris: Gallimard, 2014.

– *Individualism Old and New*. New York: Prometheus Books, 2009.

– "The Need for Social Psychology." *Psychological Review* 24, no. 4 (1917): 266–77.

Draaisma, Douwe. "Echos, Doubles, and Delusions: Capgras Syndrome in Science and Literature." *Style* 43, no. 3 (2009): 429–41.

Dumit, Joseph. *Picturing Personhood: Brain Scans and Biomedical Identity*. Princeton, NJ: Princeton University Press, 2004.

Dumont, Louis. *Homo aequalis. Genèse et épanouissement de l'idéologie économique*. Paris: Gallimard, 1977.

Dumouchel, Paul, and Luisa Damiano. *Vivre avec les robots. Essai sur l'empathie artificielle*. Paris: Seuil, 2016.

Dupont, Jean-Claude. *Eléments d'histoire de la neurotransmission*. Paris: Presses universitaires de France, 1999.

'Durkheim, Émile. *The Elementary Forms of the Religious Life: A Study in Religious Sociology.* London: G. Allen & Unwin, 1915.

Dyson, Freeman. "How to Dispel Your Illusions." Review of *Thinking, Fast and Slow,* by Daniel Kahneman. *New York Review of Books,* 22 December 2011.

Eack, Shaun M., Nina R. Schooler, and Rohan Ganguli. "Gerard E. Hogarty (1935–2006): Combining Science and Humanism to Improve the Care of Persons with Schizophrenia." *Schizophrenia Bulletin* 33, no. 5 (2007): 1056–62.

Economist. "The Computer Will See You Now," 16 August 2014.

– "Therapist Free Therapy," 3 March 2011.

Edelman, Gerald M. *Biologie de la conscience.* 1988. Reprint, Paris: Odile Jacob, 1992.

– *Bright Air, Brilliant Fire: On the Matter of the Mind.* New York: Basic Books, 1992.

– "Building a Picture of the Brain." *Daedalus* 127, no. 2 (1998): 37–69.

Edelman, Gerald M., and V.M. Mountcastle. *Mindful Brain: Cortical Organization and the Group-Selective Theory of Higher Brain.* New Haven, CT: Yale University, 1978.

EEGInfo. "What Is Neurofeedback?" https://www.eeginfo-europe.com/neurofeedback/what-is-neurofeedback/what-is-neurofeedback.html.

Ehrenberg, Alain. *La fatigue d'être soi: Dépression et société.* Paris: Odile Jacob, 1998.

– *La société du malaise.* Paris: Odile Jacob, 2010.

– *Le culte de la performance.* Paris: Calmann-Lévy, 1995.

– *L'individu incertain.* Paris: Calmann-Lévy, 1995.

– "Suis-je malade de mon cerveau ou de mes idées? Deux récits neuropsychanalytiques." In *Neurosciences et société: Enjeux des savoirs et pratiques sur le cerveau,* edited by Brigitte Chamak and Baptiste Moutaud, 255–87. Paris: Armand Colin, 2014.

Elias, Norbert. *Au delà de Freud. sociologie, psychologie, psychanalyse.* Paris: La Découverte, 2010.

– "The Civilizing of Parents." Translation by Robert van Krieken from German of "Die Zivilisierung der Eltern" (1980), in *The Norbert Elias Reader: A Biographical Selection,* edited by Johan Goudsblom and Stephen Mennell, 189–211. Oxford: Blackwell, 1998.

– "Le concept freudien de société et au-delà." In *Au-delà de Freud: Sociologie, psychologie, psychanalyse,* 131–86. Paris: Lá Découverte, 1990.

Elias, Norbert, Johan Goudsblom, and Stephen Mennell. *The Norbert Elias Reader: A Biographical Selection*. Blackwell Readers. Oxford: Blackwell, 1998.

Ellis, Hadyn D. "The Role of the Right Hemisphere in the Capgras Delusion." *Psychopathology* 27, no. 3–5 (1994): 177–85.

Emerson, Ralph Waldo. *Essays*. New York: Charles E. Merrill, 1907.

Estroff, Sue E., and John S. Strauss. "Epilogue: Forward." *Schizophrenia Bulletin* 15, no. 2 (1989): 323–4.

Evans, Bonnie. "How Autism Became Autism: The Radical Transformation of a Central Concept of Child Development in Britain." *History of the Human Sciences* 26, no. 3 (2013): 3–31.

Evans-Pritchard, Edward Evan. *The Nuer: A Description of the Modes of Livelihood and Political Institutions of a Nolitic People*. Oxford: Clarendon, 1940.

Evans-Pritchard, Edward Evan, Louis Evrard, and Louis Dumont. "Preface." In *Les Nuer: Description des modes de vie et des institutions politiques d'un peuple nilote*, i–xvi. Paris: Gallimard, 1968.

Favereau, Olivier. "La pièce manquante de la sociologie de l'acteur rationnel." *Revue Française de Sociologie* 44, no. 2 (2003): 275–95.

Feinberg, Todd E., and Martha J. Farah. *Behavioral Neurology and Neuropsychology*. New York: McGraw-Hill Professional, 2003.

Feuerhahn, Wolf. "Instituer les neurosciences sociales: Quelle histoire pour un nouveau label?" *Raisons pratiques* 23 (2013): 115–37.

– "Un tournant neurocognitiviste en phénoménologie? Sur l'acclimatation des neurosciences dans le paysage philosophique français." *Revue d'histoire des sciences humaines* 25 (2011): 59–79.

Foley, Paul. "The Encephalitis Lethargica Patient as a Window on the Soul." In *The Neurological Patient in History*, vol. 20, edited by L. Stephen Jacyna and Stephen T. Casper, 184–211. Rochester: University of Rochester Press, 2012.

Forest, Denis. *Histoire des aphasies: Une anatomie de l'expression*. Paris: Presses universitaires de France, 2015.

– "La frontière entre psychiatrie et neurosciences. Mécanismes et croyances délirante." In *Les maladies mentales*, edited by J.N. Missa, 147–74. Paris: Presses universitaires de France, 2008.

– *Neuroscepticisme: Les sciences du cerveau sous le scalpel de l'épistémologue*. Paris: Ithanque, 2014.

Forrester, John. *Dispatches from the Freud Wars: Psychoanalysis and Its Passions*. Cambridge, MA: Harvard University Press, 1997.

Fovet, Thomas, Natasza Orlov, Miriam Dyck, Paul Allen, Klaus Mathiak, and Renaud Jardri. "Translating Neurocognitive Models of Auditory-Verbal Hallucinations into Therapy: Using Real-Time fMRI-Neurofeedback to Treat Voices." *Frontiers in Psychiatry* 7, no. 103 (2016): 103.

Frackowiak, Richard S.J. "The Functional Architecture of the Brain." *Daedalus* 127, no. 2 (1998): 105–30.

Franck, Nicolas. "Editorial." *L'évolution psychiatrique* 74 (2009): 1.

Fraser, W.I. "Three Decades after Penrose." *British Journal of Psychiatry* 176, no. 1 (2000): 10–11.

Freedman, Robert. "Computerization of the Therapeutic Task of Working Through." *American Journal of Psychiatry* 171, no. 4 (April 2014): 388–90.

Freud, Sigmund. "The Ego and the Id." 1923. https://www.sigmundfreud.net/the-ego-and-the-id-pdf-ebook.jsp.

– *Psychopathologie de la vie quotidienne* (1904). Paris: Payot, 2004.

Frith, Christopher D., and Daniel Wolpert, eds. *The Neuroscience of Social Interaction: Decoding, Influencing, and Imitating the Actions of Others*. Oxford: Oxford University Press, 2004.

Gaillard, M. "Ce que le développement des outils d'exploration fonctionnelle du cerveau doit à la psychologie." In *L'exploration cérébrale, histoire récente, nouveaux enjeux*, edited by J.C. Dupont and C. Chérici, 175–86. Paris: Hermann, 2015.

Gautier, Claude. *L'invention de la société civile lectures anglo-écossaises: Mandeville, Smith, Ferguson*. Paris: Presses universitaires de France, 1993.

Gazzaniga, Michael S., ed. *Handbook of Cognitive Neuroscience*. New York: Springer, 2014.

– *The Social Brain: Discovering the Networks of the Mind*. New York: Basic Books, 1985.

Geller, J.L. "First-Person Accounts in the Journal's Second 25 years." *Psychiatric Services* 51, no. 6 (2000): 713–17.

Geschwind, Norman. "Disconnexion Syndromes in Animals and Man, Part 1." *Brain* 88, no. 2 (1965): 237–94.

– "Disconnexion Syndromes in Animals and Man, Part 2." *Brain* 88, no. 3 (1965): 585–644.

Gigerenzer, Gerd. "From Tools to Theories: A Heuristic of Discovery in Cognitive Psychology." *Psychological Review* 98, no. 2 (1991): 254–67.

Gilbert, Paul. "Moving beyond Cognitive Behaviour Therapy." *Psychologist* 22, no. 5 (2009): 400–3.

Girard, Vincent, Kenneth Driffin, Sandrine Musso, Jean Naudin, Michael Rowe, Larry Davidson, and Anne M. Lovell. "La relation thérapeutique sans le savoir. Approche anthropologique de la rencontre entre travailleurs pairs et personnes sans chez-soi ayant une cooccurrence psychiatrique." *L'évolution psychiatrique* 71, no. 1 (2006): 75–85.

Goffman, Erving. *Asylums: Essays on the Condition of the Social Situation of Mental Patients and Other Inmates.* New York: Doubleday, 1990.

Gorman, James. "The Brain, in Exquisite Detail." *New York Times,* 6 January 2014.

Grandin, Temple, and Richard Panek. *The Autistic Brain: Thinking across the Spectrum.* Boston: Houghton Mifflin Harcourt, 2013.

Grandin, Temple, and Richard Panek. *Dans le cerveau des autistes.* Translated by Agnès Botz. Paris: Odile Jacob, 2014.

Granovetter, Mark S. "The Strength of Weak Ties." *American Journal of Sociology* 78, no. 6 (1973): 1360–80.

Guillo, Dominique. *Sciences sociales et sciences de la vie.* Paris: Presses universitaires de France, 2000.

Hacking, Ian. "Autistic Autobiography." *Philosophical Transactions of the Royal Society B: Biological Sciences* 364, no. 1522 (2009): 1467–73.

Hagner, Michael. *Des cerveaux de génie: une histoire de la recherche sur les cerveaux d'élite.* Paris: Les Editions de la MSH, 2008.

Halévy, Elie. *La formation du radicalisme philosophique, tome III: Le radicalisme philosophique* (1901). Paris: Presses universitaires de France, 1995.

Halpern, L. "Brain Training: An Athletic Model for Brain Rehabilitation." *Psychiatric Services* 57, no. 4 (2006): 459–60.

Happé, Francesca. "Autism: Cognitive Deficit or Cognitive Style?" *Trends in Cognitive Sciences* 3, no. 6 (1999): 216–22.

Hardy-Baylé, Marie-Christine. "Sciences cognitives et psychiatrie." *L'évolution psychiatrique* 67, no. 1 (2002): 83–112.

Harvey, Philip D. "A Cognitive Neuroscience Trifecta." *American Journal of Psychiatry* 171, no. 5 (2014): 482–4.

Hebb, Donald O. "The American Revolution." *American Psychologist* 15, no. 12 (1960): 735–45.

– *The Organization of Behavior.* London: John Wiley, 1949.

Hécaen, Henri. "Editorial." *Neuropsychologie* 1 (1963): 1–6.

– "HL Teuber et la fondation de la neuropsychologie experimentale." *Neuropsychologia* 17, no. 2 (1979): 119–24.

– *Introduction à la neuropsychologie.* Paris: Larousse, 1972.

Hécaen, Henri, and Georges Lanteri-Laura. *Evolution des connaissances et des doctrines sur les localisations cérébrales*. Paris: Brouwer, 1977.

Heilman, K.M., F. Boller, and Antionio R. Damasio. "Founding of the Behavioral Neurology Society." http://the-sbcn.org/history-of-sbcn.

Henckes, Nicolas. "Attentes et promesses du risque de psychose." *L'évolution psychiatrique* 81, no. 1 (2016): 43–52.

Heukelom, Floris. "Kahnemann and Tversky and the Making of Behavioral Economics." PhD diss., University of Amsterdam, 2007.

– "Measurement and Decision Making at the University of Michigan in the 1950s and 1960s." *Journal of the History of the Behavioral Sciences* 46, no. 2 (2010): 189–207.

Hirschman, Albert Otto. *Les passions et les intérêts: justifications politiques du capitalisme avant son apogée*. 2nd ed. Paris: Presses universitaires de France, 2005.

Hochschild, Arlie Russell. *The Managed Heart: Commercialization of Human Feeling*. Berkeley: University of California Press, 2012.

Hogarty, Gerard E., and Samuel Flesher. "Developmental Theory for a Cognitive Enhancement Therapy of Schizophrenia." *Schizophrenia Bulletin* 25, no. 4 (1999): 677–92.

Houdé, Olivier. "Apprendre à résister aux automatismes." *Cahiers pédagogiques* 71, no. 527 (2016): 20–1.

Houdé, Olivier, Bernard Mazoyer, Nathalie Tzourio-Mazoyer, and Fabrice Crivello. *Cerveau et Psychologie: Introduction à l'imagerie cérébrale anatomique et fonctionnelle*. Paris: Presses universitaires de France, 2002.

Hume, David. *Dissertation sur les passions. Des passions*. Translated by Jean-Pierre Cléro. Paris: Flammarion, 1997.

– *A Treatise of Human Nature*. Oxford: Clarendon, 1896.

Hundbert, Edward J. "Sociability and Self-Love in the Theatre of Moral Sentiments: Mandeville to Adam Smith." In *Economy, Polity, and Society: British Intellectual History 1750–1950*, edited by Stefan Collini, Richard Whatmore, and Brian Young, 31–47. Cambridge: Cambridge University Press, 2000.

Hustvedt, Siri. *The Shaking Woman or a History of My Nerves*. London: Holder and Stoughton, 2010.

Hyman, Steven E. "Grouping Diagnoses of Mental Disorders by Their Common Risk Factors." *American Journal of Psychiatry* 168, no. 1 (2011): 1–3.

Idoux-Thivet, Anne. "Ecouter l'autisme." http://ecouterlautisme.blogspot.fr.

Imbert, M., P. Bertelson, R. Kempson, D. Osherson, H. Schnelle, N. Steitz, A. Thomassen, and P. Viviani, eds. *Cognitive Science in Europe: A Report from the FAST Programme of the Commission of the European Communities*. Berlin: Springer, 1987.

Insel, Thomas. "Dr. Tom Insel to Step Down as NIMH Director." https://www.nimh.nih.gov/about/dr-tom-insel-to-step-down-as-nimh-director.shtml.

– "Look Who Is Getting into Mental Health Research." NIH, 31 August 2015. https://www.nimh.nih.gov/about/directors/thomas-insel/blog/2015/look-who-is-getting-into-mental-health-research.shtml.

Insel, Thomas, Bruce Cuthbert, Marjorie Garvey, Robert Heinssen, Daniel S. Pine, Kevin Quinn, Charles Sanislow, and Philip Wang. "Research Domain Criteria (RDOC): Toward a New Classification Framework for Research on Mental Disorders." *American Journal of Psychiatry* 167, no. 7 (2010): 748–51.

Insel, Thomas R., and Russell D. Fernald. "How the Brain Processes Social Information: Searching for the Social Brain." *Annual Review of Neuroscience* 27 (2004): 697–722.

Insel, Thomas R., Nora D. Volkow, Ting-Kai Li, James F. Battey Jr, and Story C. Landis. "Neuroscience Networks." *PLoS Biology* 1, no. 1 (2003): e17.

Institute for Government and Cabinet Office. *Mindspace: Influencing Behavior through Public Policy*. Report by Paul Dolan, Michael Hallsworth, D. Halpern, Dominic King, and Ivo Vlaev, London: Cabinet Office, 2010.

Institute of Medicine. 1991. *Mapping the Brain and Its Functions: Integrating Enabling Technologies into Neuroscience Research*, edited by Joseph B. Martin and Constance M. Pechura. Washington, DC: The National Academies Press. https://doi.org/10.17226/1816.

Jääskeläinen, Erika, Pauliina Juola, Noora Hirvonen, John J. McGrath, Sukanta Saha, Matti Isohanni, Juha Veijola, and Jouko Miettunen. "A Systematic Review and Meta-Analysis of Recovery in Schizophrenia." *Schizophrenia Bulletin* 39, no. 6 (2013): 1296–306.

Jacyna, L. Stephen, and Stephen T. Casper, eds. *The Neurological Patient in History*. Vol. 20. Rochester: University Rochester Press, 2012.

James, William. *Pragmatism and Other Writings*. Introduction and notes by G. Gunn. New York: Penguin, 2000.

Jardri, Renaud, and Pierre Thomas. "Hallucinations et neurosciences de la subjectivité." *L'information psychiatrique* 88, no. 10 (2012): 792–3.

Jaume, Lucien. *Les origines philosophiques du libéralisme*. Paris: Flammarion, 2009.

Jeannerod, Marc. *La fabrique des idées*. Paris: Odile Jacob, 2011.

– *Le cerveau volontaire*. Paris: Odile Jacob, 2009.

Johnson, Amy. "How Understanding Neuroscience Helps Me Get Unstuck." *Schizophrenia Bulletin* 41, no. 3 (2015): 544–5.

Johnstone, Lucy, M. "Voice Hearers Are People with Problems, Not Patients with Illnesses." In *Psychosis as a Personal Crisis: An Experience-Based Approach*, edited by Sandra Escher and Marius Romme, 27–36. New York: Routledge, 2011.

Kahn, Herman, Anthony J. Wiener, Daniel Bell, Henriette Joële, Yves Malartic, and Laurent de Vilmorin. *L'an 2000: Un canevas de spéculations pour les 32 prochaines années*. Paris: R. Laffont, 1968.

Kahneman, Daniel. *Thinking, Fast and Slow*. New York: Macmillan, 2011.

Kahneman, Daniel, Edward Diener, and Norbert Schwarz, eds. *Well-Being: Foundations of Hedonic Psychology*. New York: Russell Sage Foundation, 1999.

Kaltenthaler, Eva, and Kate Cavanagh. "Computerised Cognitive Behavioural Therapy and Its Uses." *Progress in Neurology and Psychiatry* 14, no. 3 (2010): 22–9.

Kandel, Eric R. "Biology and the Future of Psychoanalysis: A New Intellectual Framework for Psychiatry Revisited." *American Journal of Psychiatry* 156, no. 4 (1999): 505–24.

Kay, J. "Toward a Clinically More Useful Model for Diagnosing Narcissistic Personality Disorder." *American Journal of Psychiatry* 165, no. 11 (2008): 1379–82.

Kennedy, Daniel P., and Ralph Adolphs. "The Social Brain in Psychiatric and Neurological Disorders." *Trends in Cognitive Sciences* 16, no. 11 (2012): 559–72.

Kennett, Jeanette. "Autism, Empathy and Moral Agency." *Philosophical Quarterly* 52, no. 208 (2002): 340–57.

Keshavan, Matcheri S., Sophia Vinogradov, Judith Rumsey, Joel Sherrill, and Ann Wagner. "Cognitive Training in Mental Disorders: Update and Future Directions." *American Journal of Psychiatry* 171, no. 5 (2014): 510–22.

Kiluk, Brian D., Dawn E. Sugarman, Charla Nich, Carly J. Gibbons, Steve Martino, Bruce J. Rounsaville, and Kathleen M. Carroll. "A Methodological Analysis of Randomized Clinical Trials of Computer-Assisted Therapies for Psychiatric Disorders: Toward Improved Standards for an Emerging Field." *American Journal of Psychiatry* 168, no. 8 (2011): 790–99.

Kleinmann, Arthur. *The Illness Narratives: Suffering, Healing and the Human Condition*. New York: Basic, 1988.

Klin, Ami, Warren Jones, Robert Schultz, Fred Volkmar, and Donald Cohen. "Defining and Quantifying the Social Phenotype in Autism." *American Journal of Psychiatry* 159, no. 6 (2002): 895–908.

Korn, Henri. "Neurosciences et maladies du système nerveux." *Académie des Sciences – Rapports sur la Science et la Technologie* 16, November 2003.

Kushner, Howard I. "The Cursing Patient: Neuropsychiatry Confronts Tourette's Syndrome, 1825–2008." In *The Neurological Patient in History*, vol. 20, edited by L. Stephen Jacyna and Stephen T. Casper, 129–59. Rochester: University Rochester Press, 2012.

Lamb, H. Richard. "A Century and a Half of Psychiatric Rehabilitation in the United States." *Psychiatric Services* 45, no. 10 (1994): 1015–20.

Langlitz, Nicolas. "Book Forum Introduction: Cultural Brains and Neural Histories." *BioSocieties* 6, no. 2 (2011): 262–75.

Lanteri-Laura, Georges. *Histoire de la phrénologie*, 2nd ed. Paris: Presses universitaires de France, 1993.

Lapoujade, David. *Fictions du pragmatisme. William et Henry James.* Paris: Minuit, 2008.

Leader, Darian. *What Is Madness?* London: Penguin UK, 2011.

Le Cardinal, P. "Les pair-aidants ou médiateurs de Santé-Paris: Enjeux d'un nouveau métier dans le champ de la santé mentale." *Pluriels* 85, no. 86 (2010): 85-7.

Lechevalier, Bernard, Francis Eustache, and Fausto Viader. *La conscience et ses troubles*. Paris: De Boeck Université, 1998.

Leguay, Denis, Aurore Étienne, Charles-Siegfried Peretti, Alain Cochet, Marc Simonet, Gérard Alloy, Nadine Bazin, and Marie-Christine Hardy-Bayle. "La piste cognitive." *L'information psychiatrique* 82, no. 4 (2006): 309–20.

Le Jallé, Eléonore. "Hayek lecteur des philosophes de l'ordre spontané: Mandeville, Hume, Ferguson." *Astérion. Philosophie, histoire des idées, pensée politique* 1, 2003. https://journals.openedition.org/asterion/17.

Lejeune, Philippe. *Je est un autre. L'autobiographie, de la littérature aux médias*. Paris: Le Seuil, 1978.

Lemov, Rebecca Maura. *World as Laboratory: Experiments with Mice, Mazes, and Men*. New York: Hill and Wang, 2005.

Le Ru, Nicolas. "L'effet de l'automatisation sur l'emploi: Ce qu'on sait et ce qu'on ignore." *La note d'analyse de France stratégie*, July 2016.

Lexmond, Jen, and Richard Reeves. "Parents Are the Principal Architects of a Fairer Society: Building Character." London: DEMOS, 2009.

Liberman, Robert Paul, and Alex Kopelowicz. "Rehab Rounds: Teaching Persons with Severe Mental Disabilities to Be Their Own Case Managers." *Psychiatric Services* 53, no. 11 (2002): 1377–9.

Lieberman, Matthew D. "Social Cognitive Neuroscience: A Review of Core Processes." *Annual Review Psychology* 58 (2007): 259–89.

Longden, Eleanor. 2013. "Learning from the Voices in My Head." Filmed August 2013 in Monterey, CA. TED Video, 14:05.

Lutz, Catherine, and Geoffrey M. White. "The Anthropology of Emotions." *Annual Review of Anthropology* 15, no. 1 (1986): 405–36.

MacLeod, Colin, and Emily A. Holmes. "Cognitive Bias Modification: An Intervention Approach Worth Attending To." *American Journal of Psychiatry* 169, no. 2 (2012): 118–20.

Malabou, Catherine. *Que faire de notre cerveau?* Paris: Bayard, 2004.

Malcolm, Janet. "The Not Returning Part of It." Review of *Wish I Could Be There: Notes from a Phobic Life* by Allen Shawn. *New York Review of Books* 54, no. 2 (2007): 4–6.

Mandler, George. "Origins of the Cognitive (R)evolution." *Journal of the History of the Behavioral Sciences* 38, no. 4 (2002): 339–53.

Maples-Keller, Jessica L., Brian E. Bunnell, Sae-Jin Kim, and Barbara O. Rothbaum. "The Use of Virtual Reality Technology in the Treatment of Anxiety and Other Psychiatric Disorders." *Harvard Review of Psychiatry* 25, no. 3 (2017): 103–13.

Markram, Henry, Wulfram Gerstner, and Per Jesper Sjöström. "A History of Spike-Timing-Dependent Plasticity." *Frontiers in Synaptic Neuroscience* 3, no. 4 (2011): 4.

Marks, Sarah. "Cognitive Behaviour Therapies in Britain: The Historical Context and Present Situation." In *Cognitive Behaviour Therapies*, edited by Windy Dryden, 1–24. London: SAGE Publications Ltd., 2012. http://doi.org/doi:10.4135/9781446288368.n1.

Marquis, Nicolas. *Du bien-être au marché du malaise. La société du développement personnel.* Paris: Presses universitaires de France, 2014.

Massé, Gérard. "Pour une réhabilitation psychosociale à la française." *L'information psychiatrique* 82, no. 4 (2006): 291–6.

Masson, Steve. "Pour que s'activent les neurones." *Cahiers pédagogiques* 71, no. 527 (2016): 18–19.

Mauss, Marcel. "Catégories collectives de pensée et liberté." 1921. In *Œuvres, II, Représentations Collectives et diversité des civilisations*, edited by V. Karady, 121–5. Reprint, Paris: Minuit, 1969.

– "Les techniques du corps." In *Sociologie et anthropologie*, 4th ed., 365–88. Paris: Presses universitaires de France, 1968.

– "Rapports réels et pratiques de la psychologie et de la sociologie." In
    Sociologie et anthropologie, 4th ed., 285–308. Paris, Presses universi-
    taires de France, 1968.

McGregor, Douglas. *The Human Side of Enterprise*. New York: McGraw-
    Hill Book, 1960.

McGurk, Susan R., Elizabeth W. Twamley, David I. Sitzer, Gregory J.
    McHugo, and Kim T. Mueser. "A Meta-Analysis of Cognitive
    Remediation in Schizophrenia." *American Journal of Psychiatry* 164,
    no. 12 (2007): 1791–802.

Micoulau Franchi, Jean-Arthur, Guillaume Fond, and Guillaume Dumas.
    "Cyborg Psychiatry to Ensure Agency and Autonomy in Mental
    Disorders: A Proposal for Neuromodulation Therapeutics." *Frontiers in
    Human Neuroscience* 7, no. 463 (2013): 463.

Miller, George A. "The Cognitive Revolution: A Historical Perspective."
    Trends in Cognitive Sciences 7, no. 3 (2003): 141–4.

– "Psychology as a Means of Promoting Human Welfare." *American
    Psychologist* 24, no. 12 (1969): 1063–75.

Miller, George A., Eugene Galanter, and Karl H. Pribram. *Plans and the
    Structure of Behavior*. New York: Henry Holt, 1960.

Montreuil, M., and P. North. "Apports de la neuropsychologie aux
    recherches en psychopathologie." *Encylopédie médico-chirurgicale* 37,
    no. 5 (2002).

Mottron, Laurent. "The Power of Autism." *Nature* 479, no. 7371 (2011):
    33–5.

Mountcastle, Vernon B. "Brain Science at the Century's Ebb." *Daedalus*
    127, no. 2 (1998): 1–36.

Moutaud, Baptiste. "C'est un problème neurologique ou psychiatrique?
    Ethnologie de la stimulation cérébrale profonde appliquée au trouble
    obsessionnel compulsif." PhD diss., University of Paris, 2009.

– "Un 'alien' dans le cerveau. Expérience sociale de la maladie mentale et
    idiome naturaliste des neurosciences." *Anthropologie & santé. Revue
    internationale d'anthropologie de la santé* 11 (2015): 177.

National Institute of Mental Health. "The National Institute of Mental
    Health Strategic Plan." https://www.nimh.nih.gov/about/strategic-
    planning-reports/index.shtml.

New, Antonia S., and Barbara Stanley. "An Opioid Deficit in Borderline
    Personality Disorder: Self-Cutting, Substance Abuse, and Social
    Dysfunction." *American Journal of Psychiatry* 167, no. 8 (2010): 882–5.

Newell, Allen, John C. Shaw, and Herbert A. Simon. "Report on a General
    Problem-Solving Program." In IFIP *Congress* 256 (1959): 64–79.

Newman, Judith. "To Siri, with Love: How One Boy with Autism became BFF with Apple's Siri." *New York Times*, 14 October 2014.

O'Connor, Cliodhna, and Helene Joffe. "How Has Neuroscience Affected Lay Understandings of Personhood? A Review of the Evidence." *Public Understanding of Science* 22, no. 3 (2013): 254–68.

Ogien, Albert. "Éléments pour une grammaire de la confiance." In *Les moments de la confiance. Connaissance, affects et engagement*, edited by L. Quéré, 217–32. Paris: Economica, 2006.

– "Normativité sociale et normativité neuronale." *Revue française de sociologie* 51, no. 4 (2010): 667–91.

Ogien, Albert, and L. Quéré. "Introduction." In *Les moments de la confiance. Connaissance, affects et engagement*, edited by L. Quéré, 1–5. Paris: Economica, 2006.

Oker, Ali, Elise Prigent, Matthieu Courgeon, Victoria Eyharabide, Mathieu Urbach, Nadine Bazin, Michel-Ange Amorim, Christine Passerieux, Jean-Claude Martin, and Eric Brunet-Gouet. "How and Why Affective and Reactive Virtual Agents Will Bring New Insights on Social Cognitive Disorders in Schizophrenia? An Illustration with a Virtual Card Game Paradigm." *Frontiers in Human Neuroscience* 9, no. 133 (2015): 1–11.

Olivier, F., O. Grandmontagne, L. Schmitt, and P. Moron. "Une priorité pour la réhabilitation des patients psychotiques: Le développement des compétences sociales." *Revue pratique de psychologie de la vie sociale et d'hygiène mentale* 3 (1991): 11–14.

Ortigues, Edmond. "Qu'est-ce qu'une guérison rituelle?" 1977. In *Le temps de la parole et autres écrits sur l'humanité et la religion*. Reprint, Rennes: Presses universitaires de Rennes (2012): 97–102.

Pachet, Pierre. *Le premier venu: Essai sur la politique baudelairienne.* Vol. 43. Paris: Denoël, 1976.

Passerieux, Christine, and Nadine Bazin. "La rééducation cognitive: Évaluation des résultats." *Revue française des affaires sociales* 1 (2009): 157–69.

Pétillon, Pierre-Yves. *La grand-route: Espace et écriture en Amérique.* Paris: Seuil, 1979.

Peyroux, Elodie, and Nicolas Franck. "RC2S: A Cognitive Remediation Program to Improve Social Cognition in Schizophrenia and Related Disorders." *Frontiers in Human Neroscience* 8, no. 400 (2014): 112.

PFSKLab. "Will Your Next Gadget Be Your New Guru?" *IQ*, 16 June 2014.

Phillipson, Nicholas. *Adam Smith: An Enlightened Life.* London: Penguin UK, 2010.

Pickersgill, Martyn, Sarah Cunningham-Burley, and Paul Martin. "Constituting Neurologic Subjects: Neuroscience, Subjectivity and the Mundane Significance of the Brain." *Subjectivity* 4, no. 3 (2011): 346–65.

Pillet, B. "Thérapie de remédiation cognitive et psychothérapie: Passer de handicapé à 'handicapable.'" *La lettre de reh@b* (March 2010): 3.

Pine, Daniel S., and Robert Freedman. "Imaging a Brighter Future." *American Journal of Psychiatry* 168, no. 9 (2011): 885–7.

Plas, Régine. "Aux origines des thérapies comportementales et cognitives: Psychanalyse, behaviorisme et scientisme aux États-Unis 1906–1970." In *Psychothérapie et société*, edited by F. Champion, 143–66. Paris: Armand Collin, 2009.

– "La psychologie cognitive française dans ses relations avec les neurosciences. Histoire, enjeux et conséquences d'une alliance." *Revue d'histoire des sciences humaines* 2 (2011): 125–42.

Pocock, John Greville Agard. *Virtue, Commerce, and History: Essays on Political Thought and History, Chiefly in the Eighteenth Century.* Vol. 2. Cambridge: Cambridge University Press, 1985.

Powers, Richard. *The Echo Maker.* New York: Farrar, Straus and Giroux, 2006.

– Interview by Alec Mitchod. "An Interview with Richard Powers." *Believer*, 1 February 2007. https://believermag.com/an-interview-with-richard-powers/.

– Interview by Andrea Lynn. "A Powers-ful Presence: Novelist and Writer-in-Residence Richard Powers Wins National Book Award." http://www.las.illinois.edu/news/article/?id=17042&key=news/2006/powers.

Premack, David, and Guy Woodruff. "Does the Chimpanzee Have a Theory of Mind?" *Behavioral and Brain Sciences* 1, no. 4 (1978): 515–26.

Price, Bruce H., Raymond D. Adams, and Joseph T. Coyle. "Neurology and Psychiatry: Closing the Great Divide." *Neurology* 54, no. 1 (2000): 8–14.

Project on the Decade of the Brain. "Presidential Proclamation 6158." http://lcweb.loc.gov/loc/brain/proclaim.html.

Putnam, Hilary. *The Many Faces of Realism.* LaSalle, IL: Open Court, 1987.

Quervain, Dominique J.F. de, Urs Fischbacher, Valerie Treyer, and Melanie Schellhammer. "The Neural Basis of Altruistic Punishment." *Science* 305, no. 5688 (2004): 1254–8.

Rabinow, Paul. "Artificiality and Enlightenment: From Sociobiology to Biosociality." In *Essays on the Anthropology of Reason*. Princeton, NJ: Princeton University Press, 1996.

Raichle, Marcus E. "Behind the Scenes of Functional Brain Imaging: A Historical and Physiological Perspective." *Proceedings of the National Academy of Sciences* 95, no. 3 (1998): 765–72.

Ramachandran, Vilayanur S., Sandra Blakeslee, Michèle Garène, and Oliver W. Sacks. *Le fantôme intérieur*. Paris: Odile Jacob, 2002.

Rees, Tobias. "Being Neurologically Human Today: Life and Science and Adult Cerebral Plasticity (An Ethical Analysis)." *American Ethnologist* 37, no. 1 (2010): 150–66.

Regelado, Antonio. "Why America's Top Mental Health Researcher Joined Alphabet." MIT Technology Review. https://www.technologyreview.com/s/541446/whyamericas-top-mental-health-researcher-joinedalphabet/.

Rhodes, John, and Simon Jakes. *Narrative CBT for Psychosis*. New York: Routledge, 2009.

Rieff, Philip. *The Triumph of the Therapeutic: Uses of Faith after Freud*. Chicago: University of Chicago Press, 1987.

Riesman, David, Nathan Glazer, and Reuel Denney. *La Foule Solitaire*. Abr. ed. Paris: Arthaud, 1964.

– *The Lonely Crowd: A Study of the Changing American Character*. New Haven, CT: Yale University, 2001.

Riffert, N.W. "It's a Brain Disease." *Psychiatric Services* 48, no. 6 (1997): 773–4.

Rodriguez, Lourdes, Ellen Corin, and Lorraine Guay. "La thérapie alternative: Se (re) mettre en mouvement." In *Les resources alternative de traitement*, edited by Yves Lecomte and Jean Gagné, 49–94. Montreal: Santé mentale au Québec, 2000.

Romme, M.A.J., A. Honig, E.O. Noorthoorn, and A.D.M.A.C. Escher. "Coping with Hearing Voices: An Emancipatory Approach." *The British Journal of Psychiatry* 161, no. 1 (1992): 99–103.

Romme, Marius A.J., and Alexandre D.M.A.C. Escher. "Hearing Voices." *Schizophrenia Bulletin* 15, no. 2 (1989): 209–16.

Romme, Marius, Sandra Escher, Jacqui Dillon, Dirk Corstens, and Mervyn Morris. *Living with Voices: 50 Stories of Recovery*. Herefordshire: PCCS Books, 2009.

Rose, Nikolas, and Joelle M. Abi-Rached. *Neuro: The New Brain Sciences and the Management of the Mind*. Princeton, NJ: Princeton University Press, 2013.

Rosenberg, T. "Depressed? Try Therapy without the Therapist." *New York Times*, 19 June 2015.

Ross, Dorothy. "Freud and the Vicissitudes of Modernism in the United States, 1940–1980." In *After Freud Left: A Century of Psychoanalysis in America*, edited by John Burnham, 163–88. Chicago: University of Chicago Press, 2012.

Rothstein, Aaron. "Mental Disorder or Neurodiversity?" *New Atlantis* 36 (Summer 2012): 99–115.

Roy, Jean-Michel. "L'émergence de la neuroscience cognitive." *Cahiers Alfred Binet* 2 (2001): 9–33.

Sacks, Oliver. *An Anthropologist on Mars: Seven Paradoxical Tales*. London: Picador, 1996.

– *The Man Who Mistook His Wife for a Hat and Other Clinical Tales*. New York: Simon and Schuster, 1985.

Sarfati, Yves, Marie-Christine Hardy-Bayle, Jacqueline Nadel, Jean-Francois Chevalier, and Daniel Widlocher. "Attribution of Mental States to Others by Schizophrenic Patients." *Cognitive Neuropsychiatry* 2, no. 1 (1997): 1–18.

Scassellati, Brian, Henny Admoni, and Maja Matarić. "Robots for Use in Autism Research." *Annual Review of Biomedical Engineering* 14 (2012): 275–94.

Sears, Robert R. "Psychoanalysis and Behavior Theory: 1907–1965." In *A Century of Psychology as Science*, edited by Sigmund Koch and David E. Leary, 208–20. Washington, DC: American Psychological Association, 1985.

Seigel, Jerrold. *Paris Bohême. 1830–1930* (1986). Paris: Gallimard, 1991.

Senk, P. "Les psy virtuels sont arrivés." *Le Figaro*, 11 July 2014.

Shawn, Allen. *Twin: A Memoir*. New York: Viking, 2010.

– *Wish I Could Be There: Notes from a Phobic Life*. New York: Viking, 2007.

Siegle, Greg J. "Brain Mechanisms of Borderline Personality Disorder at the Intersection of Cognition, Emotion, and the Clinic." *American Journal of Psychiatry* 164, no. 12 (December 2007): 1776–9.

Signoret, Jean-Louis. "Entre cerveau et cognition: La neuropsychologie." *Le débat* 47 (1987): 145–57.

Silbersweig, David, John F. Clarkin, Martin Goldstein, Otto F. Kernberg, Oliver Tuescher, Kenneth N. Levy, Gary Brendel et al. "Failure of Frontolimbic Inhibitory Function in the Context of Negative Emotion in Borderline Personality Disorder." *American Journal of Psychiatry* 164, no. 12 (2007): 1832–41.

Silver, Allan. "Friendship in Commercial Society: Eighteenth-Century Social Theory and Modern Sociology." *American Journal of Sociology* 95, no. 6 (1990): 1474–504.

Simonet, M. "La piste cognitive dans la prise en charge des patients souffrant de schizophrénie à l'hôpital de jour-CATTP du secteur Caen-Nord." *L'information psychiatrique* 82, no. 4 (2006): 313–15.

Simut, Ramona E., Johan Vanderfaeillie, Andreea Peca, Greet Van de Perre, and Bram Vanderborght. "Children with Autism Spectrum Disorders Make a Fruit Salad with Probo, the Social Robot: An Interaction Study." *Journal of Autism and Developmental Disorders* 46, no. 1 (2016): 113–26.

Singer, Tania, and Claus Lamm. "The Social Neuroscience of Empathy." *Annals of the New York Academy of Sciences* 1156, no. 1 (2009): 81–96.

Singer, Tania, Daniel Wolpert, and Chris Frith. "Introduction: The Study of Social Interactions." In *The Neuroscience of Social Interaction: Decoding, Imitating, and Influencing the Actions of Others*, xiii–xxvii. Oxford: Oxford University Press, 2004.

Skinner, B.F. *Beyond Freedom and Dignity*. New York: Bantam, 1971.

Smith, Adam. *The Theory of Moral Sentiments and Essays on Philosophical Subjects*. London: Alex Murray & Son, 1869.

Smith, Matthew J., Michael F. Fleming, Michael A. Wright, Neil Jordan, Laura Boteler Humm, Dale Olsen, and Morris D. Bell. "Job Offers to Individuals with Severe Mental Illness after Participation in Virtual Reality Job Interview Training." *Psychiatric Services* 66, no. 11 (2015): 1173–9.

Smith, Matthew J., Michael F. Fleming, Michael A. Wright, Molly Losh, Laura Boteler Humm, Dale Olsen, and Morris D. Bell. "Brief Report: Vocational Outcomes for Young Adults with Autism Spectrum Disorders at Six Months after Virtual Reality Job Interview Training." *Journal of Autism and Developmental Disorders* 45, no. 10 (2015): 3364–9.

Stanley, Barbara, and Larry J. Siever. "The Interpersonal Dimension of Borderline Personality Disorder: Toward a Neuropeptide Model." *American Journal of Psychiatry* 167, no. 1 (2009): 24–39.

Strauss, John S. "Psychological Interventions for Psychosis: Theme and Variations." *American Journal of Psychiatry* 171, no. 5 (May 2014): 479–81.

Strawson, Galen. "Against Narrativity." *Ratio* 17, no. 4 (2004): 428–52.

Tabibnia, Golnaz, Ajay B. Satpute, and Matthew D. Lieberman. "The

Sunny Side of Fairness: Preference for Fairness Activates Reward Circuitry (and Disregarding Unfairness Activates Self-Control Circuitry)." *Psychological Science* 19, no. 4 (2008): 339–47.

Teuber, Hans-Lukas. "The Brain and Human Behavior." In *Perception*, 879–920. Heidelberg: Springer, 1978.

Thakkar, Katharine N., Joel S. Peterman, and Sohee Park. "Altered Brain Activation during Action Imitation and Observation in Schizophrenia: A Translational Approach to Investigating Social Dysfunction in Schizophrenia." *American Journal of Psychiatry* 171, no. 5 (2014): 539–48.

Thaler, Richard H. "Public Policies, Made to Fit People." *New York Times*, 24 August 2013.

Thaler, Richard H., and Cass R. Sunstein. *Nudge: Improving Decisions about Health, Wealth, and Happiness.* New York: Penguin, 2009.

Thibierge, Stéphane. *Pathologies de l'image du corps. Études des troubles de la reconnaissance et de la nomination en psychopathologie.* Paris: Presses universitaires de France, 1999.

Tierney, John. "Do You Suffer from Decision Fatigue?" *New York Times Sunday Magazine*, 21 August 2011.

Tisseron, Serge, and Philippe Gutton. *Avatars et mondes viruels. Adolescence Collection.* Le Bouscat: L'ésprit du temps, 2009.

Tondora, Janis, Rebecca Miller, Kimberly Guy, and Stephanie Lanteri. "Getting in the Driver's Seat of Your Treatment: Preparing for Your Plan." Yale Program for Recovery and Community Health, 2009. https://cdn.ymaws.com/www.fadaa.org/resource/resmgr/files/resource_center/Getting_In_Drivers_Seat.pdf.

Tranulis, Constantin, Ellen Corin, and Laurence J. Kirmayer. "Insight and Psychosis: Comparing the Perspectives of Patient, Entourage and Clinician." *Philosophical Transaction of the Royal Society* 364 (2009): 1351–7.

Treffert, Darold A. «The Savant Syndrome: An Extraordinary Condition. A Synopsis: Past, Present, Future.» *Philosophical Transactions of the Royal Society B: Biological Sciences* 364, no. 1522 (2009): 1351–57.

Turkington, Douglas, David Kingdon, and Peter J. Weiden. "Cognitive Behavior Therapy for Schizophrenia." *American Journal of Psychiatry* 163, no. 3 (2006): 365–73.

Turner, David Trevor, Mark van der Gaag, Eirini Karyotaki, and Pim Cuijpers. "Psychological Interventions for Psychosis: A Meta-Analysis of Comparative Outcome Studies." *American Journal of Psychiatry* 171, no. 5 (2014): 523–38.

Van Goidsenhoven, Leni, and Anneleen Masschelein. "Posting Autism: Online Self-Representation Strategies in Tistje, a Flemish Blog on 'Living on the Spectrum from the Front Row.'" In *Disability and Social Media: Global Perspectives*, edited by M. Kent and K. Ellis, 255–73. New York: Routledge, 2016.

Varela, Francisco. *Connaître les sciences cognitives; tendances et perspectives*. Paris: Seuil, 1989.

Vianin, Pascal. *Programme de remédiation cognitive pour patients présentant une schizophrénie ou un trouble associé: Manuel du thérapeute*. Socrates éditions. Charleroi, Belgium: Promarex, 2007.

Vincent, Jean-Didier. *Biologie des Passions*. Paris: Odile Jacob, 1986.

Vuillaume, Dominique. "Ouvrir les débats actuels sur les drogues et les dépendances aux problématisations littéraires des addictions: L'exemple emblématique de David Foster Wallace et de son roman fleuve." *Infinite jest*. June 2017. https://www.hal.inserm.fr/inserm-01592743.

Watson, John B. "Psychology as the Behaviorist Views It." *Psychological Review* 20, no. 2 (1913): 158–77.

Wexler, Bruce E., and Morris D. Bell. "Cognitive Remediation and Vocational Rehabilitation for Schizophrenia." *Schizophrenia Bulletin* 31, no. 4 (2005): 931–41.

Will, O.A. Foreword to *Schizophrenia as a Lifestyle*, by A. Burton, Juan J. Lopez Ibor, and Werner M. Mendel, i–xiv. New York: Springer, 1974.

Winter, Mathias, and Nicolas Franck. "Remédiation cognitive et informations faciales." *L'évolution psychiatrique* 74, no. 1 (2009): 145–52.

Wolfe, Tom. "The 'Me' Decade and the Third Great Awakening." *New York Magazine* 23, no. 8 (1976): 26–40.

Wood, Angela. "Rethinking 'Patient Testimony' in the Medical Humanities: The Case of *Schizophrenia Bulletin*'s First Person Accounts." *Journal of Literature and Science* 6, no. 1 (2012): 38–54.

Zaki, Jamil, and Kevin N. Ochsner. "The Neuroscience of Empathy: Progress, Pitfalls and Promise." *Nature Neuroscience* 15, no. 5 (2012): 675–80.

Index